SAP® ERP Financials and FICO

Handbook

THE JONES AND BARTLETT PUBLISHERS SAP® BOOK SERIES

SAP® R/3® FI Transactions
V. Narayanan (978-1-934015-01-8) © 2007

Upgrading SAP®
Maurice Sens (978-1-934015-15-5) © 2008

SAP® FI/CO Questions and Answers
V. Narayanan (978-1-934015-22-3) © 2008

SAP® ABAP™ Handbook
Kogent Learning Solutions, Inc. (978-0-7637-8107-1) © 2010

SAP® ABAP™ Questions and Answers
Kogent Learning Solutions, Inc. (978-0-7637-7884-2) © 2010

SAP® MM Questions and Answers
Kogent Learning Solutions, Inc. (978-0-7637-8144-6) © 2010

SAP® SD Questions and Answers
Kogent Learning Solutions, Inc. (978-0-7637-8198-9) © 2010

SAP® ERP Financials and FICO Handbook
S. N. Padhi (978-0-7637-8080-7) © 2011

For more information on this series and its titles, please visit us online at http://www.jbpub.com. Qualified instructors, contact your Publisher's Representative at 1-800-832-0034 or info@jbpub.com to request review copies for course consideration.

SAP® ERP Financials and FICO

Handbook

S. N. Padhi

JONES AND BARTLETT PUBLISHERS
Sudbury, Massachusetts
BOSTON   TORONTO   LONDON   SINGAPORE

World Headquarters
Jones and Bartlett Publishers
40 Tall Pine Drive
Sudbury, MA 01776
978-443-5000
info@jbpub.com
www.jbpub.com

Jones and Bartlett Publishers
Canada
6339 Ormindale Way
Mississauga, Ontario L5V 1J2
Canada

Jones and Bartlett Publishers
International
Barb House, Barb Mews
London W6 7PA
United Kingdom

Jones and Bartlett's books and products are available through most bookstores and online booksellers. To contact Jones and Bartlett Publishers directly, call 800-832-0034, fax 978-443-8000, or visit our website, www.jbpub.com.

Substantial discounts on bulk quantities of Jones and Bartlett's publications are available to corporations, professional associations, and other qualified organizations. For details and specific discount information, contact the special sales department at Jones and Bartlett via the above contact information or send an email to specialsales@jbpub.com.

This publication contains references to the products of SAP AG. SAP, R/3, xApps, xApp, SAP NetWeaver, Duet, PartnerEdge, ByDesign, SAP Business ByDesign, and other SAP products and services mentioned herein are trademarks or registered trademarks of SAP AG in Germany and in several other countries all over the world. Business Objects and the Business Objects logo, Business Objects, Crystal Reports, Crystal Decisions, Web Intelligence, Xcelsius and other Business Objects products and services mentioned herein are trademarks or registered trademarks of Business Objects in the United States and/or other countries. SAP AG is neither the author nor the publisher of this publication and is not responsible for its content, and SAP Group shall not be liable for errors or omissions with respect to the materials.

Production Credits
Publisher: David Pallai
Editorial Assistant: Molly Whitman
Production Director: Amy Rose
Production Editor: Kat Crighton
Associate Production Editor: Melissa Elmore
Associate Marketing Manager: Lindsay Ruggiero
V.P., Manufacturing and Inventory Control:
    Therese Connell

Composition: diacriTech
Cover and Title Page Design: Scott Moden
Cover Image: © Gastev Roman/ShutterStock, Inc.
Interior Images: © SAP AG. All rights reserved.
Printing and Binding: Malloy, Inc.
Cover Printing: Malloy, Inc.

Library of Congress Cataloging-in-Publication Data
Padhi, S. N.
SAP ERP financials and FICO handbook/S.N. Padhi.
    p. cm.
Includes index.
ISBN 978-0-7637-8080-7 (hardcover)
1. SAP ERP 2. Financing Corporation (U.S.) 3. Accounting—Computer programs. I. Title.
HF5679.P23 2010
657.0285'53—dc22

                        2009037367

6048
Printed in the United States of America
13 12 11 10 09   10 9 8 7 6 5 4 3 2 1

This book is dedicated to my wife, Sharmistha.

ABOUT THE AUTHOR

A graduate in commerce and an associated member of the Institute of Chartered accountants of India, New Delhi, S. N. Padhi has more than 26 years of experience in accounting, finance, taxation, audit, and information technology. He is a participating SAP FICO consultant.

TABLE OF CONTENTS

An Introduction to SAP Software

SAP stands for Systems Applications and Products in Data Processing.

SAP® software is the leading enterprise information and management package worldwide. Use of this package makes it possible to track and manage, in real time, sales, production, financial accounting, and human resources in an enterprise.

SAP AG is the third-largest software company in the world. Founded in 1972, SAP now employs more than 48,500 people in more than 50 countries. SAP global headquarters is located in Walldorf, Germany, and the company is listed on several stock exchanges, including the Frankfurt DAX and the New York Stock Exchange, under the symbol SAP.

SAP has more than 2,400 partners, 26 industry solutions, and 12 million users at 140,000 installations around the world.

The following shortcuts are commonly used when working with SAP solutions.

Action	Shortcuts
Enter	<Enter>
Save	F11, Ctrl+S
Back	F3
Exit	Shift+F3
Cancel	F12
Help	F1
Execute	F8
Possible Values	F4
Current Date	F4 and F2

TABLE 1 Shortcuts

PREFACE

This book is different from other books available on the market. The main goals of this book are to provide readers with a good knowledge base, to offer a better understanding to those new to SAP® Financial Accounting (FI) and Controlling (CO), and to sharpen the skills of experienced consultants.

While writing this book, utmost care was taken to cover the most common, complex, and highly interview-oriented topics of SAP FICO. In this book, you will find almost all sections are arranged according to the FICO submodules. The screenshots are taken from SAP® R/3® Enterprise 4.70 and SAP ECC 6.0.

This book is divided into the following chapters:

- Chapter 1—Interview Questions and Answers: This chapter covers frequently asked questions and answers in an interview format. More than 224 questions and answers are presented by sub-module.
- Chapter 2—Certification Questions and Answers: This chapter contains nearly 200 "objective type certification" questions and answers. This is one of the unique attributes of this book.
- Chapter 3—Issues and Resolutions: In this chapter, I explain the probable solution of various production issues. Sometimes issues and resolutions depend on a particular SAP implementation environment. This is another one of the unique attributes of this book not found in other books.
- Chapter 4—Configuration Steps: While implementing SAP R/3 or SAP ERP Financials, consultants always look for sequential steps that need to be followed. In this chapter, I provide the most common object-oriented configuration steps in a sequence with path and transaction codes.
- Chapter 5—User Transaction Codes: In this chapter, I provide the most common user transaction codes. It is expected that a FICO consultant know commonly used transaction codes.
- Chapter 6—FICO Quick Tour: In this chapter, I recap various sub-modules of FICO in bullet-point format. This gives readers a high-level understanding of various sub-modules of FICO and is a valuable feature of this book.

- Chapter 7—Special Areas: This chapter covers various areas of FICO that are highly important from an interview and implementation perspective.
- Chapter 8—New G/L: The concept of the New G/L came into existence from SAP ECC 5.0 versions. It has many advantages compared to earlier versions of SAP software. In this chapter, I give a high-level overview of the New G/L and how it is different from G/L.
- Chapter 9—Tables in the SAP System: As you are aware, all transactional data and configuration data is stored in various database tables. In this chapter, I provide various tables important to SAP FICO modules.
- Chapter 10—SAP MM Configuration: SAP ERP is characterized by one-point data entry. Once data is entered in one module, it flows to and affects other modules. As a FICO consultant, if you are working in a project where an SAP Materials Management (MM) module is also implemented, you should have a basic understanding of MM configuration. In this chapter, I cover some basic configuration steps.
- Chapter 11—SAP SD Configuration: Similar to Chapter 10, in this chapter, you will find basic configuration steps of the SAP Sales and Distribution (SD) module.

I hope you will enjoy this book. All the best!

S. N. Padhi

Chapter 1

INTERVIEW QUESTIONS AND ANSWERS

1.1 SAP-GENERAL

1. **What is the SAP® implementation roadmap and what steps are involved in it?**

The SAP implementation roadmap is a standard process provided by SAP AG for smooth SAP implementation and is called the ASAP Roadmap. The ASAP Roadmap consists of five phases: (1) Project Preparation, (2) Business Blueprint, (3) Realization, (4) Final Preparation, and (5) Going Live and Support.

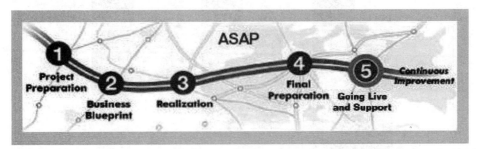

FIGURE 1.1

- *Project Preparation*—In this phase of the ASAP Roadmap, decision-makers define clear project objectives and an efficient decision-making process. Here, project organization and roles are defined and implementation scope is finalized.

- *Business Blueprint*—In this phase, the scope of the R/3 implementation is defined and the Business Blueprint is created. The Business Blueprint is a detailed documentation of the customer's requirements.

- *Realization*—The purpose of Phase 3 is to configure the R/3 system. The configuration is carried out in two steps: baseline configuration and final configuration.

1

- *Final Preparation*—The purpose of this phase is to complete the final preparation of the R/3 system for going live. This includes testing, user training, system management, and cutover activities to finalize your readiness to go live.
- *Going Live and Support*—During this phase, the first early watch session should be held, where SAP experts analyze the system's technical infrastructure. The aim is to ensure the system functions as smoothly as possible.

2.   What does system landscape mean?

The system landscape represents the SAP system deployment at your implementation site. Ideally, in an SAP environment, a three-system landscape exists, consisting of the development server (DEV), quality assurance server (QAS), and production server (PRD). This kind of setup is not primarily designed to serve as a server cluster in case of system failure; rather, the objective is to enhance "configuration pipeline management."

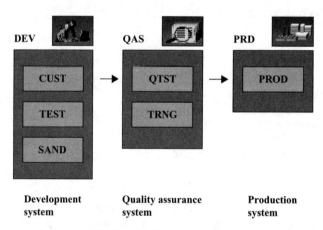

FIGURE 1.2   System landscape

The system landscape is the system structure that you have for your implementation project. For example, you might have a development system, quality assurance (QA) system, and production system. It also includes how the configuration change goes through these systems and what controls there are. System landscape mostly has to do with the systems, their servers, and so forth.

3.   What are specs?

Specs represent specifications. In an information technology (IT) environment, you will find two kinds of specifications: (1) functional specifications and (2) technical specifications. These documents contain the business requirements, such as inputs, solutions, processing logic, and so on.

Functional specification: The documentation typically describes what is needed by the system user as well as requested properties of inputs and outputs. The functional specification is business-oriented. A functional specification does not define the inner workings of the proposed system, nor does it include information for how the system function will be implemented. Instead, it focuses on what various outside agents (e.g., people using the program, computer peripherals, or other computers) might observe when interacting with the system.

Technical specification: While the functional specification is business-oriented, the technical specification is system-oriented and discusses programming.

4.   How many versions of the implementation guides (IMGs) are available in SAP? What are they?

There are three versions of the IMG available in SAP. These are:
- *Reference IMG*—The reference IMG contains all configuration transactions available for all functionalities/modules/submodules in the installed versions of SAP R/3. The reference IMG represents the base set of configuration options from which SAP functionality can be configured. All other versions of the IMG are subsets of the reference IMG.
- *Enterprise IMG*—The enterprise IMG only contains configuration transactions that are applicable to a specific company's installation of SAP software. The enterprise IMG serves the purpose of filtering out configuration options that are not required by a company if certain modules are not implemented.
- *Project IMG*—A project IMG contains a subset of the enterprise IMG configuration transactions that need to be configured to complete a specific project.

5.   In SAP solutions, is it possible to have a self-defined transaction code?

Yes, self-defined reports, transactions, and functions are possible within SAP solutions. There might be numerous reasons why a company would want customized transaction codes or reports. To cater to this demand, SAP allows the creation of user-defined transaction codes.

User-defined transaction codes allow the user to speed up access to specific reports or programs since the user no longer needs to use transaction code SE38, enter the program name or report name, and press Execute. Instead, the user can simply use a predefined transaction code that will automatically open the program. Customized T-codes can be created by using transaction code SE93. Follow these steps to create a transaction code:

1. Name your transaction code. In this case, it is ZTEST1.

FIGURE 1.3   Naming a transaction code

2. Click on the **Create** button and then select the relevant option in the screen that appears. In this case, select **Program and selection screen**.

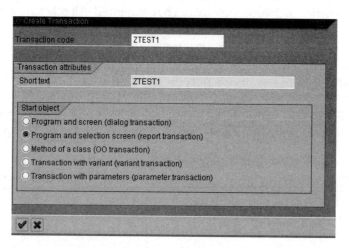

FIGURE 1.4   Creating a transaction code

3. Click on the check mark icon at the bottom left of the screen. In the next screen that appears, assign a program name and selection screen and save your work. Now your transaction code ZTEST1 is ready for execution.

Create Report transaction

Transaction code	ZTEST1
Package	

Transaction text	ZTEST1
Program	Your Program Name
Selection screen	1000
Start with variant	
Authorization object	Values

FIGURE 1.5   **Your new transaction code**

6.   What is the best practice for transporting configuration requests? How can you transport a configuration request?

In standard SAP implementation, there will be three clients: (1) Development, (2) Quality, and (3) Production. These three clients may be located within one server or on different servers for each client. Configuration will be carried out in the Development client and transported to the Testing client. After satisfactory testing of the SAP R/3 system, configuration will be transported from the Development client to the Production client.

If different servers are used for different clients, the request is generated in the Development client, which has to be released first through transaction code SE10. Then the basis consultant will move the request to QUALITY through STMS, which is really the job of the basis consultant. After thorough testing, you can again ask the basis consultant to transport through STMS to move the request to the Production client.

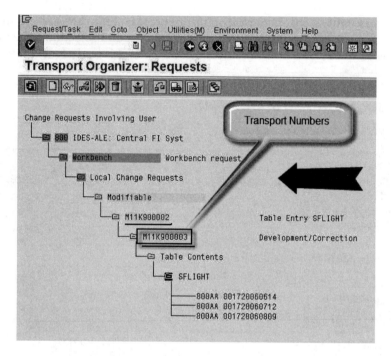

FIGURE 1.6   **Using transaction code SE10**

If clients are located on the same server, transaction code SCC1 is used to transport requests from one client to another client. For example, if in the Development server itself you have the golden client (a SAP-specific word used for a good client), i.e., DEV and one more client for Testing, you do not need to release the request in SE10. You can do this directly through transaction code SCC1 in the Testing client by giving the request number. Here, you may not require basis help.

7. After configuration you have to transport the configuration to the QAS or PRD. Can you transport number ranges of documents, assets masters, customer masters, and vendor masters in the same transport request?

No. These have to be transported separately. Number ranges are not automatically included in transport requests. It is easy to overlay number range objects and get existing ranges out of the system when you transport number ranges. It is recommended that you do not transport number ranges, and instead set them up individually in each client. This is part of the cutover activities for the go-live checklist.

8. How can you find the menu path when you know the transaction code?

There are two ways to find the application menu when you know the transaction code. Note that this is valid for the Easy Access Menu, not the IMG menu.

The first way is to enter **SEARCH_SAP_MENU** in OK and Command box and press **Enter**. In the next screen, enter your desired transaction code and click on the check mark. Now you will see the Search for a Transaction Code or Menu Title screen, which shows the menu path. To reach your desired location, read the screen from the bottom up.

Search for a Transaction Code or Menu Title

Node	Transaction code	Text
Nodes	FS00	Centrally
Preceding node		Individual Processing
Preceding node		G/L Accounts
Preceding node		Master Records
Preceding node		General Ledger
Preceding node		Financial Accounting
Preceding node		Accounting

FIGURE 1.7 **System menu path**

Figure 1.7 shows the menu path for transaction code FS00.

Another way to find the menu path is to press **Ctrl+F** on the SAP Easy Access screen, and enter the transaction code in the pop-up screen; the system will lead you to the menu path.

9. How can you extend the SAP Easy Access Menu?

User groups may ask you to extend the SAP Easy Access Menu to include menus or submenus within the SAP standard menu. For example, if a client has a large amount of customer reports for their day-to-day use, they may want to include these reports in the SAP menu.

Follow these steps to include a report menu in the SAP Easy Access Menu:

1. Create your own area menu using transaction code SE43. While saving, you will need to assign the proper development class. The system will then create a transport request for your area menu.

2. Now you will need to include your new area menu in the SAP Easy Access area menu (transaction code S000). Use transaction code SE43, enter transaction code **S000** in the Area menu field, and click on the Change icon. A pop-up window will appear with three options: Extend, Change, and Cancel. Choose **Extend** and click on ▢ to create a new enhancement ID or use an existing enhancement ID.

3. In the Edit Area Menu S000 screen, use the ▣▣ icons to add your area menu and save. The system will create another transport request.

4. Now log off and log on again; you will find your new menu in the SAP Easy Access Menu.

Similarly, you can extend the IMG menu through transaction code S_IMG_EXTENSION.

10.   What do you do with errors in batch data conversion (BDC) sessions?

You use BDC to post data into SAP solutions with the help of the system. Sometimes, while posting data through BDC, the system will encounter problems and cannot post data. When the system encounters a problem, it will create BDC error sessions. The following are common reasons for BDC error sessions:

- Posting periods are locked
- Changes in master data, e.g., in general ledger (G/L) accounts, profit centers are locked for posting
- Changes in screen layout of SAP program

These scenarios are only examples; there may be several reasons for errors. To process incorrect BDC sessions, you need to find out the reasons for these error sessions. The easiest way to do this is to analyze the BDC log. In transaction code SM35, select the BDC sessions in question and click on the log. The Batch input: Log Overview screen will appear; double-click on any of the rows of the Log Overview tab to see an error screen. After analyzing the error, fix it and process the BDC sessions.

11. Where do you find all of the transaction codes, including custom transaction codes?

In SAP R/3, the TSTC table stores all of the transaction codes. Through transaction code SE16, you can browse all of the transaction codes. The TSTC table stores the standard SAP transaction codes, as well as custom transaction codes.

12. What is gap analysis?

The SAP R/3 system comes with predefined packages. Sometimes these pre-defined packages may not suit a client's business requirements. In the first phase of implementation, the implementation team will gather all business requirements. A thorough analysis of the business requirements will lead to a gap between the business requirements and the SAP standard package. There are two ways to reduce the gap: (1) by changing the business process or (2) by developing new programs (customizing) to accommodate the client's business process. Before the second phase of implementation, the SAP implementer will try to reduce these gaps by adopting either of these options or both.

13. What is SAP Business One?

In 2002, SAP AG purchased an Israel-based developer of business applications called TopManage Financial Systems; SAP renamed its product Business One. SAP Business One is targeted for small and medium enterprises (SME). Due to its low implementation cost and SAP support, most SME find Business One affordable compared to SAP R/3 or mySAP ERP. SAP Business One consists of the following core modules:

1. *Administration Module*—This module is similar to the IMG menu in SAP R/3, where configuration is performed.
2. *Financials Module*—This module takes care of an entity's accounting needs; this is similar to FICO of R/3.
3. *Sales Opportunities Module*—This is where existing customers and potential accounts are structured and tracked.
4. *Sales Module*—Module where orders are entered, shipped, and invoiced; this is similar to the SD module of R/3.
5. *Purchasing Module*—Module where purchase orders are issued and goods are received into inventory; this is similar to the MM module of R/3.
6. *Business Partners Module*—Module where business partners (customers, vendors, and leads) are contacted and maintained.
7. *Banking Module*—Like the SAP R/3 banking module, this module records payments and receipts.

8. *Inventory Module*—This module, integrated with the purchase module, helps inventory evaluation.

9. *Production Module*—Module that takes care of production processes.

10. *MRP Module*—Module that determines purchase requirements and checks product or material availability.

11. *Service Module*—This sub-module handles contact management for after-sale service.

12. *Human Resources Module*—Module where employee information is kept; similar to the HR module in R/3.

13. *Reports Module*—Helps to build new reports. Here we will find delivered reports.

14.   How can you configure the FICO module without using the IMG menu?

As a functional consultant, you will have authorization to use the IMG menu, subject to your user role. However, from an academic point of view, it is good to know how you can configure the FICO module without using transaction code SPRO. You can do so by invoking the following transaction codes, which are area menu transaction codes. You may find these types of transactions through transaction code SE43.

- ORFB (Financial Accounting [FI])
- ORFA (Asset Accounting [AA])

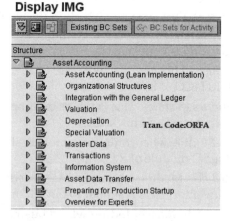

FIGURE 1.8   AA

SAP Easy Access Cost and Revenue Element Accounting: Configuration Me

			🔲 Other menu			▼ ▲	🗋 Create role	Assign users	🗋 Documentation

▽ 🗀 Favorites
    ⊞ SE16 - Data Browser
▽ 🗀 SAP menu
    ▷ 🗋 Environment
    ▷ 🗋 Master Data
    ▷ 🗋 Planning
    ▷ 🗋 Actual Postings   Tran.Code:ORKL
    ▷ 🗋 Information System
    ▷ 🗋 Tools

FIGURE 1.9   **Cost and revenue element accounting**

15.   What is the International Demonstration and Education System (IDES)?

IDES is a sample application with sample master data and standard configuration provided for faster learning and implementation. For example, the following FI company codes are in IDES. (These are just examples; there are many more.)

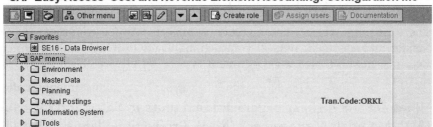

Co...	Company Name	City	Country	Crcy	Langua
0005	IDES AG NEW GL	Frankfurt	DE	EUR	DE
0006	IDES US INC New GL	New York	US	USD	EN
0007	IDES AG NEW GL 7	Frankfurt	DE	EUR	DE
0008	IDES US INC New GL 8	New York	US	USD	EN
0100	IDES Japan 0100	Tokyo	JP	JPY	JA
0110	IDES Japan 0110	Tokyo	JP	JPY	JA

FIGURE 1.10   **IDES company codes**

16.   Describe the major areas within the SAP environment.

The SAP environment consists of (1) configuration and (2) application.

1. *Configuration*—Configuration represents maintenance of settings to support business requirements through the IMG menu.
2. *Application*—This supports the handling of day-to-day activities through the SAP Easy Access Menu.

17.   Describe the data types that can be used in SAP solutions.

There are three types of data in SAP: (1) Master data–Customer master, Vendor Master, and Assets Master, (2) Transactional Data–Purchase, Sale, Payment and Receipts, and (3) Table Data–Document Type SAP Delivered Data, and so on.

18.   What are the highest organizational units in Sales and Distribution (SD), Materials Management (MM), Production Planning (PP), Financial Information (FI), and Controlling Area (CO)?

1. *SD*—Sales Organizations
2. *MM*—Plant
3. *PP*—Plant
4. *FI*—Company Code
5. *CO*—Controlling Area

1.2 FI-GENERAL

19.   When you copy the chart of accounts (COA), only one financial statement version (FSV) is being copied. However, a COA can have more than one FSV. Why does copying the COA allow only one FSV?

An FSV corresponds to the COA, wherein individual (operational) accounts are assigned to corresponding financial statement items on the lowest level of the FSV. However, in case of rollup of the account, it is not possible to copy all of the FSVs. You will have to manually create multiple FSVs, depending on the financial statements that are necessary for the organization.

20.   Describe some generally used FI submodules.

- *FI-G/L*—FI-G/L submodule; records all account data including all postings happening to subsidiary ledgers.
- *Accounts Receivable (FI-AR)*—This submodule records all transactions relating to the customer. FI-AR is treated as a subsidiary ledger of FI-GL. All transactions relating to this module are recorded in a summary form in FI-GL.

- *Accounts Payable (FI-AP)*—Like FI-AR, this submodule records transactions relating to vendors and is summarized in FI-GL.
- *Special Ledger (FI-SL)*—This submodule takes care of special reporting requirements of an entity by providing G/L based on user-defined fields.
- *FI-AA*—The FI-AA submodule takes care of recording transactions relating to assets. Here assets mean both tangible and intangible assets. FI-AA is also treated as a subsidiary ledger.

21. What information will not be copied to a new company code when you copy the company code?

All the organizational global master data for a company code will be copied to the new company code upon using the copy function except for the transactional data.

22. Can one group COA be assigned to two operational charts?

A COA is a variant. You can use a variant to *N* number of organizational objects. First, COA is a variant, then a group COA. You may use the same COA as an operational COA and a group COA. This assignment is done via transaction code OB13. A group COA can be assigned to any number of company codes. While creating the G/L accounts of an operational COA, you need to key the group COA. This way, you are making a relation between the operational COA and the group COA.

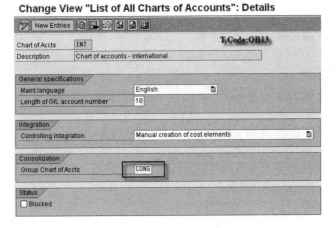

FIGURE 1.11   COA

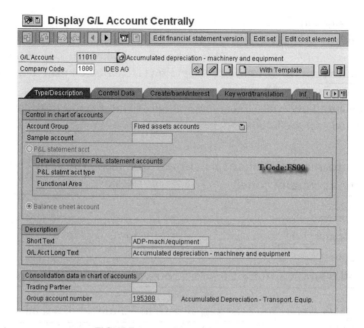

FIGURE 1.12   G/L account master

23.   What is accrued cost?

Operating expenses are often allocated differently in financial accounting than in cost accounting. If, for example, an expense incurred in external accounting covers a whole year, you must assign a proportion of such expenses to each individual cost accounting period. In this process, you distribute irregularly occurring expenses, according to cost-origin, to the months in which they are incurred. This allows you to avoid irregularities within cost accounting. Costs allocated in this manner, such as yearly bonuses, are termed accrued costs.

24.   What is the difference between the Enjoy SAP document entry screens (FB50, FB60, FB70) and the old general posting transaction?

The SAP Enjoy screens are created to expedite data entry for GL/AR/AP postings. In the old FB01 screen, users are required to manually enter document types and posting keys to determine the nature of postings. In Enjoy SAP data entry screens, these are defaulted via a configuration table so that the user just has to choose debit/credit and the system will determine whether the entry is a vendor/customer invoice/credit memo or G/L journal.

25. What is the credit control area? How is it related to the company code?

Like the company code, the credit control area is an SAP entity through which you set and control a customer's credit limit. There is one credit control area per company code. A credit control area may have more than one company code. A customer's credit limit can be set at the credit control area level or across the credit control area.

26. Explain the relationship between the Sort key and the Assignment field.

The Sort key defines the field(s) used to populate the Assignment field when a document is posted in the G/L. The Assignment field is used as a sort criterion when displaying G/L account line items.

27. Do substitution and validation work the same way when parking a document and posting a document?

No. Substitution and validation work in different ways when parking a document or posting a document.

Sequence	Posting	Parking
1	Substitution	Validation
2	Validation	Substitution

TABLE 1.1

For more information, see OSS Note: 158739.

1.3 ENTERPRISE STRUCTURE (FI-ES)

28. Tell me about the FI organizational structure.

The highest entity in the FI organization is Company, followed by Company Code. Company represents an entity that consists of one or more Company

Codes below it. Company Code represents the smallest entity for which you are preparing a financial statement of account for external reporting purposes.

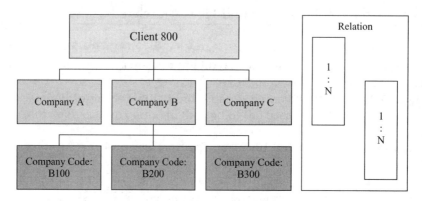

FIGURE 1.13   A company and its company code

Figure 1.13 shows a typical example of the FI organizational structure in mySAP ERP Financial.

29. How many normal and special periods will be there in a fiscal year, and why would you use special periods?

In general, there are 16 posting periods in a fiscal year. Of these 16 posting periods, there are 12 normal periods and 4 special posting periods. Special posting periods are used for book adjustments, tax adjustments, audit corrections, and so forth. Special posting periods are part of the 12th normal period.

30. Why and when would you use a year-specific fiscal year variant?

The year-specific fiscal year variants are used in two cases. The first is when the start and end dates of the posting periods differ from year to year, such as when there are 365 days in a fiscal year regardless of leap year. The second case is when one fiscal year has fewer posting periods than the others (shortened fiscal year).

31. **There is a Company field in the company code global settings. The SAP R/3 help says that it is used for consolidation. You can use the group COA to do the same. What is the significance of this field?**

A company is an organizational unit that is generally used in the legal consolidation module to roll up financial statements of several company codes. A company may have one or more company codes. If you are going for consolidation, you need to enter the six-character alphanumeric company identifier that relates to company codes for which you are consolidating accounts. Company codes within a company must use the same COA and fiscal year, and for consolidation purposes, you use the group COA where you link the operating COA by entering the G/L account number of the group COA in the G/L account of the operating COA.

In the SAP system, consolidation functions in financial accounting are based on companies. A company comprises one or more company codes. For example, Company A has four company codes, located in different states and/or countries. When Company A wants to consolidate the accounts, it will give the common list of accounts, which in turn calls the group COA. The group COA is used to define and list the G/L account uniformly for all company codes.

32. **What is the difference between the company and the company code?**

A company is the organizational unit used in the legal consolidation module to roll up financial statements of several company codes.

The company code is the smallest organizational unit for which a complete, self-contained set of accounts can be drawn up for purposes of external reporting. A company may be assigned to n number of company codes.

33. **What is a fiscal year variant?**

A fiscal year variant is a variant that holds parameters for a financial year, such as how many posting periods a fiscal year has or whether the fiscal year is year dependent. The fiscal year determines the number of posting periods, which are used to assign business transactions. The fiscal year may be year dependent or year independent. In SAP solutions, you will find four types of fiscal year variants: (1) year dependent, (2) year independent, (3) calendar year, and (4) shortened fiscal year:

Change View "Fiscal year variants": Overview

FV	Description	Year-depen...	Calendar yr	Number of posting ...	No.of special peri
24	Half periods	☐	☐	24	
C1	1st period (calendar ye...	☐	☐	1	
K1	Calendar year, 1 spec. ...	☐	☑	12	1
K2	Calendar year, 2 spec. ...	☐	☑	12	2
K3	Calendar year, 3 spec. ...	☐	☑	12	3
K4	Calendar year, 4 spec. ...	☐	☑	12	4
R1	Shortened fisc.year Jan...	☑	☐	12	4
V3	Apr.- March, 4 special p...	☐	☐	12	4
V6	July - June, 4 special pe...	☐	☐	12	4
V9	Oct.- Sept, 4 special pe...	☐	☐	12	4
WK	Calendar weeks	☑	☐	53	

Dialog Structure: Fiscal year variants — Periods, Period texts, Shortened Fiscal Yea

FIGURE 1.14   Fiscal year variant

1. *Year-dependent fiscal year*—A year-dependent fiscal year is a fiscal year that is applicable for a particular year, such as 2008 or 2009. By checking the check box in the Year-dependent column, you will mark a particular fiscal year as year dependent. In Figure 1.14, fiscal year variant R1 and WK are year dependent.

2. *Year-independent fiscal year*—A year-independent fiscal year is a fiscal year variant that is applicable for all subsequent years. All fiscal years are year independent unless you check the Year-dependent check box.

3. *Calendar fiscal year*—A calendar fiscal year is a fiscal year that starts on the first day of a year (i.e., January 1, 2009) and ends on the last day of the year (i.e., December 31, 2009). A calendar fiscal year is always year independent.

4. *Shortened fiscal year*—This is a fiscal year that has fewer normal periods. A shortened fiscal year is always year dependent.

34.   What do you mean by year dependent in fiscal year variants?

A year-dependent fiscal year variant is the financial year for which the configuration settings are valid for that particular financial year. You generally use a year-dependent financial year when the preceding financial year or succeeding financial year is a shortened financial year.

35.   What do you enter in company code global settings?

Company code global settings are populated through transaction code OBY6. Company code global settings are where you can assign different types of variants that control various parameters for a company code.

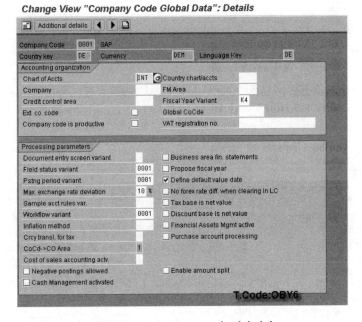

FIGURE 1.15   Company code global data

- FSV—Field status variant
- PPV—Posting period variant
- COA
- Group COA
- Enabling business-area-wise financial statement
- Negative posting allowed
- Company is productive or not productive
- Maximum exchange deviation
- Sample account variant

36. What does the screen of a COA contain?

You can create and maintain a COA through transaction code OB13. This screen
controls the following parameters for a COA:

- COA ID
- Name
- Maintenance language
- Length of the G/L account number
- CO integration
- Group COA (Consolidation)
- Block indicator

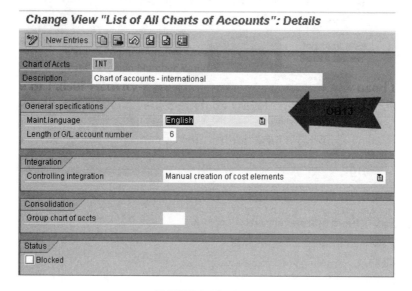

FIGURE 1.16 COA

37. What is field status group (FSG) and what does it control?

FSG represents the grouping of various fields in a certain logical way. There are various types of FSGs used in SAP solutions. These are: FSG for G/L master, FSG for customer master, FSG for vendor master, and FSG for posting a transaction.

FSG for G/L master controls which fields allow input while creating the G/L master. Similarly, vendor and customer FSG controls which fields allow input while creating the vendor and customer masters. Finally, the FSG attached to a company controls which fields allow input while posting a transaction.

A field may have one of the following statuses:

- Suppressed
  - □ Display
  - □ Optional
- Required

38.   What is an account group and what does it control?

An account group is meant for further grouping of the COA for presentation of the financial statement of account. Account groups (created using transaction code OBD4) determine which fields allow input while creating the G/L master record. It is necessary to have at least two groups, such as one for balance sheet (B/S) and another one for profit and loss (P&L) A/C. It controls:

- Number ranges of G/L A/C
- Field status of the G/L master record

Change View "G/L Account Groups": Overview

Chrt/Accts	Acct Group	Name	From acct	To account
INT	60	AR60/Fixed assets accounts	10000000	10999999
INT	ANL.	Fixed assets accounts		999999999
INT	AS	Fixed assets accounts		999999999
INT	AS60	AR60/Fixed assets accounts	10000000	10999999
INT	CASH	Liquid funds accounts		999999999
INT	ER60	AR60/Income statement accounts	15000000	15999999
INT	ERG.	P&L accounts		999999999
INT	FIN.	Liquid funds accounts		999999999
INT	GL	General G/L accounts		999999999
INT	GL60	AR60/General G/L accounts	10000000	10999999

FIGURE 1.17   G/L account groups

Figure 1.17 shows the account group configuration of the SAP standard INT COA. You can observe that account groups are defined for chart of account INT, and you can see the number range of the G/L Master assigned to the account group. To find out the attached field status of a particular group, select any of the groups and click Field status .

39. What are the country and operational COA? Why do you use the group COA?

The operational COA is used for accounting of business transactions for day-to-day activities. It is mandatory for a company code.

The country COA is used for specific legal requirements of each country. It is optional.

The group COA is used for consolidation of company codes.

Depending upon the configuration, the same COA may be an operational COA, a country COA, or a group COA.

40. What does the FSG assigned to a G/L master record control?

An FSG consists of grouping various field statuses. It controls what fields are ready for input while posting a transaction. A particular field may be required, suppressed, or optional.

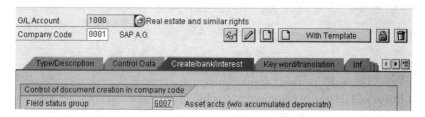

FIGURE 1.18   G/L Account master

41. What is a business area? Can you assign it to a company?

The business area is an organizational unit of financial accounting that represents a separate area of operations or responsibilities within an organization and to which value changes recorded in financial accounting can be allocated.

Business areas are used in external segment reporting (over and above company codes) based on the significant areas of operation (for example, product lines) of a business enterprise. A segment is an isolated area of activity.

The business area will not be assigned to any company code. It is available at the client level. All company codes under the same client can use the same business areas. You can restrict a business area for a company code through validation.

42. What are FSVs?

A balance sheet or profit and loss statement is called an FSV. FSV represents a variant that is configured to portray the financial statement. The FSV provides a picture of the financial position of an entity at a particular point in time (usually at the end of a reporting period). The transaction code for configuring FSV is OB58.

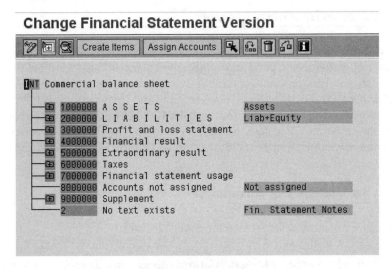

FIGURE 1.19   FSV

43. How are year-dependent fiscal year variants usually used?

The year-dependent fiscal year variants are used when the start and end dates of the posting periods differ from year to year and when one fiscal year has fewer posting periods than the others (shortened fiscal year).

44.   What is the difference between a participating and nonparticipating currency?

A participating currency is the currency of a country participating in the European Economic and Monetary Union (EMU). Those countries currently include Austria, Belgium, Cyprus, Finland, France, Germany, Greece, Ireland, Italy, Luxembourg, Malta, the Netherlands, Portugal, Slovakia, Slovenia, and Spain.

A nonparticipating currency is the currency of a country not participating in the EMU.

1.4 G/L ACCOUNTING (FI-G/L)

45.   What is open item management?

Open item management means that a line item needs to be cleared against another open item. At a particular point, the balance of an account is the sum of all open items of that account. Generally, you make these settings in the G/L Master for all clearing accounts, such as a Goods receipts and Invoice receipts (GR IR) account, customer account, vendor account, or bank G/L account, or all accounts except the main bank account. Open item managed accounts always have line item management. You can switch open item management on and off through transaction code FS00.

46.   What are the types of currencies?

The following currencies are used in SAP solutions:

- *Local currency*—This is company code currency, which is used for generating financial statements for external reporting. Sometimes it is called operating currency.
- *Group currency*—Group currency is the currency that is specified in the client table and used for consolidation purposes.
- *Hard currency*—Hard currency is a country-specific second currency that is used in countries with high inflation.
- *Index-based currency*—Index-based currency is a country-specific fictitious currency that is required in some countries with high inflation for external reporting (for example, tax returns).
- *Global company currency*—Global company currency is the currency that is used for an internal trading partner.

47. Are any FI documents created during purchase order (PO) creation? If yes, what is the entry?

During PO creation (using transaction code ME21N), no FI document will be created. However, in CO, there can be a commitment posting to a cost center according to configuration. The offsetting entry is posted at the time of GR.

48. There are many banks in a house bank. If a payment is to be made from a particular bank G/L account, how is it carried out?

There can be several accounts in one house bank. A house bank is represented by a house bank ID and a bank account is represented by an account ID. While creating the account ID, you are assigning a G/L account for outgoing payment. When making payment, you will select the house bank ID and account ID, which in turn determines from which G/L account payment will be disbursed.

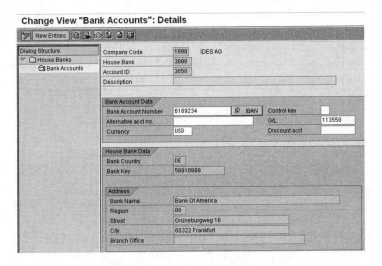

FIGURE 1.20   **House bank**

49. What is the difference between Account Assignment Model (AAM), recurring entries, and sample documents?

AAM: A reference for document entry that provides default values for posting business transactions. An AAM can contain any number of G/L account items and can be *changed or supplemented at any time*. Unlike sample documents, the G/L account items for AAMs may be incomplete.

Recurring entries: A periodically recurring posting will be made by the recurring entry program on the basis of recurring entry original documents. The procedure is comparable to a standing order by which banks are authorized to debit rent payments, payment contributions, or loan repayments.

Sample documents: A sample document is a special type of reference document. Data from this document is used to create default entries on the accounting document entry screen. Unlike an accounting document, a sample document does not update transaction figures but merely serves as a data source for an accounting document.

50. In the G/L master you have the options Only balances in local crcy and Account currency. What do these mean?

Account currency is the currency assigned to the G/L account. If you decide that you want to maintain company code currency, then you can post a transaction in any currency in that account. If you want to maintain separate currency for that G/L, note that there will be a difference because of the conversion rate.

Some G/L accounts can't be maintained on an open item basis and can't be in a foreign currency, such as clearing accounts or discount accounts, etc. In that case, you can specify Only balances in local crcy to show the balance in local currency.

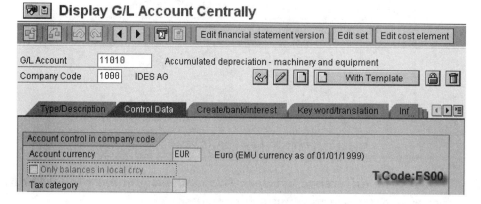

FIGURE 1.21   **G/L Account master**

51.   How many charts of account can be attached to a company code?

A maximum of three charts of account can be assigned to a company code: (1) operational COA, (2) group COA, and (3) country COA.

52.   What are substitutions and validations? What is the precedent?

Validations are used to check the presence of certain conditions. It returns a message if the prerequisite check condition is not met.

Substitutions are similar to validations. They actually replace and fill the field with values behind the scenes without the user's knowledge, unlike validations that create on-screen messages for the user.

53.   What are special periods used for?

The special periods in a fiscal year variant can be used for posting audit or tax adjustments to a closed fiscal year. The logic behind the use of special periods is to identify and have control over transactions after the closing of normal posting periods.

54.   What is a shortened fiscal year? When is it used?

A shortened fiscal year is a financial year that has fewer than 12 normal posting periods. This type of financial year is used for shifting an accounting period from one financial period to another financial period. For example, say Company X was following accounting period Apr xxxx to Mar xxxx+1, and has now decided to follow accounting period Jan xxxx to Dec xxxx. Now the current accounting period duration is only 9 months, i.e., from Apr xxxx to Dec xxxx, which is less than 12 months. This type of fiscal year is called a shortened fiscal year.

55.   What are posting periods?

A posting period is a period of time in which you are posting a transaction. It may be a month or a week. In the fiscal period configuration, you define how many posting period a company may have. A posting period controls both normal and special periods for each company code. It is possible to have a different posting period variant for each company code in the organization. The posting period is independent of the fiscal year variant.

56.   What are document types and what are they used for?

Document type is nothing but types of vouchers containing line items. Several business transactions can be identified within a particular document type. The document type controls:

- Document number ranges
- Header part of document
- Line item level of the document
- Filing of physical document

    Figure 1.22 shows the standard document types for SAP solutions.

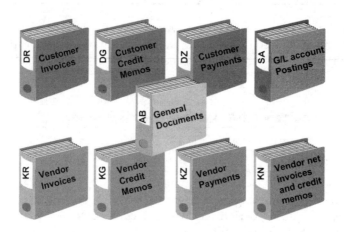

FIGURE 1.22   Document types

However, if SAP standard document types are not sufficient, you can create your own using transaction code OBA7.

57.   What is an employee's tolerance group? Where is it used?

An employee's tolerance group controls the amount that is to be posted. Tolerance groups are assigned to user IDs, which ensures that only authorized persons can make postings. By defining the employee's tolerance group, you are restricting employees from entering certain transactions for which they are not authorized. This basically controls who is authorized for what amount.

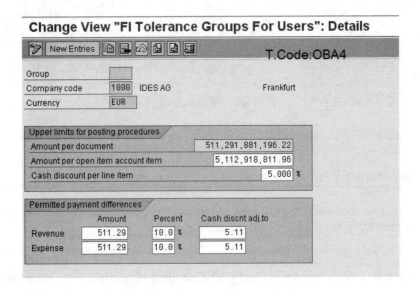

FIGURE 1.23   **User tolerance group**

An employee's tolerance group limit controls:

- Up to what amount per line item an employee can post
- Up to what amount per document an employee can post
- Allowable payment difference an employee can accept

58.   What are posting keys and what is the purpose of defining them?

Posting keys determine whether a line item entry is a debit or a credit, as well as the possible field status for the transaction. Posting keys are delivered in the SAP solution. If you want to change posting keys, such as making additional fields optional on payment type, the best possible action is to copy the posting key that needs to be modified and then modify it. Figure 1.24 shows the standard posting keys in SAP solutions.

Customers			Vendors			G/L	
01	11		21	31		40	50
02	12		22	32		80	90
03	13		23	33		81	91
04	14		24	34		83	93
05	15		25	35		84	94
06	16		26	36		85	95
07	17		27	37		86	96
08	18		28	38			
09	19		29	39			

FIGURE 1.24   Standard posting keys

59.   How many FSVs can be assigned to the company code?

There is no such restriction of assignment of FSV to company codes. You can assign as many FSVs as you want to the company code.

60.   What is a reconciliation ledger? Can you directly enter documents in that A/C?

Reconciliation ledgers are control ledgers of sub ledgers. When you post items to a subsidiary ledger, the system automatically posts the same data to the G/L. Each subsidiary ledger has one or more reconciliation accounts in the G/L. You can't use reconciliation accounts for direct postings. The sum of balances of sub ledgers will be equal to the total in the reconciliation ledgers.

61.   What are the segments of the G/L master record?

There are two segments in the G/L master: (1) COA segments and (2) company code segments. COA segments hold data that can be used by any company codes using the same COA. Company code segments contain information that is specific to a company code.

COA tabs are:

- Type/Description
- Keyword/Translation
- Information

Company code segment tabs are:

- Control Data
- Create/Bank/Interest
- Information

62. What are residual payment and part payment?

Residual payment: This clears the original invoice with the incoming amount and creates a new open line item for the remaining outstanding amount.

Part payment: This leaves the original invoice amount and creates a new line item for the incoming amount. In case of partial payment, both the original (invoice) entry and the payment entry will appear as open items.

These situations arise when you don't receive full payment against an invoice.

63. What are internal and external number ranges? Why is it generally not a good idea to have external numbering on transactions?

Internal number ranges: The document number will be generated by the system automatically in serial order and will allot the next available progressive number. This reduces the manual involvement of the user. The number must be numerical.

External number ranges: While entering a transaction, the document number needs to be keyed in by the end user. The system will not automatically insert a number in this case. The user can pick the number randomly. Note that it can be alphanumeric.

Maintain Number Range Intervals

📇 Interval	📇				

NR Object		Accounting document				

Intervals

No	Year	From number	To number	Current number	Ext	▦
01	1992	0100000000	0199999999	0	☐	
01	1993	0100000000	0199999999	0	☐	
01	1999	0100000000	0199999999	100013204	☐	
01	2000	0100000000	0199999999	100001663	☐	
01	2004	0100000000	0199999999	100013926	☐	
01	2005	0100000000	0199999999	100003609	☐	
01	2006	0100000000	0199999999	100000776	☐	
01	2007	0100000000	0199999999	100000000	☐	▲
01	2008	0100000000	0199999999	100000000	☐	▼

FIGURE 1.25   Using document number ranges

A number range can be either year dependent or year independent. In Figure 1.25, all the number ranges are year dependent. For year-dependent number ranges, you will define the document number range for each new accounting year as a year-end activity.

You can define a number range as year independent by keying 9999 in the Year column of a number range.

Entering the document number manually for each SAP financial posting is time consuming and risky for booked transactions. The transaction code for configuring the document number range is FBN1.

64.   What are the customization steps for cash journals?

The following steps are required for customizing cash journals:

1. Create a G/L account for cash journals (T-code FS00).
2. Define the document type for cash journals (T-code OBA7).
3. Define the number range intervals for cash journals (T-code FBCJC1).
4. Set up the cash journals (T-code FBCJ0).

5. Create, change, and delete business transactions (T-code FBCJ2).

6. Set up print parameters for the cash journals.

With transaction code FBCJ0, you are assigning G/L accounts to the cash journal. You can assign multiple cash journals to one G/L account where cash journal currencies are different. Otherwise, the assignment will be 1 to 1.

65. What is the main purpose of parking a document? Why would you use this?

Parking documents is used to temporarily park or store a document until it is approved by an authorized person. The following two cases demonstrate how a parked document is usually used:

1. When the end user has no authorization to enter a particular document like vendor payment, vendor invoice, etc., into the system, he can temporarily save the document in the system's memory.

2. When the end user doesn't have enough information, he can park documents in the system's memory until he has the information to complete the document.

The document number for the parked document will be generated in the same way as for a regular document. A parked document can be deleted from the system's memory if you feel that what you entered is wrong. Once you post the parked document into books of accounts as a normal document, the document number will become the regular document. The T-code for creating a parked document is F-65.

66. What is a baseline date? Where is it used? Can it be changed?

A baseline date is used to determine the due date of a line item, and is used for dunning programs, interest calculation, and automatic payment programs. You can configure the baseline date with T-code OBB8. The baseline date can be one of the following dates:

- Transaction date
- Posting date
- Document date
- Entry date

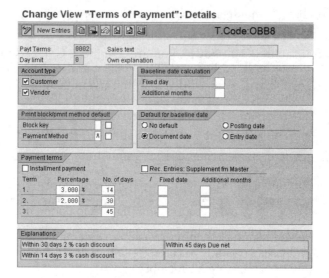

FIGURE 1.26   Payment terms

While entering a transaction, the baseline date is automatically populated from the payment terms; however, you can change it by entering another date.

67.   What is a special G/L transaction?

Special G/L transactions are transactions that are not normal business transactions with your business partners. These are generally shown in different control ledgers and are not grouped with the normal transactions. They include bills of exchange, down payments, bank guarantees, and provisions for doubtful debts.

68.   Why do you use special-purpose ledgers (SPLs)?

SPLs are used for customer-defined ledgers, and contain information for reporting purposes. The customer-defined ledger can be used as the G/L or as a sub ledger and may contain the account assignments desired. The account assignments can be either SAP dimensions from various applications or customer-defined dimensions. You can use the SPL for statutory reporting or management reporting purposes. It also helps in doing single-entry, adjustment posting, such as income tax depreciation.

69. After entering a document, can you delete the entry? Can you change the document? Which fields cannot be changed?

After posting a document, you cannot delete the document. However, you can change certain fields like cost objectives, reference texts, etc.

70. Why and when would you use business areas?

Business areas in SAP solutions are used to differentiate transactions originating from different points/lines/locations in business. Take a look at an example:

Company ABC has three company codes. These three company codes are doing similar business selling TVs and laptops but on different continents. Now ABC wants to have a balance sheet and P&L account based on products. In this case, ABC will create a product-wise business area, which will solve its requirement.

The advantages of using the business area are:

■ You can use these business areas if other company codes require the same business areas.

■ The configuration is simpler, as in the case of the company code, you would be required to go through the entire configuration of creating COAs, fiscal year variants, posting period variants, and so on. With the business area option, you just need to attach it to the company code and the rest of the details in the business area are attached by default from the company code you are using it in.

■ Using the options in CO (Enterprise CO, Profit Center Accounting [EC-PCA]), you can even draw up balance sheets and PL statements for the business areas.

This example demonstrates when the company wants to separate entries according to the lines of business it operates. Another case could be when the company wants to find out the profitability of its operations in various cities and differentiates these cities into business areas.

71.   How does FI-MM integration take place? Please explain in detail.

FI-MM integration is how the G/L account will be updated when you are carrying an inventory-related transaction. For convenience, you may divide the process into three areas: (1) Organization structure dependent, (2) material master dependent, and (3) transaction dependent. Account determination will be carried out depending upon these three factors.

Organization structure dependent:

- *Valuation level*—It is an organization structure, which determines at which level valuation will be done for material. Valuation can be done at plant level or company code level. Valuation must be at plant level if you want to use the application component PP or Costing, or if the system is an SAP Retail system. The decision you make is valid for the entire client. It is recommended that you set material valuation at plant level.

- *Valuation area*—The valuation area is a component of valuation level. Suppose you have created the valuation level at the plant level and there are several plants at the company code level; each plant is a valuation area for the purpose of inventory.

- *Valuation grouping code*—The valuation grouping code is a set of valuation areas that are grouped together for the purposes of accounting. Through the account determination process, it will be related to the COA. The valuation grouping code makes it easier to set automatic account determination. Within the COA, you assign the same valuation grouping code to the valuation areas you want to assign to the same account. Valuation grouping codes either reflect a fine distinction within a COA or correspond to a COA. Within a COA, you can use the valuation grouping code.

Material master dependent:

- *Valuation class*—This is the assignment of a material to a group of G/L accounts. Along with other factors, the valuation class determines the G/L accounts that are updated as a result of valuation-relevant transactions or events, such as a goods movement. The valuation class makes it possible to:

  - Post stock values of materials of the same material type to different G/L accounts

  - Post stock values of materials of different material types to the same G/L account

- *Material type*—This groups together materials with the same basic attributes, such as raw materials, semifinished products, or finished products. When creating a material master record, you must assign the material to a material type. The material type you choose determines:
    - Whether the material is intended for a specific purpose, such as a configurable material or process material
    - Whether the material number can be assigned internally or externally
- *Account category reference*—The account category reference is a combination of valuation classes. Exactly one account category reference is assigned to a material type. The link between the valuation classes and the material types is set up via the account category reference. In the standard system, an account reference is created for each material type. The account category reference is in turn assigned to exactly one valuation class. This means that each material type has its own valuation class.

Transaction Dependent:

- *Movement types*—This is a classification key indicating the type of material movement (for example, goods receipt, goods issue, or physical stock transfer). The movement type enables the system to find predefined posting rules determining how accounts of a financial accounting system (stock and consumption accounts) are to be posted and how the stock fields in the material master record are to be updated.
- *Transaction/Event key*—This is a key allowing the user to differentiate between the various transactions and events (such as physical inventory transactions and goods movements) that occur within the field of inventory management. The transaction/event type controls the filing/storage of documents and the assignment of document numbers. Some important transaction keys are BSX, GBB, and WRX.

Using the organization dependent, material master dependent, and transaction dependent areas, you determine the inventory management requirements, which are:

- Whether changes in quantity are updated in the material master record.
- Whether changes in value are also updated in the stock accounts in financial accounting.

FI-MM integration mapping is stored in table T030. For a better understanding, use transaction code SE16.

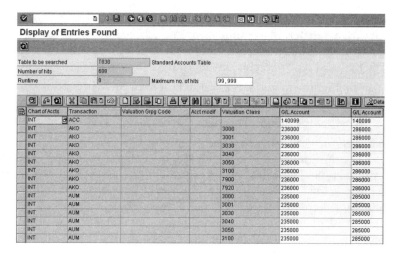

Display of Entries Found

Table to be searched	T030	Standard Accounts Table
Number of hits	608	
Runtime	0	Maximum no. of hits 99,999

Chart of Accts	Transaction	Valuation Grpg Code	Acct modif	Valuation Class	G/L Account	G/L Account
INT	ACC				140099	140099
INT	AKO			3000	236000	286000
INT	AKO			3001	236000	286000
INT	AKO			3030	236000	286000
INT	AKO			3040	236000	286000
INT	AKO			3050	236000	286000
INT	AKO			3100	236000	286000
INT	AKO			7900	236000	286000
INT	AKO			7920	236000	286000
INT	AUM			3000	235000	285000
INT	AUM			3001	235000	285000
INT	AUM			3030	235000	285000
INT	AUM			3040	235000	285000
INT	AUM			3050	235000	285000
INT	AUM			3100	235000	285000

FIGURE 1.27   **Table T030**

Figure 1.27 shows how G/L accounts are assigned to various combinations of MM transactions.

72.   What does the FSG assigned to the G/L master record control?

It controls what fields are displayed at the time the G/L master is created. Specifically, the FSG controls whether or not particular fields need to be filled. The available options are: Required, Optional, and Suppressed.

73.   What is a house bank, bank key, bank ID, and account ID?

A **house bank** represents a branch of a bank or a bank itself. A house bank may consist of more than one account.

A **bank key** is a unique key used by a bank for the transfer of money from one bank to another online. Each key represents a particular bank branch. Generally, you will use SWIFT codes as the bank key.

A **Bank ID** is an ID for house banks that the company code uses for transacting business.

An **Account ID** represents a particular account at a particular branch. Let us assume you have three accounts at the ICICI Bank Vashi, Mumbai. In this situation, the house bank will be ICICI Bank, Vashi, Mumbai. Individual accounts represent an account ID.

74. How do you identify a document? How many line items can one document have?

A document is identified through the company code, document type, and document number. Every document in FI must have at least 2 line items, with a maximum of 999 line items. However, this limitation has been removed in SAP ECC 6.0.

75. What are some examples of standard document types?

The standard document types provided in SAP solutions are: SA—General entry, DA—Customer document, KA—Vendor document, DZ—Customer payment, and KZ—Vendor payment. You can create new document types using T-code OBA7.

76. How do you control document line item fields?

The document line item fields are controlled through the field status group assigned to the G/L master and the field status of posting keys.

77. Can several companies use one posting variant?

Yes, since the posting period is a variant that can be used by one or more company code. If one posting period variant is used by several company codes, they should follow the same opening and closing of posting periods.

78. What is a tolerance group?

A tolerance group is a variant that restricts the user from posting certain transactions that they are not authorized to do. On the other side, a tolerance limit for customers and vendors determines what variations would be allowed while clearing an open item. There are four types of tolerance group: (1) employee tolerance, (2) G/L account tolerance limit, (3) customer tolerance limit, and (4) vendor tolerance limit.

79. When the currency of the cash journals are the same, is it possible to attach more than one cash journal to one G/L account?

No. When cash journal currencies are the same, you must assign a separate G/L account for each cash journal. However, when cash journal currencies are different, you can use one G/L account for more than one cash journal.

80.   How do you reverse cleared documents?

A cleared document cannot be reversed until you make it an open item. To reverse a clear document, follow these steps:

1. Reset and reverse the cleared document by breaking the document relationships and reversing it. The path is: Accounting → Financial Accounting → C/L → Document → Reset Cleared items. (Use T-code FBRA.)

2. If you have cleared the open item through an automatic payment program, you need to execute T-code FCH8.

81.   Can you configure cash discount terms?

Yes, this is configurable through payment terms. While configuring payment terms, you will define the cash discount if payment is made within the defined date. You can configure payment terms using T-code OBB8.

82.   What is a parked document and a held document? What are the differences between the two?

Held document: When a user is posting a document and does not have the requisite data in his possession, he can hold the document until he gets all of the information. When a user holds the document, the system will ask to assign a number to it for easy identification. This number can be numeric or alphanumeric.

Parked document: When the user does not have authorization for posting a document, he can prepare the document and park it for his superior to approve. When it is approved, the posting of the document will be completed.

In the case of a holding document, the FI document *may be incomplete* in respect to debits = credits, while a parking document is a complete document by itself.

In both cases, the G/L account balances will not be affected until the document is posted.

83.   What additional setup is required if more than one cash journal is maintained in a location?

These are the additional steps required if an entity wants to have more than one cash journal:

- Creation of a cash journal G/L account: An additional cash G/L account is required if you want to maintain more than one cash journal in the same currency.
- Cash journal setup: This is where you assign the document type of the G/L account to the cash journal.

84. Explain the document currency and local currency fields when posting a document in SAP FI.

Document currency is the currency in which transactions are carried out by the entity. It may or may not be the company code currency or local currency. Let us assume the company code currency is USD, and you are posting a transaction in INR (the currency code for Indian Rupees). If document currency is different from company code currency (local currency), the document currency will be translated into local currency. However, it is possible to overwrite the system proposed values manually.

85. What configurations steps are required for a special-purpose ledger?

These are the following steps for a special-purpose ledger:

1. *Define table group (T-code GCIN)IMG menu path*—Financial Accounting → Special Purpose Ledger → Basic Settings → Tables → Definition → Define Table Group
2. *Maintain field movement (T-code GCF2)IMG menu path*—Financial Accounting → Special Purpose Ledger → Basic Settings → Master Data → Maintain Field Movements
3. *Maintain ledger for statutory ledger (T-code GCL2)IMG menu path*—Financial Accounting → Special Purpose Ledger → Basic Settings → Master Data → Maintain Ledgers → Copy Ledger
4. *Assign company code (T-code GCB3)IMG menu path*—Financial Accounting → Special Purpose Ledger → Basic Settings → Master Data → Maintain Company Codes → Copy Company Code Assignments
5. *Assign activities (T-code GCV3)IMG menu path*—Financial Accounting → Special Purpose Ledger → Basic Settings → Master Data → Maintain Activities → Display Activity
6. *Define versions (T-code GCW1)IMG menu path*—Financial Accounting → Special Purpose Ledger → Periodic Processing → Currency Translation → Define Versions

7. *Set up exchange rate type (T-code OC47) IMG menu path*—Financial Accounting → Special Purpose Ledger → Periodic Processing → Currency Translation → Set Up Exchange Rate Type

8. *Create number ranges (T-code GC04) IMG menu path*—Financial Accounting → Special Purpose Ledger → Actual Posting → Number Ranges → Maintain Local Number Ranges

9. *Create currency translation document type (T-code GCBX) IMG menu path*—Financial Accounting → Special Purpose Ledger → Actual Posting → Maintain Valid Document Type

10. *Create posting period variant (T-code GCP1) IMG menu path*—Financial Accounting → Special Purpose Ledger → Actual Posting → Posting Period → Maintain Local Posting Period

86.   What is normal reversal and negative reversal?

To correct an incorrect posting, mySAP ERP Financial provides two types of reversal: (1) normal reversal and (2) negative reversal.

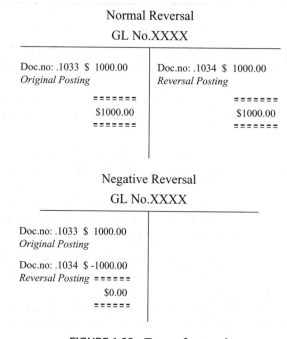

FIGURE 1.28   Types of reversal

Normal reversal: In normal reversal, mySAP ERP Financial posts the reversal document on the opposite side of the original entry. In Figure 1.28, document 1033 is the original posting, which is corrected by reversal through document 1034. This functionality does not suit the legal requirements of some countries.

Negative reversal: In negative reversal, the accounting entry is posted on the same side as the original entry with the opposite sign.

The net effect in both cases is the same. The account balance that is increased by the original posting will be reduced by the reversal posting, and vice versa.

87. Explain the reversal process in SAP solutions.

Various business situations may arise that compel a company to correct accounting documents. As you are aware, SAP R/3 and mySAP ERP Financial don't allow the deletion of an accounting entry. The only way to correct accounting entries is to reverse the incorrect accounting documents. You can reverse FI accounting document only when:

- The document that is to be reversed originated in FI.
- All additional assignments are valid at the time of reversal, i.e., cost centers, business areas, etc.
- The document to be reversed has not yet cleared.
- The FI documents are not generated through IDOCs that came from external systems.
- The accounting documents are related to G/L, AP, and AR.

During reversal, the SAP solution will create a reversal document according to the reversal document type set for the original document type. For audit tracking, you will find a reference to the reversal document number in the original document header; similarly, the reversal document header will include the original document number.

88. What is a noted item in the SAP solution?

A noted item is a special G/L transaction meant for informational purposes. A noted item reminds user groups of potential payment and creates a one-sided entry. Other advantages of noted items are access to these transactions from automatic payment programs and dunning programs.

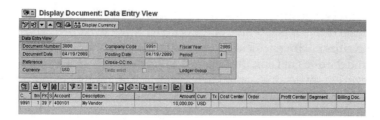

FIGURE 1.29   Noted item entry

Noted items will not update the G/L account, will not have a zero balance check, and will have a single-item account assignment. Examples of noted items include bills of exchange requests and down payment requests.

1.5 ACCOUNTS PAYABLE (FI-AP)

89.   How is the due date of a document calculated?

The due date is determined through default payment terms entered in the business partner's master data and setting a baseline date for payment terms. Payment terms can be configured through T-codes OBB8 and OBB9.

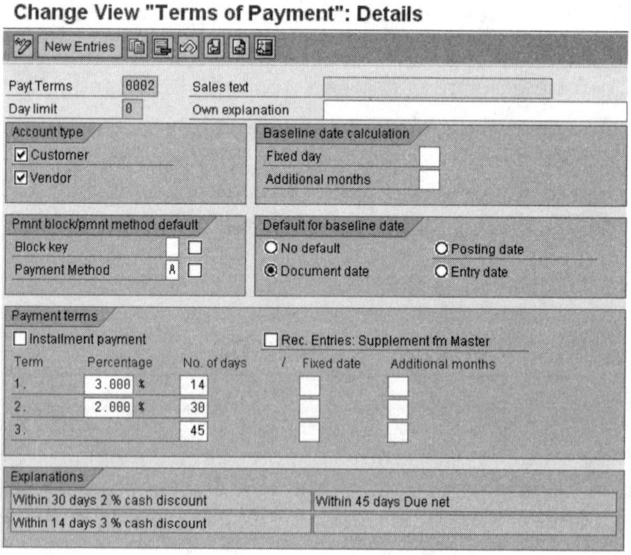

FIGURE 1.30   Due date calculation

In Figure 1.30, your baseline date will be the document date. So the due date will be the baseline (i.e., document date) + number of days (i.e., 45). For example, while posting a transaction you enter your document date as 05/01/2009. Then your due date will be 05/01/2009 + 45 days, which is 06/15/2009.

90.   What is an automatic payment program? What are the steps to configure it?

An automatic payment program is a program through which you are able to pay and generate checks for all vendors/customers you owe as per payment terms. This can be configured through T-code FBZP.

Follow these configuration steps while you customize payment terms:

1. All company codes you are defining parameters for
   a. Company code that processes payment
   b. Intercompany payment relationship
   c. Cash discount amount and percentage
   d. Tolerance days for payments
   e. Customer and vendor Special G/L transaction to be processed

2. Paying company code
   a. Minimum amount for incoming and outgoing payment
   b. Specification for bills of exchange
   c. Forms for payment advice and electronic data interchange (EDI) format

3. Payment method per country
   a. Types of payment method allowed at country level
   b. Master data lookup for payment processing
   c. Document type to be used for payment
   d. Currencies allowed for this payment method

4. Payment method per company code
   a. Minimum and maximum payment amount at company code level for a payment method
   b. Whether or not foreign payment is allowed
   c. What foreign currencies are allowed for payment
   d. Bank and postal code optimization

5. Bank determination
   a. *Ranking*—The order in which payments will be processed
   b. *Amount*—Available amount for payment
   c. *Account*—G/L account to which posting will be made for payment
   d. *Expenses and charges*—Account to be posted to if any expenses are incurred while processing payment
   e. *Value date*—Relevant for cash management module

91. What are the steps for configuration of withholding tax?

You need to configure the following steps for extended withholding tax:
- Define withholding tax types—Invoice posting
- Define withholding tax types—Payments posting
- Define withholding tax codes for withholding tax types
- Define recipient types
- Assign withholding tax types to company
- Define accounts for withholding tax
- Activate the withholding tax code and type to the company code
- Assign the withholding tax type to the vendor

92. What journal entries are passed in the system from the time of good receipt until payment is made to the vendor?

In a simple business scenario, you will pass the following accounting entries from the time of goods receipt until payment to vendor.

1. Transaction code MIGO

Material Account	debit
GR/IR Account	credit

2. Transaction code MIRO

GR/IR Account	debit
Vendor Account	credit

3. Transaction code F-28

Vendor Account	debit
Bank Account	credit

93. What is a GR/IR account? Why is it maintained?

A GR/IR account represents goods receipts and invoice receipts. This is a clearing account that is maintained to nullify the time difference between goods receipts and invoice receipts from the business partner. The balance in the GR/IR account increases because of the following:

- If the quantity received is less than the quantity invoiced. The system then expects further goods receipts for this purchase order in order to clear this balance.
- If the quantity received is more than the quantity invoiced. The system then expects further invoices for this purchase order to clear this balance.

94. What is the difference between withholding taxes and extended withholding taxes?

The differences between the classic withholding tax and extended withholding tax are described in Table 1.2.

Individual Function	Classic	Extended
Withholding tax on outgoing payment	Yes	Yes
TDS on incoming payment	Yes	
TDS at the time of invoice	Yes	Yes
TDS on partial payment		Yes
No. of withholding tax from each document	Max 1	Several
TDS basis—Net amount		Yes
Gross amount		Yes
Tax amount		Yes

TABLE 1.2   Comparison of withholding taxes

95.   What are segments in the vendor master?

A vendor master contains three segments, which control different fields for a vendor. These are:

- General data segment: This segment holds a common set of data applicable for all company code.
- Company code segment: These are company code specific data that can't be shared with other company code.
- Purchase organization segment: Like company code data, this segment contains specific purchase organization data.

96.   If a document type is configured for a vendor, can you use that document type in the line item posting key meant for a customer?

With T-code OBA7 you are defining the document type. While configuring the document type, you are defining the type of account to which it will post. If the document type is defined only for vendors and you are using it for a customer, the system will not allow us to post to the customer. Hence, the document can't be posted for a customer.

97.   What do you test in an automatic payment program? How is it done and what type of errors are you likely to get?

Use T-code F110 to test the payment program.

1. Enter data in the Parameters tab.
2. Save.
3. Edit the proposal and press **Enter**. The proposal will be completed.
4. Display the proposal.
5. Any errors will show under Exceptions.

If there is an exception, check the logs that the system displays to see what you have not done. If everything is correct, the system will show an amount in place of Exceptions.

Then you need to run the payment.

Remember that you can edit or delete the proposal before the payment is run.

Any errors may be because you have not defined the payment method in the vendor master, the vendor may be blocked for posting, or the line item might have blocked the payment.

98. What settings do you need to adjust before running the automatic payment program?

There are five steps for running the automatic payment program:

1. *Status*—In this tab page, the system will provide a message about the current status of the payment program.

2. *Parameters*—This tab page holds important parameters for the automatic payment program. These are (1) Posting date, (2) Document entered up to, (3) Company code, (4) Payment method, (5) Next payment date, and (6) Vendor or Customer numbers.

3. *Free selection*—In this tab page, you can enter additional parameters to search in the automatic payment program.

4. *Additional log*—With the help of the additional log, you can define additional information for the automatic payment program.

5. *Print out data medium*—In this tab page, you enter a variant name for the house bank. You also define the house bank, account ID, check lot, and print medium.

99. What are sensitive fields with reference to customer and vendor masters? How do they work?

Sensitive fields are a set of vendor or customer master data fields that you fill in but should not be altered frequently. In some businesses, any changes that affect these sensitive fields need to be verified by someone other than the person who makes the changes.

If you define a field in the vendor master record as "sensitive," the corresponding vendor account is blocked for payment if the entry is changed. The block is removed when a second person with authorization checks the change and confirms or rejects it.

The block will occur at the time of automatic payment program (APP) only and not for manual payments through transaction code F-53.

100. You have four house banks. The end user has to use the third bank (rank order) only for check payments. Can you make payments through the third house bank? If so, how is it possible?

Customize the priority as 1 for the third house bank. Otherwise, while posting the invoice, you can specify the house bank from which you intend to make the payment.

101. What are the steps for linking customers and vendors?

When the customer is also a vendor, or the vendor is also a customer, you need to follow these steps:

1. Create the customer master and vendor master records.

2. Assign a customer account number in the vendor master record and a vendor account number in the customer master record.

3. In the customer master record in the company code data segment, select the Payment Transactions tab, and then select the check box labeled Clearing with Vendor.

4. In the vendor master record in the company code data segment, select the Payment Transactions tab, and then select the check box labeled Clrg with Cust.

5. Now when you try to clear using T-codes F-28 or F-53, it will show all of the transactions related to vendor and customer. You can just pay the balance amount after net off transaction between vendor and customer.

102. How do you make an advance payment to a vendor through the APP?

You need to use a down payment request to a vendor. This will create a noted item in the vendor, which you need to include with the APP. This will post the advance to the vendor as a special G/L transaction.

There are two steps to make an advance payment to a vendor:

1. Create a down payment request through T-code F-47.

2. Post the down payment through T-code F110 (APP). The system will pay for all down payment requests by check or bank transfer.

103. How can you clear two general ledgers?

You can clear two general ledgers through transaction code F-04 (posting with clearing), provided both general accounts are open item managed accounts.

104. Is it possible to update the reference field in the header of a payment document when the check numbers are generated by the system? If so, what is the procedure to do it?

Using T-code FCHU, fill out the company code, house bank, and account ID, and provide the check number and payment document number for which you want to update the check number. In the Target field selection for the check number section, select the field for which you want to update the check number and execute.

105. What is an alternative payee?

The payment program can make payment to a vendor other than the one to which the invoice was posted. The payment is made to an alternative payee, which must be specified in the master record.

You can specify an alternative payee in the general data area or in the company code data area of a vendor master. The alternative payee specified in the general data area is used by every company code. If you specify an alternative payee in both areas, the specification in the company code area has priority.

To always make vender payments to an alternative payee, proceed as follows:

1. Create a vendor master record for the alternative payee. Block this account from posting.

2. Specify the account number of the alternative payee in the Alternative payee field within the payment transactions section of the vendor master record.

3. When making payments for this vendor, the payment program will always access the name and address of the alternative payee.

In some instances, it may be better to specify a payee in the document. To do this, you have to activate this function by selecting the payee in the document indicator in the general data area of the Payment Transaction tab. When you enter documents for this account, the system displays a field in which you can enter an alternative payee.

The system always uses the payee that is most specific. This means that when you enter a payee in a document, it has priority over payees specified in the master record.

106. How can you prevent a duplicate vendor master from being created?

A check for duplicates can be configured to prevent the creation of more than one master record for the same vendor. This check is configured on address match code fields and occurs when creating new accounts or when changing the address on an existing account.

107. Your client indicates they would like to allow for alphanumeric number ranges on vendor accounts. What type of number range would you recommend? Why?

The only number range that can be alphanumeric is the external number range. An internal number range, on the other hand, can only be numeric and is automatically assigned by the system.

1.6 ACCOUNTS RECEIVABLE (FI-AR)

108. What is dunning? What is a dunning level?

Dunning means notifying business partners of their overdue outstanding balance. A dunning level determines how often an account will be dunned.

109. What factors differentiate one dunning level from another dunning level?

The most important point that differentiates dunning levels is the dunning texts. The dunning text defines the urgency of the dunning notice. Other differentiating factors are dunning charges, minimum and maximum amounts, etc.

110. What is the maximum number of dunning levels that can be created?

There is a maximum of eight dunning levels for a business partner—excluding the legal dunning level.

111. Explain the steps of dunning configuration.

Use T-code FBMP to define the dunning configuration. In the dunning procedure, you are defining the following:

- Dunning parameters
- Dunning levels
- Charges
- Minimum amount
- Dunning texts
- SPL G/L indicators

Besides the preceding settings, the following optional steps may need to be configured according to the requirements:

- Define dunning areas (T-code OB61)
- Define dunning keys (T-code OB17)
- Define dunning block reason (T-code OB18)
- Define dunning groupings (T-code OBAQ)
- Define interest rates

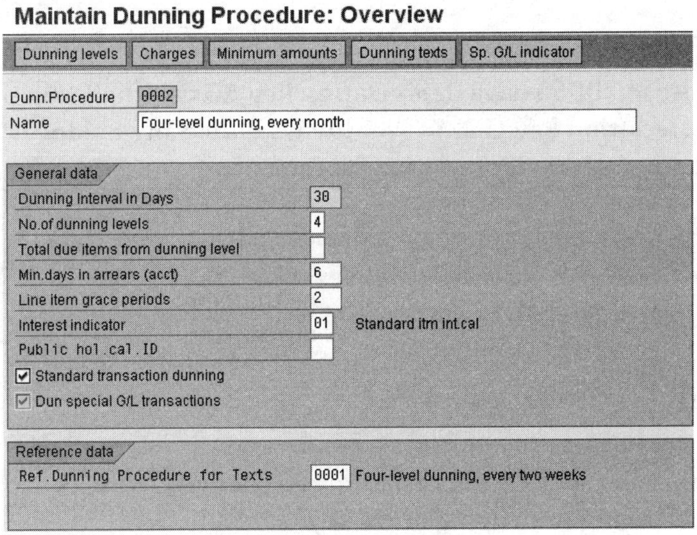

Maintain Dunning Procedure: Overview

| Dunning levels | Charges | Minimum amounts | Dunning texts | Sp. G/L indicator |

Dunn.Procedure   0002
Name   Four-level dunning, every month

General data

Dunning Interval in Days	30
No.of dunning levels	4
Total due items from dunning level	
Min.days in arrears (acct)	6
Line item grace periods	2
Interest indicator	01 Standard itm int.cal
Public hol.cal.ID	
☑ Standard transaction dunning	
☑ Dun special G/L transactions	

Reference data

Ref.Dunning Procedure for Texts   0001 Four-level dunning, every two weeks

FIGURE 1.31   Dunning procedure

112. What is a sub ledger? How is it linked to the G/L?

A sub ledger is a subsidiary ledger, which holds detailed transactions about the G/L. It is linked to G/L accounts through assignment of reconciliation accounts in the master. For example, Company X is dealing with 100 customers. The individual ledgers of these customers are called as sub ledgers. The reconciliation account attached to these 100 customers is the main ledger to these sub ledgers.

113. Why do you use "bank type" in customer/vendor master records?

The bank type is used to identify the bank through which the customer or vendor will carry out the transaction. This field is also important from the point of view of an automatic payment program. For example, Vendor X supplies materials and services. Vendor X also maintains two separate bank accounts, one for services and another one for materials. The vendor requests that payments for services be remitted to his bank account that is meant for services. In this circumstance, you may select the appropriate bank account when posting a transaction.

1.7 FI-AA

114. Suppose in 2005 I have depreciation key AB and in 2006 I have changed to depreciation key CD. In what ways would my balances be affected, e.g., accumulated depreciation, assets, etc.?

Changes in depreciation are required under varied circumstances, such as changes in law, etc. A new depreciation key certainly has an effect on the depreciation rate, the accumulated depreciation account, and the depreciation expenses account. The difference in the depreciation that was already posted with the old depreciation key and what should be posted with the new depreciation key will be posted in the current accounting period.

115. How do you calculate depreciation retroactively from its acquisition date after changing the depreciation key?

After changing the depreciation key in the asset master depreciation area, you have to execute T-code AFAB (Depreciation Run) and select the Repeat Run radio button. In the repeat run, the system posts changes to depreciation, as compared to the depreciation amounts from the previous run.

116. What is an asset class?

An asset class is the main criterion for classifying fixed assets according to legal and management requirements. The asset class controls parameters and default values for asset masters. Each asset master record must be assigned to one asset class.

117. How do you process fixed asset depreciation?

Every asset transaction immediately causes a change to the forecast depreciation. General ledgers are updated only when you run depreciation through transaction code: AFAB. It is always advisable to run depreciation in test mode to know whether any errors exist or not. Once you are satisfied with the test result, you can run depreciation in update mode/production mode. During update mode, plan or forecast depreciation and post to the general ledger along with interest and revaluation, if any.

When the system posts depreciation, it creates collective documents. It does not create separate documents for each asset.

The depreciation posting run is done via transaction code AFAB. The depreciation program creates batch input sessions for posting depreciation and interest to the G/L accounts in financial accounting and/or to CO.

118. What is an asset master? What does it control for sub asset masters?

An asset master represents the master record and information about a particular asset. According to the screen layout of the asset master, it controls the following for sub assets:

- Sub assets master number assignment
- Assignment of the depreciation key
- Determination of life of assets
- Determination of assignment of group asset

119. How many depreciation areas can be defined for a company code?

Depreciation areas are not defined for company codes. Rather, depreciation areas are defined for a chart of depreciation (COD). While creating asset management company code, you are assigning a COD to company code. Once you assign a COD to company code, all depreciation areas created in the COD will be available to the assigned company code. A maximum of 99 depreciation areas can be maintained for a COD.

120. What are the types of depreciation methods?

The following depreciation methods are used in AA:

- *Base method.*
- *Decline value method.*
- *Maximum method*—In this method, you define your maximum depreciation amount for a particular fiscal year.
- *Multilevel method*—This method helps to determine the validity of a particular depreciation rate. For example, an appropriate depreciation for assets is 5% for the first five years, and after that the depreciation rate will be 7.5% for the rest of the periods.
- *Period control method*—This determines the depreciation start date and end date of asset transactions. In this method, you determine the effective start date and end of depreciation calculation for (1) acquisition, (2) subsequent acquisitions/ postcapitalization, (3) intracompany transfers, and (4) retirements.

121. How do you upload assets in SAP solutions without creating single assets through T-code AS01?

These are possible ways of uploading the assets master:

- A legacy upload can happen through T-code AS100 (using XL), but here the group assets (used for tax purposes) future cannot be used.
- If group assets are required, using the BDC approach ensures that the legacy group assets are created prior to upload.
- For current year acquisition, use T-code ABZON.

122. What is AA company code?

Once you have assigned a COD to a company code, that company code is called AA company code.

123. What are depreciation areas?

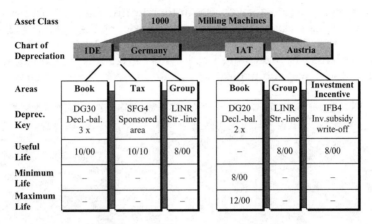

FIGURE 1.32   Depreciation areas

Depreciation areas are used to calculate depreciation values of assets. Different kinds of depreciation areas are created to take care of different kinds of legal and management requirements. SAP software provides different depreciation areas according to country-specific COD. Figure 1.33 shows the U.S.A COD.

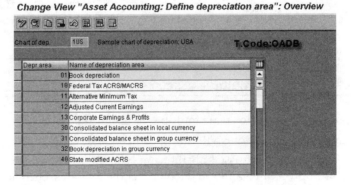

FIGURE 1.33   Depreciation areas

124. Is it possible to create an asset class automatically?

Yes, you can generate asset classes automatically. There are two ways to do so:
(1) create an asset class with reference to an existing asset class or (2) generate an
asset class through the asset class transaction code ANKL.

In the latter case, executing T-code ANKL gives you predefined steps to follow
and the system will automatically generate an asset class for each G/L account.

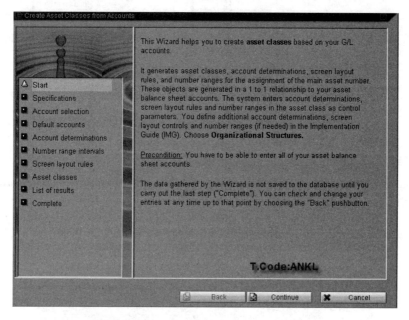

FIGURE 1.34 Automatic creation of asset classes

125. How can you create multiple assets?

There are various ways to create multiple assets for the same assets class:

- Create assets one by one with transaction code AS01.
- If the attributes of the assets are the same, you can create similar assets by enter-
  ing the appropriate values in the Number of similar assets fields.
- You can create a BDC session.

Of the preceding methods, if you want to create more than one asset of a similar kind, the second option is the best one. For example, say you have purchased three laptops and you want to create three assets (all of which are laptops).

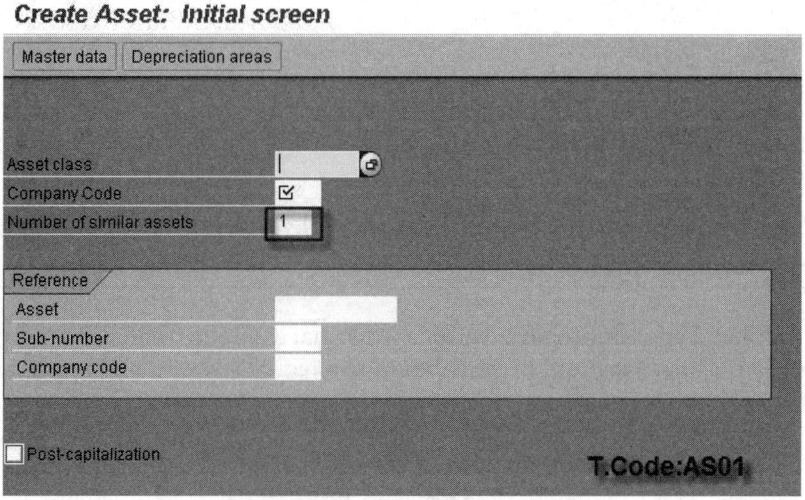

Create Asset: Initial screen

| Master data | Depreciation areas |

Asset class

Company Code ☑

Number of similar assets 1

Reference

Asset

Sub-number

Company code

☐ Post-capitalization

T.Code:AS01

FIGURE 1.35   **Asset master creation**

126. Explain various ways to acquire assets and the corresponding accounting entries.

Assets can be acquired in the following ways:

1. Outright Purchase: This is the common way for purchase of an asset. In case of outright purchase, you can acquire an asset from your supplier.

2. Assets Under Construction: These are assets that clients generate or build within their environment, i.e., construction of building, plant, and machinery.

3. Intercompany Transfer: Someone's company code transfers certain assets to another company code within a corporate group.

In all these cases accounting entries differ from others.

1. Outright Purchase:

    Debit Assets $

    Credit Vendor $

2. Assets Under Construction (AUC):

    Debit AUC $

    Credit Vendor $

3. Intercompany Transfer:

    Debit Assets $

    Credit Company $

127. Explain various ways assets may be retired and the related accounting entries.

The following chart provides various ways that assets are retired. To retire an asset, one of the following options may be considered.

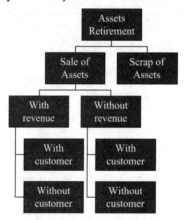

FIGURE 1.36   Asset retirement

128. What is acquisition and production cost (APC)?

Acquisition means any asset that you can acquire or purchase externally. It includes invoice price and other related expenses associated with it, like customs or freight, which you add to arrive at a total cost of acquisition for capitalization of the asset.

Production cost means any asset that is created internally within the organization. This is normally created by means of Assets Under Construction (AUC), and you go on adding cost to the AUC as you incur expenses for the same, such as an addition to the office building. Therefore, APC includes any external acquisition or internal construction expenses that need to be capitalized.

129. Explain the assets organization structure from company code to sub-assets.

The assets organization structure consists of the FI organization structure plus asset management configuration steps. Assigning a COA to company code is the first step toward creating an assets organization structure.

In asset management, you define account determination, which in turn is assigned to the G/L account. Sub-assets are created under assets, which in turn are sub-units of the asset class. The asset class is assigned to the account determination. Figure 1.37 depicts the assets organization structure.

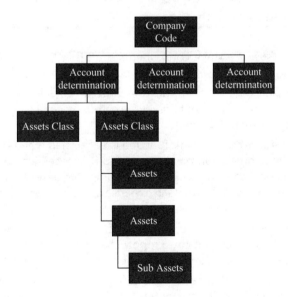

FIGURE 1.37   **Assets organization structure**

130. How do you reverse depreciation posting?

You can't reverse a depreciation posting run. Reversing posted depreciation occurs when there is a change in the depreciation parameters.

SAP solutions provide the functionality to take care of this situation. For instance, after depreciation posting you will know that there is change in the useful lives of your assets or change in the depreciation keys assigned to your assets. Asset transactions such as retirements and transfers also affect the plan. After necessary changes in configuration, you need to perform the recalculation procedure. Once you perform the recalculation procedure, the SAP solution will take care of changed parameters and recalculate depreciation from the start of the asset's life.

The difference will be posted, thereby bringing the assets in line with the plan. The only exception to this is if you change the cost center assigned to an asset. The depreciation expense is never reposted, so if you need to correct that, you have to do it with a manual adjustment in the depreciation expense accounts.

131. Which activities should be done before the production startup? Give a brief description of each of them.

1. *Check consistency*—Major components configured, e.g., COD, company codes, depreciation areas, asset classes, asset G/L accounts, and AA customizing.

2. *Reset company code*—Test application data can be deleted (asset master records and transactions of AA) but only if the company code has a test status. Customized settings are not deleted.

3. *Reset posted depreciation*—This function is performed when errors occurred while testing the depreciation posting run and it is necessary to return to the original status (includes depreciation data of an old assets data transfer). Manual adjustments in the relevant G/L expense and depreciation accounts need to be performed. The reset is possible only for a company code in a test status.

4. *Set/reset reconciliation accounts*—The G/L accounts relevant for AA are defined as reconciliation accounts by a report changing their master records. After the data transfer, these accounts can no longer be directly posted to.

5. *Transfer balances*—Balances to the G/L accounts, which have been defined as reconciliation accounts, are transferred (old data at fiscal year end).

6. *Activate company code*—This function terminates the production startup.

132. Describe the asset history sheet.

The asset history sheet is the most important and most comprehensive year-end report or intermediate report. It displays the various stages of a fixed asset's history—from the opening balance through the closing balance—including any acquisitions, retirements, or accumulated depreciation. SAP solutions supply country-specific versions of the sheet. It is often a required appendix to the balance sheet.

133. What is periodic processing, and what is it used for in AA?

Periodic processing comprises the tasks that must be performed at periodic intervals. Since only the values from one depreciation area can be automatically posted online in FI, the changes to asset values (transactions) from other areas with automatic postings have to be posted periodically to the appropriate reconciliation accounts. Period processing includes posting acquisition production cost (APC) to depreciation areas other than book depreciation areas and depreciation posting/interest posting for all other depreciation areas.

134. What are the three direct types of depreciation that are supported by the system?

Ordinary depreciation is the planned reduction in asset value due to normal wear and tear. Therefore, the calculation of depreciation should be based on the normal expected useful life.

Special depreciation represents depreciation that is solely based on tax regulations. In general, this form of depreciation allows depreciation by percentage within a tax concession period without taking into account the actual wear and tear of the asset.

Unplanned depreciation is concerned with unusual circumstances, such as damage to the asset that leads to a permanent reduction in its value.

135. Define derived depreciation area.

A derived depreciation area is a calculated depreciation from two or more real areas using a calculation formula. You can use derived depreciation areas, for example, to calculate special reserves as the difference between tax and book depreciation. The book value rule in a derived depreciation area is checked each time a posting is made or depreciation is changed in the corresponding real area.

136. Explain the difference between the methods for distributing forecast depreciation to the posting periods.

The **smoothing method** distributes depreciation evenly to the periods from the current depreciation period to the end of the fiscal year (regardless of the value date of the transaction).

With the **catch-up method**, the depreciation on the transaction (from the start of capitalization up to the current period) is posted as a lump sum. The depreciation posting program posts this amount in the posting period in which the value date of the transaction lies.

137. How many ways can you create the asset master record?

There are three ways to create your asset master record: (1) through an asset class, (2) with reference to an asset, and (3) using the number functionality for similar assets.

1. Through transaction code AS01, you can create a new asset master by using an asset class. In this case, you will provide all information with respect to the asset master.
2. Use an existing asset as a reference for creating the new asset master record.
3. You can use number functionality to create more than one similar master. For example, if you purchased 100 laptops, you can create 100 asset masters at a time instead of creating asset masters one by one using this functionality.

138. Is it possible for an asset acquisition to be posted in two steps? How do the two entries clear?

When the asset acquisition is posted in two steps or two different departments, you normally post to a clearing account. This case arises when supplier is not known while capitalizing assets. In the first step, assets value credited to an open item managed account. In the second step, you are giving credit to vendor by debiting a clearing account. Either the FI department includes this clearing account in their periodic run of SAPF123 (automatic clearing program) or the clearing account has to be cleared in an additional step (menu path: Posting → Acquisition → External acquisition → Clearing offsetting entry).

139. What is the difference between the COA and the COD?

The COA is the index of G/L accounts. The COA can be global, country specific, or industry specific, based on the needs of the business. The COD is the index of depreciation areas. The COD is only country specific. The charts are independent of each other.

140. Describe the function of depreciation areas.

The COD is the index of depreciation areas. You are maintaining different depreciation areas to fulfill different accounting needs, e.g., for IAS requirement, IFS requirements, or tax requirements. In a COD, you should have at least one depreciation area, e.g., book depreciation areas. A depreciation area contains depreciation keys, which control how assets will be depreciated.

141. What significance does depreciation key 0000 have?

Depreciation key 0000 is an SAP-delivered key that ensures depreciation and interest are not calculated and posted. This key can be used for the assets under construction, such as land.

1.8 GENERAL CO

142. What is a controlling area?

The controlling area is the central organizational unit within the CO module. It is representative of a contained cost accounting environment where costs and revenues can be managed.

143. Define the relationship between a controlling area and a company code.

A controlling area may include one or more company codes, which must use the same operative COA as the controlling area. A controlling area can contain multiple company code assignments, but a single company code can be assigned to only one controlling area.

144. What is an operating concern?

An operating concern is an organizational unit. An operating concern can be assigned to one or more controlling areas; whereas a controlling area will have only one operating concern.

145. How many statistical objects can be selected when you post an FI document where cost center accounting (CCA), PCA, and internal order (IO) are active?

When posting an FI transaction, you can choose a maximum of two statistical objects, whereas real posting can be made to one cost object. Posting to a profit center is always statistical, depending on internal order, and the cost center may have real or statistical posting.

146. What is accrual?

Accrual is a process whereby you are accumulating expenses in CO on a pre-defined constant rate throughout the financial year. These expenses arise and are posted in FI in a random fashion. It is used for revenues or expenses that have already been posted in FI and revenues or expenses that are to be posted. For example, bonuses arise at the end of the year and are posted in FI at the end of the year, but through the process of accrual, the bonus is collected in CO on a periodic basis.

147. Describe the major differences between managerial accounting and FI.

Table 1.3 describes some differences between managerial accounting and FI.

Managerial Accounting	FI
Generally no constraints	Constrained be GAAP and/or IAS
Future orientation	Past orientation
Data is used by managers at various levels within the company	Data is used by outside parties such as banks, investors, and other stockholders
Meant for internal reporting	Meant for external reporting

TABLE 1.3   Management accounting versus FI

148. Define the term cost object.

A cost object is a responsibility center, project, product, or other item for which a separate measurement of cost is desired. Cost objects are defined by management and can include cost centers, projects, and activities.

149. Describe overhead costs and provide an example.

Overhead costs are indirect costs that cannot be directly assigned to a manufacturing process. Utilities, rent, and telephone expenses are examples of overhead costs.

150. What are the two major components of CO?

Configuration and application. The purpose of configuration is to customize CO to meet the specific needs of the client. The application component supplies the tools necessary for internal reporting and analysis.

151. List the five CO submodules.

These are the five submodules of CO:

- *CO-CCA*—The management of a company frequently looks for ways to reduce overhead costs. CCA, along with IO, provides a solution to this issue. CCA tracks costs in an organization where these costs are incurred.

■ *Cost Element Accounting (CO-CEL)*—CEL describes the costs that occur within an organization. It classifies them on the point of occurrence: (1) primary cost element, (2) revenue cost element, and (3) secondary cost element.

■ *Product Cost Accounting (CO-PC)*—This is used to estimate what it will cost to produce a product (or a service). It also has capabilities to track the actual costs of production, and provides extensive tools for cost analysis.

■ *Profitability Analysis (CO-PA)*—Very often, management is interested in knowing which products and which geographical areas are performing well. This module provides this information to management.

■ *CO-PCA*—This module tracks cost and revenue from the point of responsibility accounting.

152. True or False? Activity-based costing (ABC) is primarily used to capture the costs of internal events, such as travel costs and trade fairs.

False. ABC is a sub-module of controlling, which captures cost and usage of resources at each and every activity for further analysis. Whereas an IO is used to capture cost, related to a particular event or product.

153. True or False? PCA is generally used for margin reporting and cost of sales accounting.

False. PA is used for margin reporting and cost of sales accounting. PCA is used for period-based accounting and complete financial statements.

154. What is the primary integration point between the CO and FI modules?

G/L expense accounts are the primary cost elements in CO. Primary cost element is the carrier of cost within CO. Every primary cost will have a G/L account, therefore the relationship between primary cost element and G/L account is 1:1.

155. What are the differences between business areas and profit centers?

Business areas and profit centers are both used for management reporting, i.e., internal purposes only. The main differences are:

■ A profit center is a master data, whereas a business area is not.

- A profit center is assigned to a controlling area and internally to a company code. A business area is not assigned to either of these.
- Reposting is possible from one profit center to another, whereas reposting is not possible from one business area to another until or unless you pass an entry in FI.
- In ECC 5.0 onward, online splitting is possible. That is, online derivation of a profit center is possible, but not for a business area.

156. What is the work breakdown structure (WBS)?

WBS is used in the Project Systems module. It is a node of a project. There is a hierarchical structure under the project, similar to tasks/subtasks on the project plan. WBS is used to collect costs from various resources such as POs, direct allocation to project, etc. At the end of the month when the project settlement runs, the cost collected at WBSs is transferred to other cost objects such as cost centers, assets, etc. Revenues can also be assigned to WBS elements by linking it with sales orders in SD. And since it is linked to the project in the project system, profitability of the project can be derived.

157. How can you tell an FI document from a CO document?

There are two ways to tell FI documents from CO documents:
1. Execute transaction code KSB5. Select the CO document for which you want to see the FI document, then go to Environment → accounting document.
2. If you want to find FI documents for a number of CO documents, then browse the COBK table using transaction code SE16 and look for the field COBK-REFBN.

158. How many documents are created when primary costs are posted to CO from another module?

Two documents are created when primary costs are posted to CO from another module:
- The original document in FI, AM, or MM.
- A parallel document in CO that displays the data from a cost accounting viewpoint. The CO document is summarized according to cost element and cost object.

1.9 CO-CEL

159. What are the different types of cost elements? What is the difference between primary and secondary cost elements?

There are two types of cost elements: (1) primary cost elements and (2) secondary cost elements.

Primary cost elements are cost elements whose costs originate outside of CO. These elements correspond to a G/L account in FI.

Based on usage, primary cost elements can be further divided into the categories shown in Figure 1.38.

CECt	Description
1	Primary costs/cost-reducing revenues
3	Accrual/deferral per surcharge
4	Accrual/deferral per debit = actual
11	Revenues
12	Sales deduction
22	External settlement

FIGURE 1.38   Primary cost element categories

Secondary cost elements are cost elements used to allocate costs for internal activities. Secondary cost elements do not correspond to any G/L account in FI. They are only used in CO and therefore cannot be defined in FI as a G/L account.

Secondary cost elements are divided into the categories shown in Figure 1.39.

CECt	Description
21	Internal settlement
31	Order/project results analysis
41	Overhead Rates
42	Assessment
43	Internal activity allocation
50	Project-related incoming orders: Sales r
51	Project-related incoming orders: Other r
52	Project-related incoming orders: Costs
61	Earned value

FIGURE 1.39   Secondary cost element categories

When you are creating a cost element master, you always select and create your cost element under one of the categories shown in Figures 1.38 and 1.39.

1.10 FI-CCA

160. Where do you assign the activity type in cost centers?

There is no direct assignment. You plan the output for a cost center in terms of activity using transaction code KP26. Then you have to plan the value of that cost center for which you have planned activity for a period using transaction code KP06. A planned activity expenditure or planned activity quantity will give you the planned activity rate, which you can use to valuate the activity confirmations in manufacturing orders. You can also define your own prices, but you have to run the price revaluation if you want to revaluate the actual activity prices.

161. For statistical key figures, what is the significance of sender and receiver cost elements and cost centers?

Statistical key figures are not real account assignments. In simple terms, they are used to allocate or define proportions with which the cost is allocated to various cost objects. Statistical key figures are used to calculate the debit on a receiver object. These values can be used for assessing common costs, which are used by all the other cost centers.

162. What is periodic reposting?

Periodic reposting is the function that lets us correct postings to cost centers. Periodic reposting is an allocation method that uses rules defined in the form of cycles to credit allocation cost centers. These allocation cost centers are used to collect the postings relevant to cost accounting.

Periodic reposting enables you to adjust postings made to your cost centers, business processes, IOs, or WBS elements. They lead to the same result as transaction-based reposting. The results of transaction-based reposting have a direct effect on the actual costs of the sender and the receiver, whereas periodic reposting has a one-time effect on actual costs at period-end closing.

163. What is the difference between periodic reposting, distribution, and assessment? And which would you use under what situations?

You use periodic reposting for primary cost allocation. In case of periodic reposting, you can't see the actual transfer between cost object. It just reclassifies cost between cost objects. It is used to rectify incorrect posting.

You use distribution for primary cost allocation. The amount appeared at credit side in sender cost center and amount appeared at debit side in receiver cost center. This is used to distribute cost to different cost objects, which earlier were collected in the distribution cost center.

You use assessment for primary cost allocation through a secondary cost element. Amount appeared at credit side in sender cost center and amount appeared at debit side in receiver cost center. This is used to share costs between various cost objects based on service received. You use assessment for both primary and secondary code. During assessment process, the system groups together primary cost and secondary cost allocations through the assessment cost element.

164. What is allocation structure?

It is a template that contains one or more segments called assignments to allocate the costs incurred on a sender by cost element or cost element group. The allocation structure is used for settlement as well as for assessment. In the allocation structure you set the relation between sender and receiver cost objects.

165. What is the difference between reposting and allocation?

In reposting, the debit side of the sender is reduced and a new line is created on the debit side of the receiver. In allocation, the debit side remains unchanged, but a separate credit entry is made on the sender A/C.

166. What is the standard hierarchy?

Standard hierarchy represents the structural arrangement of cost centers and cost center groups. It is a tree structure containing all of the cost centers in a controlling area from the CO standpoint. You assign a cost center to an end node of the standard hierarchy in the master data maintenance of the cost center or in the enterprise organization. This ensures that the standard hierarchy contains all of the cost centers in that controlling area. When you define the controlling area, you specify the name of the top node of the standard hierarchy in that controlling area. Use transaction code OKEON to build your cost center hierarchy.

167. What is the basic difference between cost centers and IOs?

A cost center is an organizational element that is responsible for its expenses. It is used for internal reporting for a long time span as part of the company structure. A cost center generally represents a department or work center.

An IO is used to accumulate cost for a specific project or task for a specific time period. An IO is therefore used for a short period with a specific deadline.

IOs usually settle to cost centers (and not vice versa) according to the settlement rule in the order setup.

An IO can therefore be used to group all of the expenses incurred in relation to a specific business activity. The order can be settled on a monthly basis to cost centers.

When the business object is finished, the order can finally be settled to cost centers.

168. What is a statistical key figure?

An SKF is a unit of measurement used for internal allocation of cost between various cost centers that utilizes services of other cost centers. For example, an SKF may be a machine hour, the head count of a cost center, etc.

169. What is reposting?

Reposting is a posting aid in which primary costs are posted to a receiver object under the original cost element (the cost element of the sender object). Reposting is used to rectify incorrect postings. The following methods are available:

- **Transaction-related reposting**: Each posting is made in real time during the current period.
- **Periodic reposting**: The costs being transferred are collected on a clearing cost center and then transferred at the end of the period according to

allocation bases defined by the user. This method produces the same results as transaction-related reposting.

170. What is the difference between assessment and reposting?

Assessment is a method of internal cost allocation by which you allocate (transfer) the costs of a sender cost center to receiver CO objects (orders, other cost centers, and so on) under an assessment cost element.

Reposting is a posting aid with which primary costs are posted to a receiver object through original cost element (the cost element of the sender object).

Under assessment, costs are allocated to the sender cost center under the assessment cost element. The sender cost center receives costs under the assessment cost element, which does not reveal the actual cost elements. In reposting, however, costs are transferred under the original cost elements.

171. It is said that both activity type and SKF act as a tracing factor for cost allocations. Explain what the difference is between these two and when each is used.

An SKF is set up within the cost centers and values are assigned to them as part of the allocation process. Activity types have absorption rates linked to them and dollars are consumed out of a cost center based on a specific amount of activity that has been consumed.

For example, you can have activity types for people hours and machine hours being consumed out of a manufacturing cost center. You calculate a rate in the planning processes that is loaded at the beginning of the year. Then for every hour used to produce a product, you will consume dollars from the cost center into the production order or cost object based on the hourly rate you set at the beginning of the year.

Activity type is used where the sender cost center produces certain output, such as machine hours, that is utilized by other cost objects, while SKF is used to distribute cost among various cost objects.

172. How are cost centers populated with financial data?

Cost centers get financial data in the following ways:

- While posting a transaction you are entering the cost object at the line item level.

- Instead of entering a cost object, you assign a default cost center to G/L accounts by assigning a cost center to a cost element.
- Cost centers also get financial data through settlement of IOs, assessment, and distribution of cost center.

173. How can you allocate depreciation expenses to multiple cost centers?

There are two ways to transfer depreciation cost to cost centers: (1) through default cost center assignment to the asset master and (2) through default cost center assignment to the primary depreciation cost element.

When an organization uses its assets for various cost centers, it is better to use the second option. In the second option, you can assign a distribution cost center as the default to the primary depreciation cost element. As a period-end process, you can distribute depreciation expenses to various cost centers through cost center distribution.

174. What are segments and cycles?

Cycles and segments are utilized by the SAP system to perform automated allocations, such as distributions, assessments, and reposting (covered in Chapter 5) of both planned and actual costs.

A cycle may be defined as a holding place for the various rules that will define an automated allocation. Cycles are comprised of segments, and each segment represents one set of data needed to complete the automated allocation.

A segment consists of the following:

- *Allocation Characteristics*—Identification of sending and receiving cost centers.
- *Sender Values*—The types of costs that will be allocated, whether they are planned or actual amounts, and what percentage of total sender costs will be allocated.
- *Receiver Values (Tracing Factors)*—The basis for allocation, which can be percentage, fixed amount, or SKF.

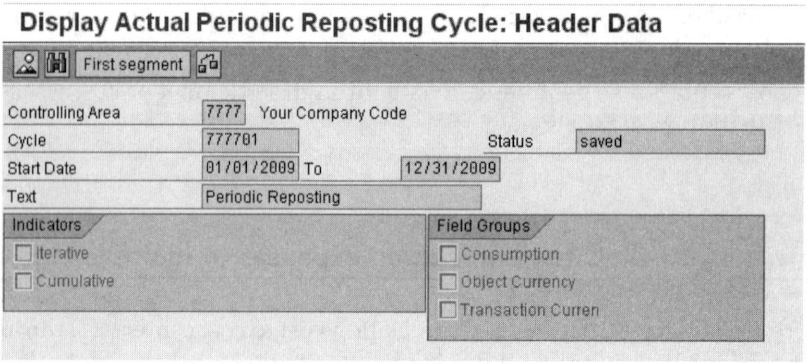

Display Actual Periodic Reposting Cycle: Header Data

Controlling Area	7777	Your Company Code		
Cycle	777701		Status	saved
Start Date	01/01/2009	To	12/31/2009	
Text	Periodic Reposting			

Indicators	Field Groups
☐ Iterative	☐ Consumption
☐ Cumulative	☐ Object Currency
	☐ Transaction Curren

FIGURE 1.40   Cycle

Figure 1.40 shows a cycle. Cycles are controlling areas dependent and valid for a period of time. All postings occurring in the cycle periods will be processed through one or more segments.

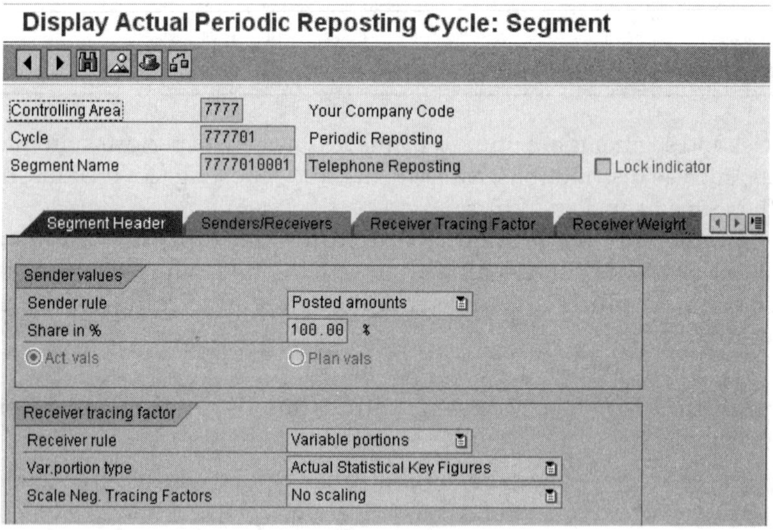

Display Actual Periodic Reposting Cycle: Segment

Controlling Area	7777	Your Company Code	
Cycle	777701	Periodic Reposting	
Segment Name	7777010001	Telephone Reposting	☐ Lock indicator

Segment Header	Senders/Receivers	Receiver Tracing Factor	Receiver Weight

Sender values

Sender rule	Posted amounts
Share in %	100.00 %
⦿ Act. vals	○ Plan vals

Receiver tracing factor

Receiver rule	Variable portions
Var.portion type	Actual Statistical Key Figures
Scale Neg. Tracing Factors	No scaling

FIGURE 1.41   Segments

You create segments within a cycle. Segments determine the sender and receiver relation and distribution methods.

175. What is the purpose of variance analysis?

Variance analysis is used to calculate and interpret differences between planned costs and actual costs within a cost center or cost center group. It also provides vital information that can be used to modify and improve planning in subsequent periods.

176. List the two main types of actual postings to CO.

There are two types of actual postings to CO: (1) transaction-based postings and (2) periodic allocations.

Transaction-based postings (also known as transaction-based allocations) are posted on a real-time basis from other modules or within CO. This enables up-to-the-minute reporting of costs incurred on the cost centers at any time during the period. There are four transaction-based postings to CO:

- From other modules:
  - □ Direct postings to cost centers from other modules, such as FI, AM, and MM
- Within CO:
  - □ Reposting
  - □ Activity allocation
  - □ Posting of SKFs

Periodic allocations exist entirely within CO. They occur at the end of the period after all primary postings have been completed. Periodic allocations require cycles and segments to be executed. There are five main types of periodic allocations:

- Periodic reposting (periodic transfers)
- Distribution
- Assessment
- Imputed cost calculation
- Indirect activity allocation

177. Define direct internal activity allocation.

Direct internal activity allocation is the process of recording activities performed by a cost center and simultaneously allocating those activities to receiving cost centers based on consumption. In the case of direct activity allocation, the sender (output) and the receiver (consumption) activity volumes are known.

178. Explain both the iterative and cumulative form of cycle processing.

In iterative processing, the iterative sender/receiver relationships (sender is also among the receivers) are considered when this cycle is processed. The iteration is repeated until each sender is fully relieved of costs provided. Cycles may be set to iterative processing for both plan and actual data.

In cumulative processing, all posted sender amounts since the first period are accumulated and allocated based on the tracing factors accumulated since this period. The difference between the accumulated amount and the posted amounts in previous periods is posted in the current period. The postings in previous periods remain unchanged. Cycles may be set to cumulative processing for actual data only.

179. Describe the use of the reconciliation ledger.

The reconciliation ledger keeps track of transactions between company codes within one controlling area, since such cross-company allocations result in an imbalance between CO totals and FI totals. Because legal reporting is based in FI, all transactions that cross company codes in CO must be reflected in FI.

180. Describe imputed cost calculation in CO.

Imputed cost calculations are used to smooth the effect on cost centers for large, one-time charges, such as insurance premiums or employee bonuses. By smoothing one-time expenses in CO, price fluctuations from period to period can be avoided. There are two methods for calculating imputed costs in the R/3 system: (1) cost element percent method and (2) target = actual method.

181. Define activity dependent cost, activity independent cost, and mixed cost.

Activity dependent costs are variable costs that fluctuate based on activity. The greater the activity, the greater the cost. For example, direct labor costs increase as production increases.

Activity independent costs are fixed costs. Activity independent costs do not fluctuate based on activity. For example, regardless of output, insurance premiums will not change.

Mixed costs are a combination of both fixed and variable costs, and display the characteristics of both. For example, the basic cost of heating a building (fixed portion) would increase as production increases (variable portion).

1.11 CO-PCA

182. What is a dummy profit center?

A dummy profit center is created to take care of any missing configuration or assignments in CO area. For example, if you do not assign some of the cost centers to a profit center, they will be assigned to the dummy profit center so that the configuration is automatically completed while making consolidations for reporting/decisional purposes. Every item that goes to the dummy profit center will be adjusted at month end to their actual profit centers as well. Because the dummy profit center absorbs all types of costs, it has to be adjusted to its actual profit center at month end. Use transaction code KE59 to create a dummy profit center.

183. What is a cost center and a profit center?

A cost center is an organizational unit within a controlling area that represents a defined location of cost incurrence. The definition can be based on:

- Functional requirements
- Allocation criteria
- Physical location
- Responsibility for costs

A profit center is an organizational unit within a controlling area that represents a defined location for revenue recognition. The definition can be based on:

- Functional requirements
- Allocation criteria
- Physical location
- Responsibility for costs

184. Describe how cost and revenue flow to PCA.

Depending upon business requirements, profit centers are mapped to various business objects in the following ways:

- *Through material master*—In this case, any transaction affecting material will update the profit center.
- *Through cost center*—Assignment of profit center to cost center master.
- *Through IOs*—Like Cost center, you can assign profit center to internal order master.
- *Through transaction code OKB9*—In this case, you are mapping the profit center with a combination of company code, cost element, and profit center.

1.12 CO-IO

185. What is IO?

IO is a cost object that collects costs for the management information system and, in some instances, revenues for an organization. IOs can be used to:

- Monitor the costs of short-term measures
- Monitor the costs and revenues related to a specific service
- Monitor ongoing costs

  IOs are divided according to function into the following categories:
- *Overhead Orders*—Overhead orders monitor subareas of indirect costs arising from short-term measures. They can also be used for detailed monitoring of ongoing plans and actual costs independent of organizational cost center structures and business processes.
- *Capital Investment Orders*—Capital investment orders monitor investment costs, which can be capitalized and settled to fixed assets.
- *Accrual Orders*—Accrual orders monitor period-based accrual between expenses posted in FI and accrual costs in CO.
- *Orders with Revenues*—Orders with revenues monitor the costs and revenues arising from activities for partners outside the organizational boundaries, or from activities not belonging to the core business of the organization.

186. What is order type? What are the parameters it controls for IO?

An order type contains many kinds of control information important for managing orders. This includes many default values that can be called upon when you create a new order with this order type. You must assign each order to an order type that transfers specified parameters to the order.

The order type is client specific, which means that an order type can be used in all controlling areas.

The order type controls/determines the following fields for an order:

- Order Category
- Number Assignment
- Control Indicator
- CO Partner Updating
- Order Classification
- Commitment Management
- Revenue Posting
- Integrated Planning
- Settlement Profile
- Planning Profile
- Budget Profile
- Status Management

187. What is an order category?

An order category is a technical classification criterion for IOs. The order category determines the SAP application to which an order belongs, and controls the functions with which an order can be processed. The standard order categories are:

- 01—IO (CO)
- 02—Accrual Calculation Order (CO)
- 03—Model Order (CO)
- 04—CO Production Orders
- 05—Product Cost Collector

188. What is a settlement profile?

In a settlement profile you will specify a range of control parameters that define how the order will be settling to other cost objects. You must define the settlement profile before you can enter a settlement rule for a sender.

In a settlement profile, you define the following parameters:

- Permitted settlement receivers (such as cost center or asset)
- Default values for the settlement structure and the PA transfer structure
- Allocation bases for defining the settlement shares (using percentages and/or equivalence numbers)
- Maximum number of distribution rules
- Retention period of the settlement documents
- Document type for settlements relevant to accounting, or, more specifically, to the balance sheet
- Definitions for the settlement of actual costs or the cost of sales

189. What is a planning profile?

A planning profile contains parameters and default values for overall planning. You can also assign an order type to the planning profile at a later date. You need planning profiles for the following planning methods:

- Overall planning for IOs
- Hierarchy cost planning for projects
- Preliminary costing for production orders that do not have a quantity structure (CO production orders)
- Cost planning for investment programs or investment measures, and for appropriation requests
- Financial budgeting

190 What is a budget profile?

Budgeting within SAP solutions provides the user with enhanced project management capabilities not provided by IO planning. Where an IO planning is an estimate of expenditures made at the beginning of the fiscal year, a budget represents the actual approved amount of funding for a given order. Because the budgeted amount is maintained separately you have an opportunity to do plan versus budget comparisons. This profile contains parameters and default values for budgeting. You can also assign an order type to a budgeting profile at a later date.

191. What are reference orders and model orders?

A model order is not a real order in the commercial sense. It is customized with certain default values to reduce time and effort while creating real IOs. Model orders contain default values for the orders in an order type. You need to enter the model order as the reference order in the order type. When you create a new order, all of the active fields in the relevant order type are copied from the model order to the new order. Model orders make the work of entering new orders considerably easier. The data that recurs in orders from a particular order type is already defined. This reduces the likelihood of errors.

192. What is a settlement rule?

The settlement rule determines what portions of a sender's costs are to be settled to which receiver(s). You specify this by assigning one or more distribution rules to each sender. Typically there is one distribution rule for each receiver. This is carried out at order level.

193. What is availability control in IO?

Availability control is a process where users of IOs will issue a warning when the order cost reaches a particular stage. The idea behind availability control is that the SAP solution should alert you when you are about to exceed some predefined percentage of the budgeted amount. This activity is carried out through the establishment of spending tolerance levels associated with each budget profile/controlling area relationship.

194. What is a budget manager?

A budget manager is a person who will be informed when an IO reaches a particular spending level. When you are maintaining the action setting for availability control, you are given a choice of whether to return a warning with or without an email message. If you have chosen a warning with an email, you must have established the proper budget manager setting before the email process will work.

195. What is IO status management?

Status management is an act of determining and managing which transactions are valid for an order at any given time within its life cycle. In SAP solutions, the term life cycle refers to an order's fluid existence, moving from one phase to another until it is closed. There are two types of status management available: (1) general status management and (2) order status management.

196. What settlement types are available for IO?

IO may be settled to other CO objects and/or to G/L in the following ways:

- 100% validation
- % settlement
- Equivalence number
- Amount settlement

197. Define statistical IOs.

A statistical IO can be defined to collect costs for informational purposes only and therefore needs a real cost assignment (e.g., to a cost center) at the same time. The costs posted to a statistical IO are not settled.

1.13 CO-PA

198. What are the characteristics of PA?

The characteristics of an operating concern represent objects or market segments that can be used as a basis for performing evaluations. The characteristics also represent reference objects for allocating costs in PA. This enables source-related cost allocation at the level responsible, according to direct costs and contribution margin accounting. Some of the SAP-delivered characteristics are: Country, Material group, State, and Customer group.

199. What are value fields?

Value fields are key figures that represent the lines in a report in CO-PA drill-down reporting. The values contained in the fields can be aggregated with reference to the characteristics available or displayed at a lower level. Some of the value fields are: Sales quantity, Outgoing Freight, Revenue, and Qty discount.

200. What is characteristic derivation?

Characteristic derivation is a process through which you will derive values of other characteristics. Derivation lets you find values for certain characteristics automatically based on the known values of other characteristics, where these characteristics are logically dependent on one another.

When an operating concern is generated, the system produces a standard derivation strategy containing all known dependencies between characteristics. You can display these by choosing *View → Display all steps*.

If you use the Derivation rule in derivation step type, some additional entry options are available:

- Under Maintain rule values, you will enter which values in the target fields must be placed in which characteristic values of the source fields.

- Under Characteristics, you can make additional entries that, for example, make it possible to enter a validity date for the step.

201. What are the differences between account-based CO-PA and costing-based CO-PA?

Table 1.4 shows the differences between account-based CO-PA and costing-based CO-PA.

Costing-Based CO-PA	Account-Based CO-PA
1. Uses characteristics and value fields to display reports.	1. Uses cost and revenue elements to display reports.
2. In costing-based CO-PA, you can calculate anticipated cost.	2. Takes real cost and revenue from FI; hence you cannot calculate anticipated cost.
3. Uses tables specific to CO-PA, which may or may not agree with FI.	3. Uses CO application tables.
4. Revenue and cost of sales are posted when the billing document is posted.	4. Revenues are posted when the billing document is posted, while cost of sales is posted when FI posting occurs for goods issue.
5. At a given point in time, it may or may not reconcile with FI.	5. Always reconciles with FI.

TABLE 1.4   Costing-based COPA Vs. Account-based COPA

1.14 PRODUCT COSTING (CO-PC)

202. What are costing variants?

The costing variants in PC play a very important role in product cost calculation. Unless you maintain this, the system can't calculate the cost of the product. It is through this variant that you tell the system where to obtain the cost of material, labor, activity prices, and Overhead (OH).

The costing variant has five tabs:

1. *Costing Type*—Here, you maintain the cost estimate like std cost, modified cost for different purposes, etc.

2. *Valuation Variant*—This plays an important role, as it determines prices that the SAP system selects to valuate the quantity structure of the material cost estimate. It has five tabs.

   - First tab for material valuation gives priority of prices for material cost.
   - Second tab determines activity prices for process cost.

- Third tab determines subcontracting price for subcontracting cost estimate.
- Fourth tab determines external processing cost price.
- Fifth tab determines which costing sheet you want to use for overhead costs.

3. *Date Control*—This maintains the costing date for when this costing variant applies.
4. *Quantity Structure*—bills of material (BOM) application for cost estimation.
5. *Transfer Control*—In cross-company code costing, you use this to avoid repetitive costing.

203. List several major functions of the PC module.

Product cost planning enables:
- Calculation of standard internal cost for manufactured goods
- Calculation of works in progress (WIP) during month-end closing
- Calculation of period-end variances
- Settlement of product costs

1.15 SD

204. What is a credit control area? What relationship exists between credit control areas and company codes?

Within an R/3 system, the credit control area is an organizational entity that monitors and controls the credit limit of various customers. A credit control area may have more than one company code, but one company code can't be assigned to more than one credit control area.

Note: You are assigning the credit control area to the company code, not vice versa.

205. What is the difference between an inquiry and a quotation?

An inquiry is a request from your customer for availability of stock and price. A quotation represents your responses to a customer inquiry.

206. What is a condition technique in SAP solutions?

In SAP R/3, a condition technique refers to the procedures or system through which R/3 determines the price of the material. During sales order processing, R/3 uses a condition technique to determine the price of a product.

207. What is the item category group? Where do you maintain it?

An item category group represents the grouping of similar items into one group. The item category group determines how material will be processed in SAP solutions. When processing sales and distribution documents, the system uses the item category group to determine the item category. The item category is an attribute of material master, which determines what type of transaction is allowed for this item category.

208. What is the access sequence in SD?

You use various combinations, i.e., customer, material, etc., in SD to determine the correct account to be posted. The Standard Access sequence consists of following combinations: (1) Cust. Grp/Material Grp/Acct Key, (2) Cust. Grp/Acct Key, (3) Material Grp/Acct Key, (4) General, and (5) Acct Key.

209. Which three organizational elements make up a sales area? Briefly explain their function.

A sales area is a combination of the following three organizational entities:

1. *Sales organization*—An organizational unit that sells and distributes products, negotiates terms of sale, and is responsible for these transactions.

2. *Distribution channel*—A channel through which salable materials or services reach customers. Typical distribution channels include wholesale, retail, and direct sales. You can assign a distribution channel to one or more sales organizations.

3. *Division*—Product groups can be defined for a wide-ranging spectrum of products. For every division, you can make customer-specific agreements on, for example, partial deliveries, pricing, and terms of payment. Within a division, you can carry out statistical analyses or set up separate marketing.

1.16 MM

210. What is meant by materials requirements planning (MRP)?

MRP is used to procure material in time and/or produce material in time. This process monitors incoming and outgoing stock within the Inventory Management (IM) module. MRP considers existing stock, sales orders, purchase orders, and production orders while creating material recommendations to fulfill the company's commitment to its customers.

211. What are special stocks in SAP MM?

In the SAP MM module, you are managing stocks as special stocks. The attributes of special stocks are controlled through a special stock indicator. You are assigning special stock characteristics to stock, while processing stock movement in the SAP MM module. Broadly, there are two types of special stock from the IM point of view:

- A company's own special stocks:
  - Stock of material provided to vendor
  - Consignment stock at customer
  - Returnable packaging stock at customer
- Externally owned special stocks:
  - Vendor consignment
  - Returnable transport packaging
  - Sales order stock
  - Project stock

212. What is meant by consignment stock?

Consignment stocks are special stocks that are in your possession but ownership lies with the vendor. In the case of consignment stock, physical material is at your premises, while the vendor retains ownership of these materials. Your liabilities arise when you are issuing consignment materials to production orders or consuming them.

213. What is the difference between a contract and a scheduling agreement?

In the SAP IM module, a contract represents an agreement between buyer and seller for the supply of material or services. There are two types of contracts: (1) quantity contract and (2) value contract.

A scheduling agreement represents how material will be delivered during a period of time.

You can create a contract through transaction code ME31K and a scheduling agreement through transcation code ME31L.

214. What is the use of configurable material?

Typically, the concept of configurable material is used for a made-to-order environment. This concept is useful where a lot of permutations and combinations exist for a product. For example, in the case of a laptop, there are various combinations possible with respect to hard drive capacity, processor, and other features. For configurable material, you will use a super BOM, which takes care of all possible alternative materials. A routing is also maintained, consisting of all possible operations that could be used. Configurable materials are either created in a material type that allows the configuration (in the standard system, the material type KMAT) or they are given the indicator Configurable in the material master record.

215. Is it possible to generate a purchase requisition (PR) with reference to a scheduling agreement?

You can create a PR with reference to another PO. A PR can't be created with a PO or scheduling agreement. POs and scheduling agreements are outcomes of PR. You can create a PO with reference to a PR through transaction code ME21N.

216. What is a standard price and a moving average price?

A standard price and a moving average price are two different methods of valuating inventory. In the case of a standard price, inventory will be valuated at a fixed price, where in the case of a moving average price, the valuation price changes. Generally, you will use a moving average price for raw materials, spare parts, and traded goods. Standard prices are used for the valuation of finished and semifinished goods. Table 1.5 shows how SAP R/3 calculates the moving average price (MAP).

Date	Receipts		Issues		Balance		
	Qty	Price	Qty	Price	Qty	Price	MAP
01/01/2009	100	1000			100	1000	10.00
01/10/2009	150	1300			250	2300	9.20
01/20/2009			80	900	170	1400	8.24

TABLE 1.5 Calculating the moving average price

1.17 TECHNICAL QUESTIONS

217. What is Open SQL versus native SQL?

Open SQL consists of a set of Advanced Business Application Programming (ABAP) statements that run across the database. In other words, Open SQL is not database dependent. Thus, Open SQL provides a uniform syntax and semantics for all of the database systems supported by SAP solutions. Open SQL statements can only work with database tables that have been created in the ABAP dictionary. ABAP native SQL allows you to include database-specific SQL statements in an ABAP program. Most ABAP programs containing database-specific SQL statements do not run with different databases. If different databases are involved, use Open SQL. To execute ABAP native SQL in an ABAP program, use the statement EXEC.

218. What is a workflow and what is its importance?

The SAP Business Workflow is a tool that automates business processes within SAP solutions. You can use the SAP Business Workflow for simple business processes like approval procedures or more complex processes like month-end and year-end closing. The main advantages of the SAP Business Workflow are:

- Reduction of time, i.e., no waiting time

- Increase in transparancy of the business process since you can store process documentation within the workflow
- Increase in quality through the reduction of manual processes

You can configure the SAP Business Workflow through transaction code SWDD.

219. How can you find out what transaction codes a user used within a particular time span?

You can use transaction code STAT to find out what activities or transaction codes were used by a user on a particular day.

220. What is structure and what are its advantages?

A structure is like a table in SAP solutions, but it does hold data. You are creating structure in the ABAP/4 dictionary like a table and it can be accessed from ABAP/4 programs. During program run time, structure is used to transfer data between various objects. Any change to the definition of the structure in the ABAP/4 dictionary is automatically implemented in all programs.

While data in tables is stored permanently in the database, structures only contain data during the run time of a program.

221. What are internal tables?

Internal tables are tables used only at run time that take data from other tables and store that data in working memory in ABAP. In ABAP, internal tables fulfill the function of arrays. While running an ABAP program, you are using internal tables to append, insert, delete, and manipulate data, which you extracted from other tables. Using internal tables increases system efficiency. A particularly important use for internal tables is for storing and formatting data from a database table within a program. They are also a good way of including very complicated data structures in an ABAP program.

222. What is IDOC?

An IDOC is an intermediate document, which is used to exchange data between SAP R/3 and non-SAP systems. IDOCs are created through message types. IDOCs consist of three components: (1) control record, (2) data segments, and (3) status records.

1. Control records consist of a sender's name, a receiver's name, the IDOC type, and the message type.
2. The data segment consists of a sequential segment number, a segment type description, and a field containing the actual data of the segment.
3. The status record shows the information status of the IDOC, i.e., whether it was processed or is to be processed.

223. What is application linking and enabling (ALE)?

ALE is a communication tool between SAP systems and/or non-SAP system. It integrates various distributed systems through its intelligent mechanisms. ALE technology facilitates rapid application prototyping and application interface development, thus reducing implementation time.

Chapter 2   CERTIFICATION QUESTIONS AND ANSWERS

2.1 QUESTIONS

1. **Where do you define the length of general ledger (G/L) account numbers?**

    a. Transaction code OBC4
    b. Transaction code OB13

2. **When is a G/L master complete?**

    a. After the chart of account (COA) segment data is created
    b. After the company code segment data is added to the COA segment data

3. **State True or False for the following statements, with respect to whether the same chart of account is being used by multiple company codes.**

    a. All company codes will use the same COA data and company code segment data.
    b. All company codes will use the same COA segment data and different company code segment data.

4.   **State True or False for the following statements, with respect to the appearance of the G/L account master. The appearance of the company code segment of a G/L account is based on:**

    a. The account group under which G/L masters are created.

    b. Group account number/alternative account number that are assigned to G/L accounts.

5.   **Account numbers control the appearance of the G/L master. (True/False)**

6.   **How can you prevent duplicate vendors from being created?**

    a. Checking the match code before creating a new vendor

    b. Switching on automatic duplication check in the vendor master

7.   **State True or False for the following statements, with respect to document type.**

    a. The document type controls what account types are allowed for posting.

    b. Field status of document header text and reference field.

    c. The document type indicates whether or not batch processing is allowed.

    d. None of the above.

8.   **Posting keys are defined at:**

    a. Client level

    b. Company code level

    c. Controlling area level

9. **What would be the effect if multiple company codes used the same posting period variant?**

   a. Individual company codes can close or open posting periods for their respective company code.
   b. Opening and closing can be done centrally and will apply to all company codes.

10. **Generally, under what circumstances are two period ranges open for posting?**

    a. During month end
    b. During year end
    c. For daily transactions

11. **What determines the posting period and fiscal year?**

    a. Document entry date
    b. Document posting date

12. **Which of the following would be the baseline date?**

    a. Document date
    b. Posting date
    c. Entry date
    d. None of the above

13. **The clearing document updates the clearing document number and the clearing document date fields of the open items that it clears. (True/False)**

14.   You should have a separate cash journal for each currency. (True/ False)

15.   A down payment request updates and changes the G/L balance of the vendor/customer. (True/False)

16.   Employee tolerance and G/L tolerance limits work together. (True/ False)

17.   You can post to a reconciliation ledger. (True/False)

18.   An SAP R/3 system only contains a database server. (True/False)

19.   A database server contains all data and programs. (True/False)

20.   You can open more than six sessions of a particular system at a time. (True/False)

21. You can only have a year-dependent fiscal year. (True/False)

22. A fiscal year normally has 12 normal periods and one or more special posting periods. (True/False)

23. A shortened fiscal year will have exactly 12 posting periods. (True/False)

24. State True or False for each of the following statements.

   a. A company code can have more than one currency as a local currency.
   b. A company code can only have one local currency.
   c. None of the above.

25. A retained earnings account is a company code–specific G/L account. (True/False)

26. State True or False for each of the following statements. The business area is:

   a. Company code specific (True/False)
   b. Client specific (True/False)
   c. None of the above

27.   Posting into a G/L account is controlled by the field status group (FSG) assigned to the G/L master. (True/False)

28.   State True or False for each of the following statements.

    a. You can have at least one retained earning account.

    b. The configuration of a retained earning account is optional.

29.   State True or False for each of the following statements.

    a. The G/L account group controls the document field status.

    b. The G/L account group controls the G/L account number ranges.

    c. All of the above.

30.   State True or False for each of the following statements.

    a. The G/L account ID and house bank ID should be the same.

    b. A G/L account can be assigned to more than one house bank.

31.   State True or False for each of the following statement.

The G/L account for a bank is linked to

    a. A house bank is created under chart of account.

    b. A G/L account can be assigned to more the one bank key.

32.   State True or False for each of the following statements.

    a. A company code may have an operating COA and n number of group COAs.

    b. A company code should have only one operating COA.

33.   State True or False for each of the following statements.

   a. The relation between the operating COA G/L and the group COA G/L is 1:n.
   b. The relation between the operating COA G/L and the group COA G/L is n:1.
   c. The relation between the operating COA G/L and the country COA G/L is 1:1.

34.   The G/L master consists of which of the following segments?

   a. Sales area data
   b. Purchase area data
   c. COA data
   d. Company code data

35.   State True or False for each of the following statements.

   a. You can assign two number ranges to a document type.
   b. Document number ranges are defined at the client level.
   c. Different company codes can have the same number of range intervals with respect to documents.
   d. You can use alphanumeric document number ranges for internal number ranges.

36.   State True or False for each of the following statements.

   a. You can define account groups at the client level.
   b. You can define account groups at the COA level.

37.   State True or False for each of the following statements.

   a. One or more reconciliation accounts can be assigned to a vendor or customer.
   b. The number range and account groups always have a 1:1 relation.

38. State True or False for each of the following statements.

    a. Customer or vendor masters are company code–dependent masters.

    b. Customer or vendor masters are client-dependent masters.

39. The customer master has which of the following segments:

    a. COA segment and company code segment

    b. General data segment, company code segment, and sales area segment

    c. General data segment, company code segment, and purchase organization segment

40. A document is uniquely identified by:

    a. Document number, company code, and fiscal year

    b. Company code, fiscal year, and document types

    c. Company code, fiscal year, and posting periods

41. State True or False for each of the following statements.

    a. Document numbers can be alphanumeric and year specific.

    b. The document type controls account types to be posted and number ranges to be used.

42. State True or False for each of the following statements.

    a. The relationship between the house bank and account ID is 1:1.

    b. The relationship between the house bank and account ID is 1:n.

    c. The relationship between the house bank and account ID is n:1.

43. State True or False for each of the following statements.

    a. You can use sample accounts as reference documents.

    b. Sample accounts are created at the client level.

44. **State True or False for each of the following statements.**

   a. A G/L account can be blocked for posting at company code level or at the COA level.
   b. A G/L account is always blocked at the COA level.
   c. A G/L account that has been blocked can't be opened for posting.

45. **State True or False for each of the following statements.**

   a. You create all relevant information while posting for a one-time vendor.
   b. You maintain one-time vendor master records in SAP solutions.
   c. A one-time vendor master always has an external number range.

46. **State True or False for each of the following statements.**

   a. A customer can be blocked from creating company codes.
   b. A customer can be blocked from posting in all company codes.
   c. A customer can be blocked from posting in selected company codes.

47. **One G/L account may appear in multiple groups in the same COA. (True/False)**

48. **If multiple company codes use the same COA, G/L accounts are available for all company codes. (True/False)**

49. **Do you need an account group for the creation of a vendor/customer master? (Yes/No)**

50. **Is a company code mandatory for the creation of a customer/vendor master? (Yes/No)**

51. **Should all G/L masters have the same FSG within an account group? (Yes/No)**

52. **Can you track G/L master, customer master, vendor master, and assets master changes in mySAP ERP? (Yes/No)**

53. **In an automatic payment program (APP), mySAP ERP selects open items to be paid, posts payment documents, and clears open items by printing payment media. (True/False)**

54. **State True or False for each of the following statements.**

   a. In an APP, you can edit a payment proposal.
   b. You can block and unblock line items due for payment.

55. **State True or False for each of the following statements.**

   a. The steps in an APP are: (1) parameter, (2) proposal, (3) payment run, and (4) printout.
   b. The steps in an APP are: (1) post payment document and (2) print payment medium.
   c. Payment run is identified by payment run ID.

56.   State True or False for each of the following statements.

    a. One company will be sending company and paying company code in APP.
    b. You can only pay vendors through an APP.
    c. You can't pay a down payment request through an APP.
    d. Checks lots are maintained through the SAP application menu.

57.   State True or False for each of the following statements.

    a. All company codes in a payment run must belong to the same country.
    b. You can't edit payment proposals after a payment run.

58.   State True or False for each of the following statements.

    a. A dunning run updates customer/vendor master data with the last dunning running date.
    b. You can't edit dunning data at the proposal stage.
    c. You can't dun a one-time customer/vendor.

59.   What is the maximum number of dunning levels that can be configured?

60.   A dunning program considers all line items that have reached the due date + grace period. (True/False)

61.   State True or False for each of the following statements.

    a. A dunning run updates the last dunning run date in the customer master record.

    b. A dunning run updates the dunning level in the customer master record.

    c. You can set a minimum amount for dunning charges on each dunning level.

62.   State True or False for each of the following statements.

    a. A financial statement version consists of a maximum of nine hierarchy levels.

    b. A financial statement version can be used by one company code.

    c. In a financial statement version, you can assign the debit balance and credit balance to different nodes.

    d. Foreign currency valuation is only possible for customer/vendor open items, not for G/L.

63.   State True or False for each of the following statements.

    a. Depreciation can be posted through background processing (batch input session) in SAP R/3.

    b. Depreciation can be posted through dialog mode in mySAP ERP.

64.   State True or False for each of the following statements.

    a. You can post transactions to an account in any currency only if that account currency is the same as the company code currency.

    b. The carry forward of an account balance is a month-end process.

    c. Exchange rate type M is the default exchange rate during FI posting.

    d. You can clear open items if the open items have the same dimensions in every respect.

65.   Sample accounts and account assignment models are used for reference templates while posting a FI document. (True/False)

66. Posting keys are used to decide which account type will be used for posting. (True/False)

67. Cross-company document numbers consist of the document number of the first company code + the first company code + fiscal year. (True/False)

68. The reversal document always has an external document number. (True/False)

69. Financial statements can be generated in any currency. (True/False)

70. The vendor master record consists of general data, company code data, and purchasing data. (True/False)

71. A special G/L transaction can be posted into a normal reconciliation account. (True/False)

72. A down payment request is a noted item and does not update the G/L balance. (True/False)

73. The regrouping of AR and AP reclassifies AR with a credit balance and vice versa. (True/False)

74. The dunning area is used to distinguish dunning areas within an entity. (True/False)

75. Line layout is used to display desired fields in the vendor line item display screen. (True/False)

76. State True or False for each of the following statements.

   a. Business areas are used across company codes.
   b. Business areas are assigned to company codes.
   c. When the business area balance sheet is enabled, the business area is a required entry during posting.
   d. Use of the business area is optional.

77. State True or False for each of the following statements.

   a. The company code is assigned to a plant.
   b. A COA can be assigned to multiple company codes.
   c. A plant can be assigned to multiple company codes.

78. The three tiers in an SAP R/3 system are the presentation server, application server, and database server. (True/False)

79.   The company code is the entity in SAP R/3 that provides financial statements for external reporting. (True/False)

80.   State True or False for each of the following statements.

   a. A company code can be assigned to many plants.
   b. A company code and a company have a 1:*n* relationship.
   c. A controlling area may have multiple company codes.
   d. A company code can be assigned to an operating concern.

81.   The implementation of business area entities is optional for FICO implementation. (True/False)

82.   The main menu, application menu, and task menu represent the menu hierarchy in an SAP R/3 system. (True/False)

83.   On the logon screen, only the client, user ID, and password field appear. (True/False)

84.   Which of the following is seen by the user in the message bar?

   a. Transaction code
   b. Program names
   c. Screen variants
   d. Information, error, and warning messages

85. When a user has multiple sessions open, the system saves all opened sessions when he saves. (True/False)

86. A business area is directly assigned to a company. (True/False)

87. ABAP stands for Advanced Business Application Programming. (True/False)

88. The configuration menu resides within the application menu. (True/False)

89. There are three data types within SAP: master data, table data, and transaction data. (True/False)

90. All company codes within a controlling area should have a COA. (True/False)

91. A parked document changes G/L balances. (True/False)

92. When you cancel/delete a parked document, another number is created. (True/False)

93. The document number range in FI is shared by all company codes within a client. (True/False)

94. GR/IR clearing has to be done manually. (True/False)

95. Through an APP, you can pay the vendor as well as the customer. (True/False)

96. State True or False for each of the following statements.

   a. You create the bank master at the country level.
   b. Once the address of the company code is configured, you can't change it.
   c. It is possible to configure installment payments based on amount.
   d. An SAP solution first posts to the G/L, and then to sub ledgers

97. State True or False for each of the following statements.

   a. All of the data and programs are stored in the database server in SAP R/3.
   b. You use /o to end the current session.
   c. You can execute a program directly from the command box.
   d. The assignment of company codes and business areas is 1:1.

98. State True or False for each of the following statements.

    a. The G/L master consists of two segments: (1) general data and (2) company code data.

    b. A COA can be assigned to more than one company code within a client.

    c. A year-dependent fiscal year needs to be configured each year.

99. State True or False for each of the following statements.

    a. Customer/vendor master data is client-dependent master data.

    b. FI document header data is stored in table BKPF.

    c. Company code segment data of the G/L master is stored in table SKB1, while general data is stored in table SKA1.

    d. Document number ranges are either internal or external for all document types of a company code.

100. State True or False for each of the following statements.

    a. A fiscal year is either year dependent or year independent.

    b. Many sales organizations can be assigned to a company code.

    c. A document number range can be assigned to more than one document type.

    d. Posting keys are company code–dependent data.

101. State True or False for each of the following statements.

    a. An asset class is client-dependent master data.

    b. A line item managed account must have open item management activated.

    c. An SD payment term has priority over an FI payment in cases where the document originated from the SD module.

    d. All company code within a client must use the same COA.

102. State True or False for each of the following statements.

    a. The document posting date determines the baseline date of a line item.

    b. You can't override payment terms assigned to a customer/vendor master while posting a transaction.

c. You can assign more than one payment term to a customer/vendor master.

d. The document type determines the reversal document type.

103. State True or False for each of the following statements.

a. SAP R/3 always assigns document number in case of internal number range.

b. A purchase order creates an accounting document within SAP R/3.

c. You can see all linked documents in SAP R/3.

104. State True or False for each of the following statements.

a. An APP selects all vendors/customers to be paid.

b. An APP selects open items to be paid for defined customers/vendors.

c. An APP clears the open items, which are paid.

105. State True or False for each of the following statements.

a. You can block or remove any payment block in the payment proposal edit phase of an APP.

b. You can remove a payment block from the vendor/customer master during the APP edit phase.

c. Line items that can be paid are listed in the exception list.

106. An automatic payment run is identified by run date and identification. (True/False)

107. As per best practice, the payment run date should be the current date. (True/False)

108. State True or False for each of the following statements.

    a. A dunning program is meant for dunning of regular customers, not for a one-time account.

    b. You can assign more than one dunning program to a customer.

    c. You can set the minimum limit for transactions to be dunned.

    d. A dunning program posts dunning interest to G/L accounts.

109. A customer can have a maximum of nine dunning levels in a standard SAP-delivered program. (True/False)

110. State True or False for each of the following statements.

    a. You can calculate balance interest with interest type "P."

    b. You assign an interest ID to line items while posting a transaction.

111. State True or False for each of the following statements.

    a. You can configure a financial statement version up to 10 levels.

    b. In a G/L external number range, the G/L number can be more than 10 characters.

    c. It is possible to reclassify a customer under a different group.

112. A doubtful receivable is a special G/L transaction. (True/False)

113. You can run foreign currency valuation only for customers or vendors, not for G/Ls. (True/False)

114. State True or False for each of the following statements.

    a. You can't clear an open item by reversing it.
    b. Profit center accounting (PCA) is part of the FI module in mySAP ERP.
    c. You can settle an IO to the G/L through external settlement.

115. State True or False for each of the following statements.

    a. Depreciation posting happens through a batch input session in SAP R/3.
    b. Depreciation posting happens through direct posting in mySAP ERP.
    c. A transaction can be posted to G/L account, which doesn't have company code segment.
    d. Even if a G/L account is blocked at a COA level, you can post it.

116. State True or False for each of the following statements.

    a. You can select a reconciliation ledger while posting to a vendor.
    b. Payment terms are company code dependent.
    c. A down payment request clears open items in AP and AR.
    d. When you are clearing a debit item with a credit item, the SAP system doesn't create a clearing document.

117. State True or False for each of the following statements.

    a. The down payment due date is determined by the SAP solution.
    b. The G/L master is a company code–dependent master.
    c. You can have alphanumeric characters in an external number range.
    d. All special G/L transactions are posted to the normal reconciliation account of the vendor/customer.

118. State True or False for each of the following statements.

    a. The company code is part of the line item information in an FI document.
    b. You can see document currency and company code currency during line item display.

119. R/3 stands for real-time three-tier architecture. (True/False)

120. The FI module in mySAP ERP consists of the GL, AP, AR, AA, and PCA modules. (True/False)

121. A controlling area can be assigned to multiple operational concerns. (True/False)

122. More than one purchase organization can be assigned to a company code. (True/False)

123. Costing-based CO-PA shares tables with other CO modules. (True/False)

124. The creation of company codes is an IMG activity. (True/False)

125. The selection variant helps to standardize selection criteria for repetitive use. (True/False)

126. The credit control area provides integrated solutions for the SD and AR components of SAP solutions. (True/False)

127. A company code can be assigned to an operating COA, country COA, or group COA. (True/False)

128. The G/L account groups control number range and G/L master field status. (True/False)

129. The G/L account and primary cost element have a 1:1 relationship. (True/False)

130. In addition to the standard hierarchy, you can have an alternative profit center hierarchy. (True/False)

131. Statistical order permits external settlement. (True/False)

132. The SD billing document generates an FI document. (True/False)

133. A purchase order creates a commitment posting into CO if commitment posting is active in the controlling area. (True/False)

134. An FI document has the following areas: header section, line item section, and template areas. (True/False)

135. The FI document number range is assigned to document types. (True/False)

136. Standard SAP delivered account types are A, D, K, M, and S. (True/False)

137. Posting keys determine account types, debit and credit logic, and line item field status. (True/False)

138. In mySAP ERP, leading and nonleading ledgers will have the same fiscal year variant. (True/False)

139. A normal fiscal year can have a maximum of 12 regular posting periods and 4 special periods. (True/False)

140. Negative reversal posts a transaction with a negative sign on the same side of the G/L account. (True/False)

141. The customer and vendor masters can only be created in the FI module. (True/False)

142. The customer master is divided into four parts: (1) general data, (2) company code data, (3) sales organization data, and (4) credit control area data. (True/False)

143. The employee tolerance limit determines the allowable line item tolerance limit for clearing open items. (True/False)

144. Posting keys determine the document types to be used while posting a business transaction. (True/False)

145. The document type is company code dependent. (True/False)

146. Posting keys 01 and 11 are used for G/L posting. (True/False)

147. The document date determines the posting period and fiscal year. (True/False)

148. When you are creating the vendor master centrally, the system allows you to create all segments of the vendor master. (True/False)

149. The house bank ID is always a numeric ID. (True/False)

150. When the controlling (CO) module is active, you can post an expense without a cost object. (True/False)

151. In the standard system, the posting key 40 refers to G/L credit. (True/False)

152. While posting to a one-time vendor, the user needs to enter vendor information like vendor name, address, etc., at the line item level. (True/False)

153. A parking document is always a balanced document, i.e., debits = credits. (True/False)

154. A shortened fiscal year is always a year-dependent fiscal year. (True/False)

155. In order to get the opening balance in a new fiscal year, you need to carry forward GL, AR, and AP. (True/False)

156. A user can enter the currency transaction rate if the document currency is different from the company code currency. (True/False)

157. The tax category dictates whether or not a tax code is required for a line item. (True/False)

158. If you want to display a document line item based on the posting date, then you should use short key "001." (True/False)

159. All open item managed accounts should have the line item activated. (True/False)

160. If line item management is activated, then you can drill down to the line item level from the G/L balance. (True/False)

161. In SAP R/3, you can post up to 999 line items in a document. (True/False)

162. For AP, AR, and AA, you use reconciliation accounts, which are updated through batch processing. (True/False)

163. Validation checks for conditions and updates the required fields. (True/False)

164. For every G/L account, you should have a cost element. (True/False)

165. A company code should have one G/L account. (True/False)

166. For a reconciliation account, you should always set up an external number range. (True/False)

167. The field status group is created at the company code level. (True/False)

168. Once you cross a posting period, the system closes the posting period automatically. (True/False)

169. While posting to a vendor, you are selecting the vendor group and vendor. (True/False)

170. A tax procedure is a client-level configuration. (True/False)

171. A special G/L transaction always posts to an alternative reconciliation account. (True/False)

2.2 ANSWERS

1. b
2. b
3. a-False, b-True
4. a-True, b-False
5. False
6. b
7. a-True, b-True, c-True, d-False
8. a
9. b
10. a, b
11. a
12. a, b, c
13. True
14. False
15. False
16. True

17. False
18. False
19. False
20. False
21. False
22. False
23. False
24. a-False, b-True, c-False
25. False
26. a-False, b-True, c-False
27. True
28. a-True, b-False
29. a-True, b-True, c-True
30. a-False, b-True
31. a-False, b-True
32. a-False, b-True
33. a-False, b-True, c-False
34. c, d
35. a-False, b-False, c-True, d-False
36. a-False, b-True
37. a-False, b-False
38. a-False, b-True
39. b
40. a
41. a-True, b-True
42. a-False, b-True, c-False
43. a-False, b-False
44. a-True, b-False, c-False
45. a-True, b-False, c-False
46. a-False, b-True, c-True
47. False
48. False

49. Yes
50. No
51. No
52. Yes
53. True
54. a-True, b-True
55. a-True, b-False, c-False
56. a-False, b-False, c-False, d-False
57. a-True, b-True
58. a-True, b-False, c-False
59. 9 (Nine)
60. True
61. a-True, b-True, c-True
62. a-True, b-False, c-True, d-False
63. a-True (Up to 4.6C), b-False (After 4.6C)
64. a-True, b-False, c-True, d-False
65. False
66. True
67. True
68. False
69. True
70. True
71. False
72. True
73. True
74. True
75. True
76. a-True, b-False, c-True, d-True
77. a-True, b-True, c-False
78. True
79. True

80. a-True, b-False, c-True, d-False
81. True
82. True
83. False
84. d
85. False
86. False
87. True
88. False
89. True
90. True
91. False
92. False
93. False
94. True
95. True
96. a-True, b-False, c-False, d-False
97. a-False, b-False, c-False, d-False
98. a-True, b-True, c-True
99. a-True, b-True, c-True, d-False
100. a-True, b-True, c-True, d-False
101. a-True, b-False, c-True, d-False
102. a- Not always, b- False, c- False, d-True
103. a-True, b-False, c-True
104. a-False, b-True, c-False
105. a-True, b-False, c- False
106. True
107. True
108. a-False, b-False, c-True, d-False
109. True

110. a-False, b- False
111. a-False, b-False, c-False
112. True
113. False
114. a-True, b-True, c-True
115. a-True, b-True, c-False, d-False
116. a-False, b-False, c-False, d-False
117. a-False, b-False, c-True, d-False
118. a-False, b-True
119. True
120. True
121. False
122. True
123. False
124. True
125. True
126. True
127. False
128. True
129. True
130. True
131. False
132. True
133. True
134. True
135. True
136. True
137. True
138. False
139. True

140. True
141. False
142. False
143. False
144. False
145. False
146. False
147. False
148. True
149. False
150. False
151. False
152. True
153. True
154. True
155. True

156. True
157. True
158. True
159. True
160. True
161. True
162. True
163. False
164. False
165. False
166. False
167. False
168. False
169. False
170. True
171. True

3

ISSUES AND
RESOLUTIONS

A ticket is a generic name for claims made by the end user to technical support. At the very least, the end user has to send an email with a description of the issue, the transaction code, and the program or report name. There are some applications available to manage these jobs, such as Quality Center from HP, ClarifyCRM®, and ManageNow®, among others. The tickets usually have a priority scale: T1 (meaning the issue must be handled the same day, T2, T3, etc. The person in charge of each module for analysis and resolution handles those tickets. If it involves configuration, when you have missing e.g. cost center, currency or customized reports discrepancy or for third part as ABAP developers for debug or include functionality. Depending on the nature of the ticket and resolution, necessary code changes will be done in the development server. Once the SAP team is satisfied with unit testing, changes will be promoted to the quality environment for user testing acceptance. Once changes are approved by the user, the SAP team deploys the changes in the production environment.

This chapter presents issues that may arise while using SAP solutions and discusses ways to resolve those issues.

3.1 SAP GENERAL

Issue No.: 1
The user is trying to create a vendor for a particular company code. In the initial screen for the customer, the company code was set to the default and the user is trying to create another company code.

For rapid data entry, some important parameters such as company code and controlling area are set as the default while setting the user profile. If the security role allows, the user can reset or define his own parameters through transaction code SU01. In transaction code SU01, you will find a Parameter tab; this is where you make all default settings. Check the default value for parameter ID BUK. If you don't want any default values, remove them.

3.2 GENERAL LEDGER (G/L) ACCOUNTING

Issue No.: 2
The user is not getting the drop-down list of G/L accounts that he defined through FS00 while posting through transaction code FB50/F-02.

While entering a transaction, the user usually presses F4 to select a G/L account from the chart of account (COA). The SAP R/3 system displays all available accounts that are created for the desired company code and COA in question. If the user is not getting the G/L account in the drop-down list, try one of the following:

1. Check if the G/L accounts have been created in the company code you are posting.
2. Make sure you have selected the correct company code in T-code FB50.
3. The drop-down has a personal list and a global list. If you are in the personal list, switch to the global list.

Issue No.: 3
My client raised a PO at USD 13 for 50 qty. A goods receipt MIGO transaction was done at that price. Now my client wants to do a MIRO transaction at USD 14 for 50 qty.

This situation can be handled in two different ways: (1) price difference or (2) reversing MIGO and repost MIGO with correct price.

1. At the time of the MIRO transaction, you have an option to post a price difference. In the MIRO transaction, enter the G/L account for price difference and amount (i.e., $1).
2. Reverse the MIGO entry, make changes in the PO, then once again do the MIGO and MIRO transactions.

Issue No.: 4
How can you add a new column in an open item clearing transaction with T-code F-03? Right now you have a document number, document date, document type,

posting key, and amount. You need to add a posting key and amount in the transaction fields in the screen.

1. Go to the Clearing G/L Account Process Open Item screen using T-code F-03 from the menu bar.
2. Select **Settings** and **Change line layout**.
3. Select the **Create** button.
4. Give the line layout a name and description, and press **Enter**.
5. Select the **Insert after** button to view the available fields.
6. Select the required field by double-clicking on that field. The required field is automatically listed under your own layout.
7. Repeat the process for each field required to create your layout and save.
8. Go back to the Clearing G/L Account Process Open Item screen, and select the **Editing option** button under the line layout variant for the G/L account clearing transaction.
9. Give your variant a name and save.

Issue No.: 5
The user wants to add a trading partner as selection criteria in the F-03 screen. This does not come with the standard screen.

You are using transaction code F-03 to clear open items for a particular G/L account. While offsetting debit transactions with credits, depending upon business requirements, the user will select one of the selection options provided in that screen. The SAP R/3 system will pull all open items based on the selection criteria. The standard SAP R/3 system comes with very limited selection criteria; however, you can include a new selection field and change the sequence of the selection criteria. To add a new selection field or change the selection criteria sequence, you have to configure the SAP R/3 system through transaction code O7F1.

Issue No.: 6
There are a few G/L accounts where line item displays are not activated. The client would like to see what entries are actually hitting these accounts.

There are two possible solutions regarding this problem. SAP recommends the first solution because only standard means are used. The second solution requires the usage of a correction report and is therefore a consulting solution.

- Standard solution:

  1. Create a new account and set the options according to your require-
     ments. Be sure to set the line item display indicator (SKB1-XKRES).
  2. Transfer the items from the old account to the new account. You can
     only do this for accounts that you cannot automatically post to. As an
     alternative, you can transfer the balance completely.
  3. Lock the old account for postings.

- Consulting solution:

  1. Manipulate all documents that were posted in the past. You can use the
     correction program RFSEPA01 (contained in the standard system as
     of release 3.0D). Read the document carefully.
  2. For releases prior to 3.0D, a corresponding correction program is
     available on SAPSERV3.

While creating the G/L account, utmost care should be taken with the open
item management and line item management attributes of the G/L account.

Issue No.: 7

*While creating G/L accounts, some of the G/L accounts were wrongly kept as
open item management. Now the user wants to remove open item management
functionality through transaction code FS02, but the system is giving the
following error message: "This account does not balance to zero."*

System Response:
*You cannot switch the open item management specification on or off with this
transaction.*

Procedure:
*If you want to switch this function on retroactively for a certain account, you
should create a new account with the correct setting and use this to make a
transfer posting of existing items.*

While creating the G/L master, you have to pay utmost attention to the setting
of G/L master attributes. The situation here is changing the attribute of G/L
accounts after posting the transaction. For this, you have two options:

- Standard solution:

  1. Create a new G/L account.
  2. Transfer the account balance from the old G/L account to the new G/L
     account.

3. Switch off open item management for the old account and retransfer the G/L balance from the new account to the old account.

Without making the account balance zero, you can't switch an open item attribute of a G/L account.

▪ Consulting solution:

As an alternative, the user could try program RFSEPA03, depending on his SAP release. The user may have to copy the program to the "Z" program and remove the piece of code that prevents its use. Before adopting this procedure, make sure the user reads the program documentation and related SAP advice.

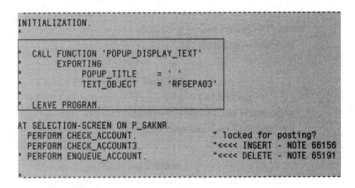

FIGURE 3.1   RFSEPA03 correction report

Issue No.: 8
The client processed a bank statement and one of the line items in the bank statement overview in transaction FEBA shows the status as "Complete." However, the client used a wrong posting rule here. How can you change to the correct posting rule and process the transaction again so that the status is changed to "Posted"?

There are two ways to handle this situation:

▪ With a reverse bank reconciliation posting document.
▪ By deleting the bank statement from the SAP R/3 system. To delete the bank statement, follow these steps:

1. In T-code SM38, enter **RFEBKA95** and execute the program. It will open the posted bank statement.

2. Deselect all and select the statement that is wrongly posted to delete it.
3. Repost the bank statement through T-code FF67.

Issue No.: 9

The user has posted the documents without a business area. Now he wants to update them. You know that once a document is posted, the business area cannot be changed in the document overview. How can you solve this issue?

To update the business area, you have two options:

- With the help of ABAP, you can update the business area in the posted document's BSIS table.
- Or you could just reverse the original entry and repost the entry with business all the necessary details.

It is advisable to use the second option.

Issue No.: 10

The user is posting monthly entries through T-code FBS1 and reversing them on the first of the next month through T-code F-81. The user wants to automate the reversal procedure.

SAP solutions do come with automatic reversal of accrual entries, but the user has to execute transaction code F-81 for accrual reversal. Accrual entries are made through transaction code FBS1. SAP R/3 includes functionality to enter reversal dates while posting transactions. Once you are executing transaction code F-81, SAP R/3 will provide a list of accrual entries to be reversed. Instead of executing transaction code F-81 manually at an interval, you can create a batch job with a suitable variant and schedule it.

Issue No.: 11

A company code was assigned to an alternative COA. While creating a new G/L, the user keyed the alternative G/L in the G/L master. But while saving, the following error occurred: "Alternative Account number already assigned to account xxxxxx, cannot save." What would be the reason and how can you solve this?

The error is due to the assignment of the operating G/L account to the country COA. You can't assign multiple operating G/L accounts to one country COA G/L account. The relation between the operating G/L and country COA G/L is 1:1. When you are creating the G/L account with reference from some existing account, the alternative COA is also copied here; however, the country COA G/L is already assigned to an operating COA G/L account. This rule is not valid for group COA G/L accounts.

Issue No.: 12

After a transaction was posted, the client learned that an account that was classified as a balance sheet account should have been a P&L account. Now the client wants to reclassify the G/L account. Is this possible?

The reclassification of G/L accounts from a balance sheet account to a P&L account or vice versa is possible. Here are the steps for such a conversion:

1. You can reclassify a G/L account when its balance is zero. So clear all open items and bring your account balance to zero.
2. Through T-code FS00, change the account type from a BS account to a P&L account. In a standard SAP system, you will get an error message. Note the message numbers.
3. Change the message control by following this menu path: **SPRO → Cross-Application Components → Bank Directory → Change Message Control** (transaction code OBA5).
4. Enter **FH** in the Area box (note that this is just an example) and press **Enter** for the next screen. In the New Entries: Overview of Added Entries screen, enter the two message numbers from step 2 and set the message to W (for Warning).

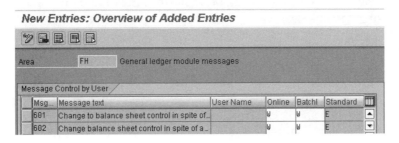

FIGURE 3.2 **Message control**

5. Once you have completed step 4, reclassify your G/L account as mentioned in step 2 This time, the system will issue a warning message and your account will be reclassified once you save your changes.
6. If your books of accounts are closed for the previous year, run program SAPF0110 to carry forward your balance to the new year.

The reclassification of G/L accounts is advisable at either the end or beginning of the year.

Issue No.: 13

While analyzing accounts, the user found that certain document numbers are not appearing or are missing. For example, number range 17 is assigned to document type KA, which has the range 1700000000–1799999999 valid up to 9999. The current status shows that the next available number is 1790000000. During analysis, the user found that documents 1780000000–1780000010 are missing.

The user wants to know why document numbers are missing.

There are several reasons for missing document numbers. Here are two scenarios for this issue:

1. One possible reason could be that these documents were initially parked and later deleted. In this case, those document numbers cannot be reused.
2. The documents probably don't exist. SAP solutions will set aside numbers for use when the system detects multiple document creation. If someone is creating documents, the system will make available, for example, the next 10 numbers, "reserving them," in essence. If the user only creates eight documents, two document numbers will be missing.

You may use the following programs/reports to find out the reason for the missing documents:

- Program RFVBER00 provides a list of transactions that failed while updating the database.
- Program RFBNUM00 shows gaps in the FI number range.

Issue No.: 14

What is ranking order in an APP?

Ranking order represents priority assignments to each house bank. This helps the APP choose the house bank for payment in case there is more than one bank account satisfying the payment program parameters.

3.3 ACCOUNTS PAYABLE (AP)

Issue No.: 15
The client printed 50 checks, of which 10 checks are spoiled or torn. Now the client wants to reprint the checks using the same APP. Is this possible? Or do you have to void those checks that are spoiled or torn?

There may be times when the payment run has successfully posted payment documents and generated checks, but for some reason or other, the checks are not valid. In this situation, you have to void all of the printed checks and reprint them. To void and reprint, follow these steps:

1. Execute transaction code **FCH7**. You may navigate to FCH7 through the payment run.
2. Execute transaction code **F110**, enter the payment run ID and run date, then follow the menu path: **Environment**→**Check information**→**Change**→ **Reprint Check** (t-codeFCH7).
3. Enter the following details:

   - Paying company ode
   - House bank
   - Account ID
   - Number of the check to be voided
   - Void reason code
   - New check number

4. Choose the path: **Check**→**Reprint** from the menu.

   You must follow this process in a situation where you have issued checks, but the checks are lost in post.

Issue No.: 16

While posting outgoing payments through T-code F-53, the client received the error message 'The entry 1210 is missing in table T043G' and the system did not allow the posting payment document.

The SAP R/3 system returns this error when it doesn't find vendor/customer tolerance for your company code. In this example, you are processing an outgoing payment for a company code for which the vendor tolerance group is not defined. Create vendor tolerance through transaction code **OBA3** (menu path: **Financial Accounting**→**Accounts Receivable and Accounts Payable**→**Business Transactions**→**Outgoing Payments**→**Manual Outgoing Payments**→**Define Tolerances** (Vendors)) for your company code.

Issue No.: 17

A vendor has requested that charges for services and materials be paid through separate bank accounts. For example, Vendor X supplies both services and materials and maintains two bank accounts—one for services and another for materials. The vendor requests that your client pay for services through bank account XXXXX and materials through bank account YYYYY. Is this possible when payments are made through an APP?

A vendor may have multiple bank accounts. The SAP system provides the functionality to store and use information from multiple vendor bank accounts in the Payment transactions screen of the vendor master general data via transaction code FK03.

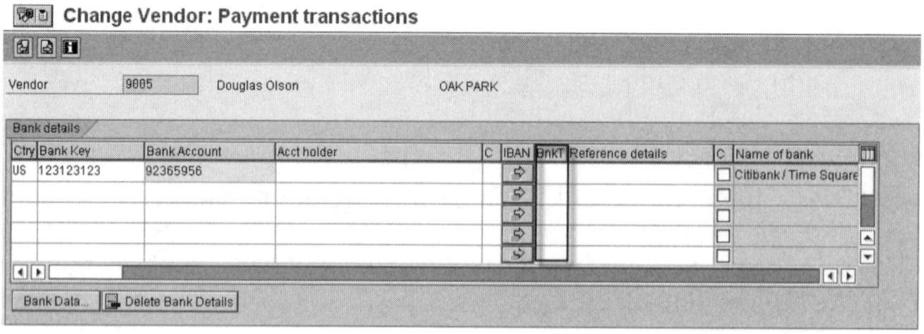

FIGURE 3.3   **Vendor bank accounts**

You can use the BnkT (bank type) field in the vendor master to enter text differentiators for identifying the vendor's bank accounts. If you leave the bank type field blank for a bank account in the vendor master, it serves as the default bank if the bank type information is missing in the vendor invoice.

In this situation, you maintain information on both banks through the identifiers XXXXX and YYYYY. While entering the vendor invoice for services, select bank identifier XXXXX and for materials, select YYYYY. Now when you are paying through an APP, you will find you are remitting payment to two different bank accounts for the vendor for different services.

Issue No.: 18

A client posted a new document using T-code FBR2. Using T-code F110, payment was also posted for this invoice.

After this transaction, it was found that the discount base was wrong and the system had taken the value based on the reference document. How can you reverse a payment posting and change the baseline date?

You have posted a vendor invoice through transaction code FBR2. This transaction code is used to post a new document with reference to an existing document. While posting a new document through transaction code FBR2, SAP R/3 will copy all of the fields from the reference document; however, you can change whatever is needed. After having posted the vendor invoice, you also processed payment for the said document. To correct the baseline date, you have to correct the vendor document. Follow these steps to resolve this:

1. Cancel the payment check via transaction code FCH8 (if the check is in your possession). This transaction voids the check, resets the clearing process, and reverses the payment document.
2. Reverse the vendor document and post a new document with the correct discount base date.

Issue No.: 19

A user made an advance payment of INR 20000 through a special G/L transaction and deducted withholding taxes, at 2% (Rs. 400.00). Later the user received an invoice for Rs. 30000. Now the client wants to deduct withholding tax on the balance amount, i.e., Rs. 10000, not on the entire amount. If the user uses T-code F-43, it deducts the tax on the full invoice value of Rs. 30000, which is Rs. 600, whereas the user wants the advance payment taken into account and wants to pay Rs. 200 (Rs. 600–Rs. 400).

The user needs to deduct the tax on the entire amount at the time of invoice posting. While adjusting the advance payment against the invoice, the SAP R/3 system will reverse the tax you have deducted.

However, the user needs to make the following configuration in the payment withholding type for this tax reversal to take place:

1. Follow the menu path: **IMG → Financial Account Global setting → Withholding tax → Extend withholding tax → Calculation → Withholding Tax Type → Define withholding tax type for payment posting**.
2. Select the withholding tax type. At the bottom is a Central invoice window, in which the user will select the last radio button—**Central inv. prop**.

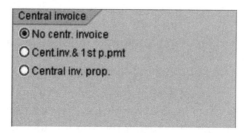

FIGURE 3.4   Configuring withholding tax

Issue No.: 20
The client needs to update a reference field in the header of a payment document with the check number generated by the system. Is there any way to update the payment document with the check number?

Normally, you follow this process when you have issued a check that is written outside of the SAP solution. To maintain the check register, you have to update the payment document with check numbers. You can achieve this through transaction code FCHU, which will update the payment document with check information. Follow these steps:

1. Go to transaction code FCHU.
2. Fill out the company code, house bank, and account ID areas and give the check number and payment document number for which you want to update the check number.
3. Now, in the Target field selection of the check number section, select the field on which you want to update the check number.
4. Then execute.

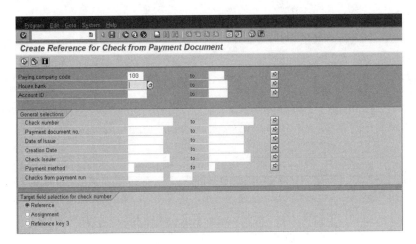

FIGURE 3.5 **Executing transaction code FCHU**

Issue No.: 21

The user wants to print a check for a vendor down payment. To use T-code F-58, the system needs an open item. When the user makes an advance payment, there will not be any open items in the vendor account.

Transaction code F-58 is used to process payment for existing open items. This transaction code can't be used for processing advance payments. You have two options to handle this situation: (1) create an advance payment request and pay through an APP or (2) create an advance payment document through transaction code F-48 and print a check through transaction code FBZ5. Here are the steps for both options:

■ Option 1:

1. Create a down payment request through transaction code **F-47**.
2. Run the payment program through transaction code **F110**.

■ Option 2:

1. Use transaction code **F-48** for advance payment to vendors.
2. Based on the posted document number, print a check using transaction code **FBZ5**.

Issue No.: 22

The user wants to make a check payment for petty expenses like stationery, travel, etc. Transaction code F-02 provides facility to capture check information. Without check information, the user can't do bank reconciliation. The user is wondering if there is any workaround to deal with this situation.

The user can use transaction code F-53 with doc type GZ (General Payments). In the Post Outgoing Payment: Header Data screen, the user has to provide bank data and the check number in the assignment field. After entering this information, the user can switch screens using F-02. To switch the screen, the user must follow these steps:

1. From the system menu, choose **Goto → Document overview** (as shown in Figure 3.6).

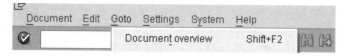

FIGURE 3.6   **Using transaction code F-53**

2. After selecting Document overview, the user will get a new screen, in which he can enter expenses by entering the posting key and expenses G/L accounts. For bank reconciliation, the user can choose internal algorithm 15 or 13 for the system to check the assignment field for check numbers.

Issue No.: 23
While posting a transaction through T-code F-58, the user sees this error message:
"Changes for vendor XXXXX not yet confirmed."

In SAP R/3 configuration, you define certain fields as sensitive to have proper control and tracking on master data changes. If the user changes these sensitive field(s), someone other than the user who changed the master data has to confirm these changes. Until such confirmation, the SAP R/3 system does not allow any transactions with that trading partner. For example, you configure payment term as a sensitive field. To accommodate business requirements, user XXXXX updates the payment term with a new payment term ID. In order to carry out any transactions with this business partner, the changes have to be approved by another user.

To confirm this change, the user has to use transaction code FK09. Follow this procedure before executing transaction code F-58.

Issue No.: 24
In transaction code F-33 (bills of exchange discounting), the user entered all data.
When this is executed, the user receives a message that A/C No. 400400 (Interest
account) requires an assignment to a CO object. What does this mean?

When a controlling area is active, the user has to assign a valid cost object while posting expenses. In this case, bank interest is an expenses account, while posting selects a valid cost object.

Issue No.: 25
The user has executed transaction code F110 to pay 50 vendors, but he only
has 20 checks left. Hence, when he ran the program, it printed the checks with
random numbers. Now the problem is he is unable to cancel the payments, as
there is no check number. How can he reprint or cancel the checks?

The check printing program generated more checks than there are available check numbers. To handle this issue, follow these steps:

1. Before proceeding, ensure that you have maintained a new check lot through transaction code FCHI. Be sure to correct your check lot before you do anything.
2. In transaction code F110, enter the payment run ID and payment run date.

3. Go to the Printout/data medium tab and place the mouse curser on variant field against print program.
4. From the system menu, choose **Environment → Maintain Variants** as shown in Figure 3.7.

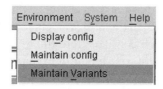

FIGURE 3.7   Using transaction code F110

5. SAP R/3 will show the Maintain variant: XXXX screen, at the bottom of which you will see the section shown in Figure 3.8.

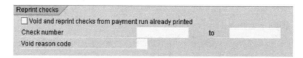

FIGURE 3.8   Using transaction code F110

6. Select **Void and reprint checks from payment run already printed**. This procedure will void all of the checks generated through this particular payment program.

If you want to void and regenerate a particular set of checks, enter the check numbers you want to void along with a void reason code.

7. Save the variant and come back to the payment run screen. Click on 🔧 Printout to generate the desired checks.

Issue No.: 26
The user defined multiple payments in the vendor master, i.e., "C" and "E." As per business requirements, if the business is paying $10,000 or less, the check will be issued to the vendor. For a payment of more than $10,000, the business will pay though wire transfer. As a FICO consultant, the user is looking to you for guidance.

You can define multiple allowed payment methods for the vendor by assigning the payment method in the vendor master.

While configuring the payment program through transaction code FBZP, you specify your allowable minimum and maximum dollar amounts for your payment method in the Payment Methods in Company Code step.

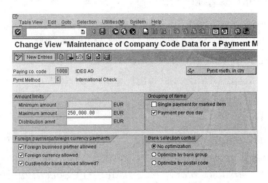

FIGURE 3.9   Using transaction code FBZP

Follow these steps to resolve this issue:

1. Set the minimum to 0 and the maximum to 10000 for payment method "C."
2. Set the minimum to 10001 and the maximum to any larger amount for payment method "E."

Issue No.: 27
It is not possible to post multiple customers in transaction code FB70. Can you use F-21?

After starting with FB70 and making as many entries as you wish, if you need to post to other customer accounts you can press F6, which switches you back to the "old-style" data entry screen where you can post to as many other customer accounts as you wish using the old "posting key" method.

3.4 ASSETS MANAGEMENT (AM)

Issue No.: 28
During data migration, the client forgot to transfer two assets whose book values are zero. Now the client wants to bring those assets to the asset portfolio for reporting purposes. The client needs both acquisition cost and accumulated depreciation in FI, including information from the AM module. As the data

migration is already done and the company code in question is already in the Go-live stage, how can you bring these two assets to FI—including the Asset module?

The solution for this ticket would be:

1. Set the company code status to **"1"Asset data transfer not yet completed**.
2. Update legacy data using T-code **AS91**.
3. Enter the acquisition cost and accumulated depreciation using T-code **OASV**.

Issue No.: 29

The user wants to transfer an asset from one asset class to another asset class. A depreciation expense of the new asset class is assigned to another account determination. The user wants to transfer APC, accumulated depreciation, and depreciation expenses to G/L accounts that are assigned to the new asset class. Transaction code ABUMN has fields for ACP and accumulated depreciation. The user is wondering how depreciation expenses will be transferred from the old accounts to the new account.

Through transaction code ABUMN, you can reclassify assets. In the reclassification process, you can only transfer APC and accumulated costs to a new asset class with immediate effect. Depreciation expenses will be transferred to the new G/L when you run depreciation. However, during the depreciation run, you can't transfer previous depreciation expenses that were already charged to the cost center. But you can transfer current-year depreciation to the new depreciation expenses account. While entering the transaction in transaction code ABUMN, enter in the value date field the date on which you want to transfer your expenses to the new account.

Issue No.: 30

After the depreciation run, the user changed the capitalized date and the depreciation start date in the asset master. After making changes in the asset master, the user once again ran depreciation in "repeat run" mode. But changes made to the asset master did not hit depreciation, and the difference value is appearing as a planned value when checked in T-code AW01N.

If you are making any changes in the asset master that affect depreciation that is already posted, you must follow this procedure:

1. Recalculate depreciation using T-code **AFAR**.
2. Repeat the depreciation run using T-code **AFAB**.

Issue No.: 31
While running the year-end closing process through transaction code AJAB, the system gives the following errors:

"Asset is incomplete and has to be completed. Message no. AU083"

Diagnosis:
The asset 000000100001-0000 is marked as incomplete. The asset was created by someone who did not have the 'asset accountant' asset view. When this is the case, the system expects that certain required fields are not maintained.

Procedure:
You can add the necessary specifications using the master data change transaction and the needed asset view.

The system gives this type of error when the asset master was not properly maintained. You can execute transaction code AUVA to get the list of incomplete assets. After getting the list of incomplete assets, maintain the necessary data for the asset master and rerun transaction code AFAB.

Issue No.: 32
The user wants to post a transaction in the year 2008 through transaction code F-90. While posting the transaction, the system returns the following error:

"You cannot post to asset in company code 9999 fiscal year 2008 Message no. AA347."

Diagnosis:
"A fiscal year change has not yet been performed in Asset accounting for company code 9999."

Procedure:
Check the asset value date.

It looks like the user entered an asset acquisition in fiscal year 2008 for company code 9999, for which the assets accounting (AA) fiscal year change has not been carried out.

For AA, it is required that the user carry out the fiscal year change before entering a transaction in the new year.

Run transaction code AJRW to change the fiscal year. The latest date you can run this transaction code is the last business day of a financial year.

Issue No.: 33

After running depreciation posting for a few months, a user found that a few assets were created in the wrong asset class. The user wants to reclassify these assets to the correct asset class.

Or

Issue No.: 34

The user wants to move assets to another class because the assets were created under the wrong asset class. The old asset is capitalized on 08/01/2008. Since the depreciation key is 000, there is no depreciation running for that asset.

Now the user wants to transfer the asset to another class, so the old asset is removed (or may be retired) with an acquisition date of 08/01/2008, so that the depreciation expenses can be calculated from 08/01/2008.

This is a case of reclassification of assets. In transaction code ABUMN, = enter the APC and the accumulated cost along with an asset value date of 08/01/2008. In the receiver asset master screen, enter the desired depreciation key and the depreciation start date.

Issue No.: 35

Is it possible to integrate the sale of assets with the SD module? It will involve some sales tax and also the client wants to generate an invoice in the SAP solution. Can the SD module be used for this?

Follow these steps for selling assets with integration with the SD module:

1. Retire the asset without customer (T-code ABAON). This will credit the APC and debit the clearing account (which is a P&L account).
2. Then take a nonvaluated material for asset sale purpose, and sell the same using SD. Make sure you have a separate pricing procedure/SD document type, etc., where the account key ERL will post to the clearing account mentioned in step 1. You can collect sales tax/excise, etc., as usual.

Issue No.: 36

While capitalizing assets, the user capitalized $10,000. During the year-end process, the user realized he has wrongly capitalized $10,000 instead of $7,000. Now the user wants to rectify this by posting a credit transaction through transaction code F-90. While crediting, SAP R/3 returns the following message: "acquisition value negative in the area 15." What does this mean? How can you solve this issue and correctly post the document? Is there any other way to decapitalize an asset?

To see the negative book value check box, you will have to first activate it in the screen layout. To do this, go to **Master Data → Screen layout for Asset depreciation areas**, select the screen layout attached to the asset class to which the asset in question belongs, and click on Field group rules. Here you can make negative values optional.

If you want to allow the negative book value for all of the assets created in that particular asset class, follow the menu path: **Valuation → depreciation areas → Determine depreciation areas in the asset class**. Select the asset class, click on the depreciation area, and check the negative book value check box.

If you want to allow negative book values only for a particular asset, you can use transaction code AS02. Go to the Depreciation tab, double-click on depreciation area 15, and then check the negative values allowed check box.

Issue No.: 37

While creating assets under asset class XXXX, the user is getting default depreciation terms and the system does not allow changing depreciation terms. The user does not want the default depreciation key. How can you resolve this situation?

It sounds as if the depreciation key has been set as the default for the asset class. Check this in the IMG by doing the following:

1. Go to the Depreciation Areas screen layout using T-code **OA21**. This transaction determines how fields of depreciation areas in the asset master behave. This transaction code controls whether or not fields are editable.
2. Determine depreciation areas in an asset class using T-code **OAYZ**. This transaction code determines screen layout of the asset class and depreciation keys assigned to that asset class.

Issue No.: 38

In AA the client has not closed the year 2005, and so 2006 cannot be closed. For 2005, there are errors and recalculations required for depreciation. However, if this is done, it will hit the FI and figures submitted for 2005 will change in the SAP solution. From an audit perspective, this cannot be permitted. How can the user remedy this?

The corrections must be made to enable you to close FI-AA for 2005 and carry forward into 2006. If these corrections will significantly change your balance sheet, you can "neutralize" them by posting manual entries to bring your overall balance sheet back to what has already been reported, and then reverse these in 2006. And convince your auditor accordingly.

Issue No.: 39

The user is trying to post unplanned depreciation for an asset for depreciation area 33, i.e., the depreciation area for group currency, using the transaction type 643 and T-code ABAA. While posting, the following message pops up: "In Dep. Area 01, you can post manual depreciation up to the amount 0.00 only." The assets explorer shows the net book value as $1800.

This error generally appears after posting the unplanned depreciation when the net book value of those assets after considering the planned depreciation becomes negative. Depreciation does not allow negative book values.

Issue No.: 40

When you retire an asset, you only want the depreciation that has been posted to be reversed, i.e., accumulated depreciation up to the last month has to be reversed. However, the system is also taking the current month's unplanned depreciation into consideration when reversing accumulated depreciation and hence the profit and loss is calculated incorrectly. How can this be changed?

You assign the period control method in the depreciation key. The period control method controls how depreciation will be calculated during acquisition, retirement, etc. Check the period control method assigned to your depreciation key, which in turn is assigned to the asset master.

Issue No.: 41

The user is trying to create an asset master using transaction code AS01. He is able to see fields in the General, Time dependent, and Allocations tabs, but is not finding fields in the Depreciation Area tab. As a result, the user is unable to specify the depreciation key and life of an asset.

1. Check your screen layout for depreciation areas (transaction code **AO21**).
2. In T-code OAYZ, make sure that the depreciation areas are activated and a depreciation key is assigned. Also, check the screen layout rule for the depreciation area. It is the last column in the table after useful life and index. This is where you enter the depreciation screen layout.

Issue No.: 42

Suppose that during year end, the period for both March and April are open and the depreciation run for April is also executed. The asset year closing for the previous year is not done. Now an adjustment in depreciation is to be made in the previous year (for the March period) and the user has to run depreciation once again for March. Is this possible?

Run a depreciation recalculation (transaction code AFAR) before you execute another depreciation run.

Issue No.: 43

Assume the following scenario in AA:

Life of the asset: 3 years

Original Cost: 60,000; Scrap Value: 15,000.

The configuration was done in such a way that the SAP solution was taking the original cost as the basis for calculating depreciation. Thus, it is calculating depreciation as follows:

1st Year: 20,000
2nd Year: 20,000
3rd Year: 5,000

However, the user requirement is that depreciation should be calculated based on original cost net of scrap value. That is, depreciation should be as follows:

1st Year: 15,000
2nd Year: 15,000
3rd Year: 15,000

This could be achieved by using T-code AFAMA in SPRO by resetting (for each depreciation key) the scrap value field as "Base Value is reduced by the Scrap Value Amount."

Issue No.: 44
The user acquired his first set of assets in the month of February 2008 and is trying to run depreciation starting from February. While running depreciation, the system returns the following message: "According to the posting cycle, you should post period 001 next. Either enter period 001, which corresponds to the posting cycle, or request an unplanned posting run explicitly for this parameter."

If your posting cycle is monthly, then your SAP solution expects depreciation to run for every period in sequential order. So, you can't run February until you have completed the January depreciation run. Since you have acquired assets in the month of February, you are not running depreciation for the month of January. However, SAP R/3 is expecting you to run depreciation for January also. To overcome this, you have to do one of the following: (1) run depreciation for the month of January and then the month of February or (2) select the unplanned posting run for February. The unplanned run lets you skip over periods (in instances like this).

Issue No.: 45
The user wants to attach JPG pictures of assets to the asset master record. How can he do this?

You can attach JPG pictures to an asset master. From the asset master record menu, choose **System → Services for Object → Create Attachment**.

Issue No.: 46
In January 2008, a user noticed that assets purchased in 2007 were not recorded in the books of account. In the meantime, the user closed the books of account

for 2007. Now the user wants to disclose this asset in his books of account from January 2008.

This issue can be handled in two different ways, depending upon user requirements, i.e., from which date the user wants to calculate depreciation expenses.

1. If the user wants to calculate depreciation from January 2008, then post the asset acquisition using transaction code F-90 with reference to a vendor or using transaction code F-91 through a clearing account.
2. If the user wants to charge depreciation starting from the original purchase date, then post the acquisition through transaction code ABNAN. Then enter that date, 07/01/2007 in this example, in the Orig. val.dat field as shown in Figure 3.10.

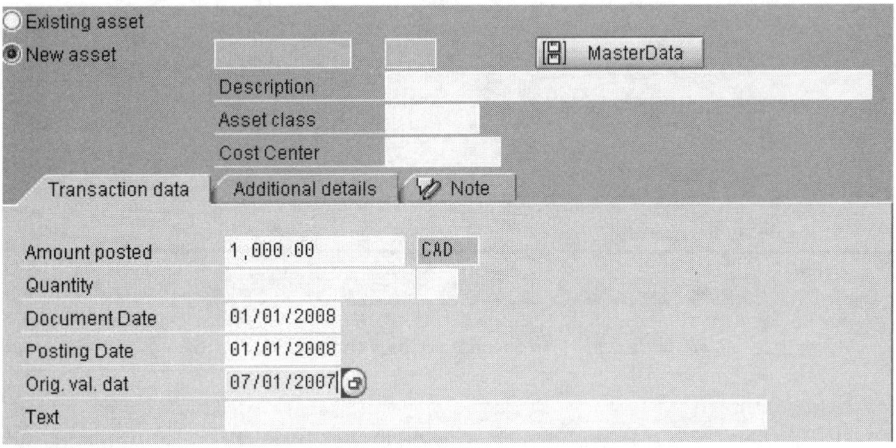

FIGURE 3.10   Using transaction code ABNAN

Issue No.: 47
The user is configuring the depreciation key. He has a unique requirement for calculating depreciation for the month of acquisition as well as retirement. Here is the requirement:

If the asset is purchased from the 1st to the 15th of a month, the depreciation should be calculated for the full month. If the assets are purchased after the 15th of a month, then no depreciation for the month of purchase is calculated. However, depreciation should be calculated for the full month for subsequent months.

The start date and end date of depreciation are controlled through the period control method. You are assigning a calendar here to control how depreciation will be calculated for the acquisition month.

See your configuration by using transaction code OAVH (menu path: **IMG → Financial Accounting → Asset Accounting → Depreciation → Valuation Methods → Period Control → Define Calendar Assignments**).

Display View ""Maint. of period control"": Overview

FV	Per.c	Name for period control	Ye...	Mo	Dy	Period	MidMon
K4	01	Pro rata at period start date	0	0	0		
K4	02	Pro rata upto mid-period at period start date	1	15	0		
K4	02	Pro rata upto mid-period at period start date	2	14	1		
K4	02	Pro rata upto mid-period at period start date	3	15	2		
K4	02	Pro rata upto mid-period at period start date	4	15	3		
K4	02	Pro rata upto mid-period at period start date	5	15	4		
K4	02	Pro rata upto mid-period at period start date	6	15	5		
K4	02	Pro rata upto mid-period at period start date	7	15	6		
K4	02	Pro rata upto mid-period at period start date	8	15	7		
K4	02	Pro rata upto mid-period at period start date	9	15	8		
K4	02	Pro rata upto mid-period at period start date	10	15	9		
K4	02	Pro rata upto mid-period at period start date	11	15	10		
K4	02	Pro rata upto mid-period at period start date	12	15	11		

FIGURE 3.11   **Additional settings for period control**

Issue No.: 48

When the user is processing asset impairment through transaction code ABMR, the system pops up with the Depreciation Areas screen. The user does not want this pop-up screen. Is there any way of turning off this pop-up and defaulting to the appropriate areas?

It is ideally advisable not to change this configuration. This pop-up window lets you select your desired depreciation areas for asset impairment. If you want to avoid this, you have to change the configuration through transaction code OA81. In this transaction code, you are setting automatic posting.

Issue No.: 49

How can the user change the screen layout for equipment masters in order to add warranty information?

If you are trying to put the warranty information on the equipment master data record itself, you can configure this in the IMG within the PM module.

Follow the menu path: **IMG → Plant Maintenance and Customer Service → Master Data in Plant Maintenance and Customer Service → Technical Objects → General Data → Set View Profiles for Technical Objects**.

The transaction code for Set View Profiles for Technical Objects controls various field layouts of the equipment master.

Issue No.: 50
A user needs help with the following situation:

Some assets will be purchased for $50 million. Then, after using them for 12 years, they can be sold for $5 million. So, the depreciable basis needs to be $45 million instead of $50 million over 12 years, or $3.750 million per year. The method will be straight line. So at the end of the 12 years, the net book value should be $5 million.

The SAP R/3 system comes with two options to handle the scrap: (1) by defining an absolute percentage or (2) by entering an absolute value.

1. You can define an absolute percentage in the scrap key and then assign the key to the asset master. To define the scrap key, use transaction code ANHAL (menu path: **IMG → Financial Accounting → Asset Accounting → Depreciation → Valuation Methods → Further Settings → Define the Cutoff Value Key**).

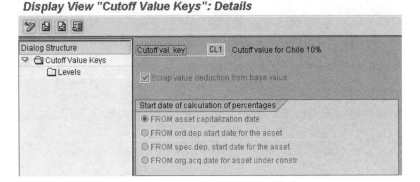

FIGURE 3.12   **Using transaction code ANHAL**

2. Instead of a scrap key, you can enter an absolute amount in the asset master as a scrap value.

Depending upon your other configurations, either the scrap value will be reduced before calculation of depreciation or the system will limit depreciation to the scrap value.

Issue No.: 51

The user posts an acquisition transaction through transaction code F-90 and expects the capitalization and depreciation start date to be filled by the system. SAP help says the capitalization date and depreciation start date will be filled by the system with the first acquisition date. But this is not happening in his case. How can this be resolved?

As per SAP standard practice, on the first acquisition, the system will populate capitalization and the first depreciation date. If this is not happening, check your configuration setting in transaction code AO73 (menu path: **IMG → Financial Accounting → Asset Accounting → Transactions → Acquisitions → Define Transaction Types for Acquisitions → Define Transaction Types for Acquisitions**).

Display View "FI-AA: Transaction types": Details

| Trans. type | 100 | External asset acquisition |
| Transaction type grp | 10 | Acquisition |

Account assignment
- ● Debit transaction
- ○ Credit transaction
- ☑ Capitalize fixed asset
  - Document type AA Asset posting

Posting type
- ○ Post to affiliated company   ○ Gross
- ● Do not post to affiliated co.   ● Net

Other features
- ☐ Cannot be used manually   ☐ Set changeover year
- Consolidation transaction type 120 Additions/Purchases
- Asst hist sheet grp 10 Acquisition
- ☐ Call up individual check

FIGURE 3.13   **Defining transaction types**

In the screen that appears, shown in Figure 3.13, check whether the Capitalize fixed asset box is checked. If not, check it.

Issue No.: 52
While posting a transaction through transaction code ABSO-Miscellaneous Transaction, the system returns an error message. After further analysis, the user finds that his company code is activated for parallel currencies. How can the user set up depreciation areas for parallel currencies?

If your company code is set up for multiple currencies and has implemented asset management, then be sure you are complying with the following steps:

1. Verify how many currencies are active for your company code. You can verify this setting in transaction code:____ (menu path: **IMG → Financial Acctg → Financial Acctg Global Settings → Company Code → Multiple Currencies → Define additional local currencies**).
2. Review your depreciation areas in AA. In case of multiple currency scenarios, you should have one additional depreciation area for each currency. You can check this setting in transaction code OADB (menu path: **IMG → Financial Acctg → Asset Accounting → Valuation → Depreciation Areas → Define Depreciation Areas**).
3. For each additional depreciation area, define the depreciation transfer rule with transaction code OABC (menu path: **IMG → Financial Acctg → Asset Accounting → Valuation → Depreciation Areas → Specify Transfer of Depreciation Terms**). You must set up the transfer values for additional depreciation areas from book depreciation area 01.
4. Similar to step 3, you have to set up the APC transfer rule. You can set up this transfer rule through transaction code OABD (menu path: **IMG → Financial Acctg → Asset Accounting → Valuation → Depreciation Areas → Specify Transfer of APC Values**).
5. Now you can set up currency for additional depreciation areas through transaction code OAYH (menu path: **IMG → Financial Acctg → Asset Accounting → Valuation → Currencies → Define Depreciation Areas for Foreign Currencies**).

3.5 COST CENTER ACCOUNTING (CCA)

Issue No.: 53

The canteen cost center costs (for example, Rs. 10,000) were to be allocated to other receiving cost centers with "No. of Employees" as the statistical key figure. The canteen cost center also has some employees, so it is becoming both the sender and the receiver for itself. The problem is that when trying to allocate the costs through the distribution method, the system is first allocating some portion of the costs (for example, Rs. 500) back to the canteen cost center and then reallocating the costs to the other cost centers, so that in the end, the debit and the credit balances for the canteen cost center is showing Rs. 10,500 (10,000 + 500). When trying the assessment method, however, the system is sending the portion of the canteen cost center costs back (Rs. 500), it is not reallocating them to the other cost center, and the debit side is showing Rs. 10,500 while the credit side is only showing Rs. 10,000.

When defining assessment, be sure to check the check box for iterative. This will repeatedly allocate the costs to other cost centers until the balance becomes zero.

Issue No.: 54

A client posted an entry to 0001 cost center instead of 4000. Now the client wants to correct the posting without revising the document. How can the correction be done without reversing the document?

Using T-code KB11N, you can repost the costs from one cost center to another cost center.

3.6 PROFIT CENTER ACCOUNTING (PCA)

Issue No.: 55

While posting the AP balance to PCA through transaction code 1KEK, the user found that some of the line items are posted to a dummy profit center. The user is expecting these to go to specific profit centers.

A customer and vendor balance consists of open items, i.e., those that are yet to offset. While transferring balances, the system looks for profit centers from the offsetting entry. In the case of open items, the system will not find an offsetting entry and will post line items to a dummy profit center. You can transfer the posting from a dummy profit center to another profit center through transaction code 4KE5.

3.7 NEW G/L

Issue No.: 56
The user has reported that the system is not splitting document type SA but is splitting other document types.

In the standard configuration, document type SA is assigned to transaction type 0000, to which no splitting rule is assigned. In these circumstances, the system is expecting that you will enter an account assignment while entering a business transaction.

See how your system is configured in the following menu path:

- **Financial Accounting (New) → General Ledger Accounting (New) → Business Transaction → Document Splitting → Classify document types for document splitting**
- **Financial Accounting (New) → General Ledger Accounting (New) → Business Transaction → Document Splitting → Classify GL account for document splitting**

Chapter 4

CONFIGURATION STEPS

Configuring SAP software is a job for a consultant, who is required to do a lot of homework before the system goes live. The configuration of an SAP solution depends upon the client's requirements and the business practices of the industry. This chapter covers the general configuration sequences that are common across industries.

To configure the SAP FI module, you can divide the configuration process as follows:

- Enterprise Structure (ES)
- General Ledger (G/L) Accounting
- Accounts Payable (AP)
- Accounts Receivable (AR)
- Bank Accounting (BA)
- Assets Accounting (AA)

Similarly, you can divide the controlling as follows:

- General Controlling (CO)
- Cost Element Accounting (CEL)
- Cost Center Accounting (CCA)
- Internal Order (IO)
- Profit Center Accounting (PCA)
- Profitability Analysis (PA)
- Product Costing (PC)

4.1 ENTERPRISE STRUCTURE (FI-ES)

The following steps are the minimum configuration requirements for FI company codes. These may vary depending upon implementation requirements.

Steps	Function Name and Path	T-code
1	**Define Company:** IMG → Enterprise Structure → Definition → Define Company	OX15
2	**Define Company Code:** IMG → Enterprise Structure → Definition → Define/Delete/ Check Company Code	OX02
3	**Assignment of Company Code to Company:** IMG → Enterprise Structure → Assignment → Financial Accounting → Assign company code to company	OX16
4	**Maintain Fiscal Year Variant (FYV):** IMG → Financial Accounting → Financial Accounting Global Settings → Fiscal Year	OB29
5	**Assign Company Code to FYV:** IMG → Financial Accounting → Financial Accounting Global Setting → Assign company code to fiscal year variants	OB37
6	**Define Variants for Open and Closing Posting Periods:** IMG → Financial Accounting → Financial Accounting Global Settings → Document → Define Posting Period	OBBO
7	**Open and Closing Posting Periods:** IMG → Financial Accounting → Financial Accounting Global Settings → Document → Open & Closing Posting Period	OB52
8	**Assign Posting Period Variants to Company Code:** IMG → Financial Accounting → Financial Accounting Global Setting → Document → Assign posting period variants to company code	OBBP
9	**Document Number Ranges:** IMG → Financial Accounting → Financial Accounting Global Settings → Document → Define Document Number Ranges → Overview	FBN1
10	**Maintain FSVs:** IMG → Financial Accounting → Financial Accounting Global Settings → Line Item → Control → Define Field Status Variants	OBC4

Continued

Steps	Function Name and Path	T-code
11	**Assign FSV to Company Code:** IMG→Financial Accounting→Financial Accounting Global Settings→Line Item→Assign FSV to company code	OBC5
12	**Define Tolerance Groups for Employees:** IMG→Financial Accounting→Financial Accounting Global Settings→Line Item→Define Tolerance groups for employees	OBA0, OBA4
13	**Edit Chart of Account (COA):** IMG→Financial Accounting→General Ledger Accounting→G/L Accounts→Master Records→Preparation→Edit Chart of account list	OB13
14	**Assign Company Code to COA:** IMG→Financial Accounting→General Ledger Accounting→G/L Accounts→Master Records→Preparation→Assign Co Code to Chart of Account	OB62
15	**Define A/C Group:** IMG→Financial Accounting→General Ledger Accounting→G/L Accounts→Master Records→Preparation→Define Account Group	OBD4
16	**Define Retained Earnings A/C:** IMG→Financial Accounting→General Ledger Accounting→G/L Accounts→Master Records→Preparation→Define Retained Earning Account	OB53
17	**Enter Global Parameters:** IMG→Financial Accounting→Company Code→Enter Global Parameters	OBY6
18	**Maximum Exchange Rate Difference:** IMG→Financial Accounting→Financial Accounting Global Settings→Maximum exchange rate difference	OB53

TABLE 4.1

4.2 GENERAL LEDGER ACCOUNTING (FI-G/L)

The following are the minimum configuration requirements for the FI-G/L submodule.

Steps	Function Name and Path	T-code
	Define Tolerance Groups for G/L Accounts: IMG → General Ledger Accounting → Business Transactions → G/L Account Posting → Open Item Clearing → Clearing Differences → Define Tolerance Groups for G/L Accounts	

Sample Accounts: If you are implementing the sample account concept in your project, you need to configure the following steps.

Steps	Function Name and Path	T-code
1	**Maintain List of Rule Type:** IMG → General Ledger Accounting → G/L Accounts → Master Records → Preparation → Additional Accounts → Sample Accounts	OB15
2	**Define Data Transfer Rule:** IMG → General Ledger Accounting → G/L Accounts → Master Records → Preparation → Additional Accounts → Sample Accounts	FSK2
3	**Assign Company Code to Rule Type:** IMG → General Ledger Accounting → G/L Accounts → Master Records → Preparation → Additional Accounts → Sample Accounts	OB67
4	**Create Sample Accounts:** IMG → General Ledger Accounting → G/L Accounts → Master Records → Preparation → Additional Accounts → Sample Accounts	FSM1

Intercompany transactions: This step is required for automatic posting of intercompany transactions.

Steps	Function Name and Path	T-code
1	**Prepare Cross-Company Code Transactions:** IMG → General Ledger Accounting → Business Transactions → G/L Account Posting → Prepare Cross-Company Code Transactions	OBYA

Continued

Function Name and Path	T-code

Foreign Currency Transactions: If you are expecting that your SAP solution will handle foreign currency transactions, then configure this step.

	Function Name and Path	T-code
1	**Define Accounts for Exchange Rate Differences:** IMG → General Ledger Accounting → Business Transactions → G/L Account Posting → Open Item Clearing → Define Accounts for Exchange Rate Differences	OB09

Payment Difference: This step is required for automatic posting of payment differences.

	Function Name and Path	T-code
1	**Create Accounts for Clearing Differences:** IMG → General Ledger Accounting → Business Transactions → G/L Account Posting → Open Item Clearing → Clearing Differences → Create Accounts for Clearing Differences	

TABLE 4.2

4.3 ACCOUNTS PAYABLE (FI-AP)

The following table lists the minimum configuration parameters for the FI-AP submodule.

	Function Name and Path	T-code
1	**Define Account Groups with Screen Layout (Vendors):** IMG → Financial Accounting → Accounts Receivable and Accounts Payable → Vendor Accounts → Master Data → Preparations for Creating Vendor Master Data → Define Account Groups with Screen Layout (Vendors)	OBD3

TABLE 4.3

Continued

	Function Name and Path	T-code
2	**Create Number Ranges for Vendor Accounts:** IMG → Financial Accounting → Accounts Receivable and Accounts Payable → Vendor Accounts → Master Data → Preparations for Creating Vendor Master Data → Create Number Ranges for Vendor Accounts	XKN1
3	**Assign Number Ranges to Vendor Account Groups:** IMG → Financial Accounting → Accounts Receivable and Accounts Payable → Vendor Accounts → Master Data → Preparations for Creating Vendor Master Data → Assign Number Ranges to Vendor Account Groups	SPRO
4	**Define Tolerances (Vendors):** IMG → Financial Accounting → Accounts Receivable and Accounts Payable → Business Transactions → Outgoing Payments → Manual Outgoing Payments → Define Tolerances (Vendors)	SPRO

Payment Difference: The following setting is required for automatic posting of payment differences.

	Function Name and Path	T-code
	Define Accounts for Payment Differences (Manual Outgoing Payment): IMG → Financial Accounting → Accounts Receivable and Accounts Payable → Business Transactions → Outgoing Payments → Manual Outgoing Payments → Overpayment/ Underpayment → Define Accounts for Payment Differences (Manual Outgoing Payment)	OBXL

Automatic Payment Program: The following configurations are required to set up automatic payments.

	Function Name and Path	T-code
	Set Up All Company Codes for Payment Transactions: IMG → Financial Accounting → Accounts Receivable and Accounts Payable → Business Transactions → Outgoing Payments → Automatic Outgoing Payments → Payment Method/Bank Selection for Payment Program → Set Up All Company Codes for Payment Transactions	FBZP

Continued

Function Name and Path	T-code
Set Up Paying Company Codes for Payment Transactions: IMG→Financial Accounting→Accounts Receivable and Accounts Payable→Business Transactions→Outgoing Payments→Automatic Outgoing Payments→Payment Method/Bank Selection for Payment Program→Set Up Paying Company Codes for Payment Transactions	FBZP
Set Up Payment Methods per Country for Payment Transactions: IMG→Financial Accounting→Accounts Receivable and Accounts Payable→Business Transactions→Outgoing Payments→Automatic Outgoing Payments→Payment Method/Bank Selection for Payment Program→Set Up Payment Methods per Country for Payment Transactions	FBZP
Set Up Payment Methods per Company Code for Payment Transactions: IMG→Financial Accounting→Accounts Receivable and Accounts Payable→Business Transactions→Outgoing Payments→Automatic Outgoing Payments→Payment Method/Bank Selection for Payment Program→Set Up Payment Methods per Company Code for Payment Transactions	FBZP
Set Up Bank Determination for Payment Transactions: IMG→Financial Accounting→Accounts Receivable and Accounts Payable→Business Transactions→Outgoing Payments→Automatic Outgoing Payments→Payment Method/Bank Selection for Payment Program→Set Up Bank Determination for Payment Transactions	FBZP

TABLE 4.3

Continued

Function Name and Path	T-code

Down Payment Configuration: The following step must be configured to define down payments.

Function Name and Path	T-code
Define Alternative Reconciliation Account for Down Payments: IMG → Financial Accounting → Accounts Receivable and Accounts Payable → Business Transactions → Down Payment Made → Define Alternative Reconciliation Account for Down Payments	OBYR

Interest Calculation: The following steps must be followed for interest calculation.

Function Name and Path	T-code
Define Interest Calculation Types: IMG → Financial Accounting → Accounts Receivable and Accounts Payable → Business Transactions → Interest Calculation → Interest Calculation Global Settings → Define Interest Calculation Types	SPRO
Define Number Ranges for Interest Forms: IMG → Financial Accounting → Accounts Receivable and Accounts Payable → Business Transactions → Interest Calculation → Interest Calculation Global Settings → Define Number Ranges for Interest Forms	SPRO
Prepare Interest on Arrears Calculation: IMG → Financial Accounting → Accounts Receivable and Accounts Payable → Business Transactions → Interest Calculation → Interest Calculation Global Settings → Prepare Interest on Arrears Calculation	SPRO
Prepare Item Interest Calculation: IMG → Financial Accounting → Accounts Receivable and Accounts Payable → Business Transactions → Interest Calculation → Interest Calculation Global Settings → Prepare Item Interest Calculation	SPRO

Continued

Function Name and Path	T-code
Prepare Account Balance Interest Calculation: IMG → Financial Accounting → Accounts Receivable and Accounts Payable → Business Transactions → Interest Calculation → Interest Calculation Global Settings → Prepare Account Balance Interest Calculation	SPRO
Prepare Special G/L Transaction Interest Calculation: IMG → Financial Accounting → Accounts Receivable and Accounts Payable → Business Transactions → Interest Calculation → Interest Calculation Global Settings → Prepare Special G/L Transaction Interest Calculation	SPRO
Define Reference Interest Rates: IMG → Financial Accounting → Accounts Receivable and Accounts Payable → Business Transactions → Interest Calculation → Interest Calculation Global Settings → Define Reference Interest Rates	OBAC
Define Time-Based Terms: IMG → Financial Accounting → Accounts Receivable and Accounts Payable → Business Transactions → Interest Calculation → Interest Calculation Global Settings → Define Time-Based Terms	OB81
Enter Interest Values: IMG → Financial Accounting → Accounts Receivable and Accounts Payable → Business Transactions → Interest Calculation → Interest Calculation Global Settings → Enter Interest Values	OB83
Interest on Arrears Calculation (Vendors): IMG → Financial Accounting → Accounts Receivable and Accounts Payable → Business Transactions → Interest Calculation → Interest Posting → Interest on Arrears Calculation (Vendors)	OBV9

TABLE 4.3

Continued

Function Name and Path	T-code
Interest on Account Balance (Vendors): IMG → Financial Accounting → Accounts Receivable and Accounts Payable → Business Transactions → Interest Calculation → Interest Posting → A/P: Balance Interest Calculation	OBV4

TABLE 4.3

4.4 ACCOUNTS RECEIVABLE (FI-AR)

The following table lists the minimum configuration parameters for the FI-AR submodule.

Function Name and Path	T-code
Define Account Groups with Screen Layout (Customers): IMG → Financial Accounting → Accounts Receivable and Accounts Payable → Customer Accounts → Master Data → Preparations for Creating Customer Master Data → Define Account Groups with Screen Layout (Customers)	OBD2
Create Number Ranges for Customer Accounts: IMG → Financial Accounting → Accounts Receivable and Accounts Payable → Customer Accounts → Master Data → Preparations for Creating Customer Master Data → Create Number Ranges for Customer Accounts	XDN1

Continued

Function Name and Path	T-code
Assign Number Ranges to Customer Account Groups: IMG → Financial Accounting → Accounts Receivable and Accounts Payable → Customer Accounts → Master Data → Preparations for Creating Customer Master Data → Assign Number Ranges to Customer Account Groups	OBAR
Define Tolerances (Customers): IMG → Financial Accounting → Accounts Receivable and Accounts Payable → Business Transactions → Incoming Payments → Manual Incoming Payments → Define Tolerances (Customers)	OBA3

Payment Terms: The following steps may be configured for payment terms configuration.

Maintain Terms of Payment: IMG → Financial Accounting → Accounts Receivable and Accounts Payable → Business Transactions → Maintain Terms of Payment	OBB8
Define Terms of Payment for Installment Payments: IMG → Financial Accounting → Accounts Receivable and Accounts Payable → Business Transactions → Define Terms of Payment for Installment Payments	OBB9

Payment Difference: The following steps may be configured to handle payment differences.

Define Reason Codes: IMG → Financial Accounting → Accounts Receivable and Accounts Payable → Business Transactions → Incoming Payments → Incoming Payments Global Settings → Overpayment/Underpayment → Define Reason Codes	SPRO

TABLE 4.4

Continued

Function Name and Path	T-code
Define Accounts for Payment Differences: IMG→Financial Accounting→Accounts Receivable and Accounts Payable→Business Transactions→Incoming Payments→Incoming Payments Global Settings→Overpayment/Underpayment→Define Accounts for Payment Differences	SPRO

Dunning: The following steps may be configured to send dunning letters to customers/vendors.

Function Name and Path	T-code
Define Dunning Areas: IMG→Financial Accounting→Accounts Receivable and Accounts Payable→Business Transactions→Dunning→Basic Settings for Dunning→Define Dunning Areas	OB61
Define Dunning Keys: IMG→Financial Accounting→Accounts Receivable and Accounts Payable→Business Transactions→Dunning→Basic Settings for Dunning→Define Dunning Keys	OB17
Define Dunning Block Reasons: IMG→Financial Accounting→Accounts Receivable and Accounts Payable→Business Transactions→Dunning→Basic Settings for Dunning→Define Dunning Block Reasons	OB18
Define Dunning Procedures: IMG→Financial Accounting→Accounts Receivable and Accounts Payable→Business Transactions→Dunning→Dunning Procedure→Define Dunning Procedures	FBMP
Define Dunning Groupings: IMG→Financial Accounting→Accounts Receivable and Accounts Payable→Business Transactions→Dunning→Dunning Procedure→Define Dunning Groupings	OBAQ

TABLE 4.4

4.5 BANK ACCOUNTING (FI-BL)

Function Name and Path	T-code
Minimum Configuration: **Define House Banks:** IMG→Financial Accounting→Bank Accounting→Bank Accounts→Define House Banks	**FI12**
Define Number Ranges for Checks: IMG→Financial Accounting→Accounts Receivable and Accounts Payable→Business Transactions→Outgoing Payments→Automatic Outgoing Payments→Payment Media→Check Management→Define Number Ranges for Checks	**FCHI**
Define Void Reason Codes: IMG→Financial Accounting→Accounts Receivable and Accounts Payable→Business Transactions→Outgoing Payments→Automatic Outgoing Payments→Payment Media→Check Management→Define Void Reason Codes	**FCHV**

Lockbox Processing: The following steps may be configured for lockbox processing.

Function Name and Path	T-code
Define Lockboxes for House Banks: IMG→Financial Accounting→Bank Accounting→Bank Accounts→Define Lockboxes for House Banks	**SPRO**
Create and Assign Business Transactions: IMG→Financial Accounting→Bank Accounting→Business Transactions→Payment Transactions→Manual Bank Statement→Create and Assign Business Transactions	**SPRO**

TABLE 4.5

Function Name and Path	T-code

Processing Bank Statement: The following steps may be configured for processing bank statements.

Define Posting Keys and Posting Rules for Manual Bank Statement: SPRO

IMG→Financial Accounting→Bank Accounting→Business Transactions→Payment Transactions→Manual Bank Statement→Define Posting Keys and Posting Rules for Manual Bank Statement

- Create Account Symbols
- Assign Accounts to Account Symbol
- Create Keys for Posting Rules
- Define Posting Rules

Define Variants for Manual Bank Statement: OT43

IMG→Financial Accounting→Bank Accounting→Business Transactions→Payment Transactions→Manual Bank Statement→Define Variants for Manual Bank Statement

Make Global Settings for Electronic Bank Statement: SPRO

IMG→Financial Accounting→Bank Accounting→Business Transactions→Payment Transactions→Electronic Bank Statement→Make Global Settings for Electronic Bank Statement

Define Control Parameters: OBAY

IMG→Financial Accounting→Bank Accounting→Business Transactions→Payment Transactions→Lockbox→Make Global Define Control Parameters

Continued

Function Name and Path	T-code
Define Posting Data: IMG → Financial Accounting → Bank Accounting → Business Transactions → Payment Transactions → Lockbox → Define Posting Data	OBAX

Cash Journal: The following steps may be configured for a cash journal.

Function Name and Path	T-code
Create G/L Account for Cash Journal: IMG → Financial Accounting → Bank Accounting → Business Transactions → Cash Journal → Create G/L Account for Cash Journal	SPRO
Create G/L Account for Cash Journal: IMG → Financial Accounting → Bank Accounting → Business Transactions → Cash Journal → Create G/L Account for Cash Journal	SPRO
Define Document Types for Cash Journal Documents: IMG → Financial Accounting → Bank Accounting → Business Transactions → Cash Journal → Define Document Types for Cash Journal Documents	SPRO
Define Number Range Intervals for Cash Journal Documents: IMG → Financial Accounting → Bank Accounting → Business Transactions → Cash Journal → Define Number Range Intervals for Cash Journal Documents	SPRO
Set Up Cash Journal: IMG → Financial Accounting → Bank Accounting → Business Transactions → Cash Journal → Set Up Cash Journal	SPRO
Create, Change, Delete Business Transactions: IMG → Financial Accounting → Bank Accounting → Business Transactions → Cash Journal → Create, Change, Delete Business Transactions	SPRO
Set Up Print Parameters for Cash Journal: IMG → Financial Accounting → Bank Accounting → Business Transactions → Cash Journal → Set Up Print Parameters for Cash Journal	SPRO

TABLE 4.5

4.6 ASSETS ACCOUNTING (FI-AA)

Depending on business requirements, the following steps may be configured for assets accounts.

Function Name and Path	T-code
Minimum Configuration:	
Check Country-specific Settings: IMG → Financial Accounting → Assets Accounting → Organizational Structures → Check Country Specific Settings	OA08
Copy Reference Chart of Dep./Dep. Areas: IMG → Financial Accounting → Assets Accounting → Organizational Structures → Copy Reference Chart of Dep./Dep. Areas	EC08
Specify Description: IMG → Financial Accounting → Assets Accounting → Organizational Structures → Copy Reference Chart of Depreciation/Dep. Area	EC08
Copy/Delete Depreciation Areas: IMG → Financial Accounting → Assets Accounting → Organizational Structures → Copy Reference Chart of Depreciation/Dep. Area	OADB
Assign COD to Co. Code: IMG → Financial Accounting → Assets Accounting → Organizational Structures → Chart of Depreciation to Co Code	OAOB
Define Number Range Interval: IMG → Financial Accounting → Assets Accounting → Organizational Structures → Assets Class → Define Number Range Interval	AS08
Specify Account Determination: IMG → Financial Accounting → Assets Accounting → Organizational Structures → Assets Class → Specify Account Determination	SPRO

Continued

Function Name and Path	T-code
Define Assets Class: IMG → Financial Accounting → Assets Accounting → Organizational Structures → Assets Class → Define Assets Class	OAOA
Define How Depreciation Areas Post to General Ledger: IMG → Financial Accounting → Assets Accounting → Integration with General Ledger → Define how depreciation areas post to general ledger	OADX
Assign Input Tax Indicators for Non-taxable Acquisitions: IMG → Financial Accounting → Assets Accounting → Integration with General Ledger → Assign input tax indicators for Non-Taxable Acquisitions	OBCL
Specify Fin Stat Version for Assets Reporting: IMG → Financial Accounting → Assets Accounting → Integration with General Ledger → Specify Fin. Stat. version for assets reporting	OAYN
Specify Document Types for Posting Depreciation: IMG → Financial Accounting → Assets Accounting → Integration with General Ledger → Post depreciation to the general ledger → Specify document types for posting of dep.	OA71
Specify Intervals and Posting Rule: IMG → Financial Accounting → Assets Accounting → Integration with General Ledger → Post depreciation to the general ledger → Specify intervals and posting rule	OAYR
Determine Depreciation Areas in the Assets Class: IMG → Financial Accounting → Assets Accounting → Valuation → Determine Depreciation areas in the assets class	OAYZ

TABLE 4.6

Continued

Function Name and Path	T-code
Specify Maximum Amount for Low Value Assets + Assets Class: IMG→Financial Accounting→Assets Accounting→Valuation→Amount Specification (Company Code/Chart of Depreciation)→Specify Max. Amount for low value assets + Assets Class	OAY2
Specify the rounding of net book value and/or depreciation: IMG→Financial Accounting→Assets Accounting→Valuation→Amount Specification (Company Code/Chart of Depreciation)→Specify the rounding of net book value and/or depreciation	OAYO
Determine Depreciation Areas: IMG→Financial Accounting→Assets Accounting→Depreciation→Ordinary Depreciation→Determine Depreciation Areas	OABN
Define Base Method: IMG→Financial Accounting→Assets Accounting→Depreciation→Valuation Method→Depreciation Key→Calculation Method→Define Base Methods	SPRO
Define Decline Balance Method: IMG→Financial Accounting→Assets Accounting→Depreciation→Valuation Method→Depreciation Key→Calculation Method→Define Decline Balance Method	SPRO
Maintain Period Control: IMG→Financial Accounting→Assets Accounting→Depreciation→Valuation Method→Depreciation Key→Calculation Method→Maintain Period Control Methods	
Main Depreciation Key: IMG→Financial Accounting→Assets Accounting→Depreciation→Valuation Method→Depreciation Key→Maintain Depreciation Key	AFAMA

TABLE 4.6

4.7 CONTROLLING AREA (CO)

Configuration of the following steps are required for general controlling area setup.

Function Name and Path	T-code
Maintaining the CO Area: IMG→Controlling→General Controlling→ Organization→Maintain Controlling Area→Maintain Controlling Area (Selection Menu)	OKKP
Maintaining Versions: IMG→Controlling→General Controlling→Organization→Maintain Versions	OKEQ
Maintain Number Ranges for CO Documents: IMG→Controlling→General Controlling→Organization→Maintain Number Ranges for Controlling Documents	KANK

TABLE 4.7

4.8 COST CENTER ACCOUNTING (CO-CCA)

The following steps are required for cost center accounting.

Function Name and Path	T-code
Cost Center Categories: IMG→Controlling→Cost Center Accounting→Master Data→Cost Centers→Define Cost Center Categories	OKA2

TABLE 4.8

Continued

Function Name and Path	T-code

Plan Accrual Calculation:

| **Plan Cost Accrual Calculation:**
IMG → Controlling → Cost Center Accounting → Planning → Planning Aids → Accrual Calculation → Percentage Method → Maintain Overhead Structure | KSAZ |

Plan Distribution:

| **Planning Cost Distribution:**
IMG → Controlling → Cost Center Accounting → Planning → Allocations → Distribution → Define Distribution | KSV7 (KSV8) |

Plan Reposting:

| **Planning Periodic Reposting:**
IMG → Controlling → Cost Center Accounting → Planning → Planning Aids → Periodic Reposting → Define Periodic Reposting | KSW7 (KSW8) |

Plan Assessment:

| **Planning Cost Assessment:**
IMG → Controlling → Cost Center Accounting → Planning → Allocations → Assessment → Define Assessment | KSU7 (KSU8) |

Actual Reposting:

| **Actual Period Reposting:**
IMG → Controlling → Cost Center Accounting → Actual Postings → Period-End Closing → Periodic Reposting → Define Periodic Reposting | KSW1 |

Actual Accruals:

| **Cost Accrual Calculation (Percentage Method):**
IMG → Controlling → Cost Center Accounting → Actual Postings → Period-End Closing → Accrual Calculation → Percentage Method → Maintain Overhead Structure | KSAZ |

Continued

Function Name and Path	T-code
Actual Distribution:	
Actual Cost Distribution: IMG → Controlling → Cost Center Accounting → Actual Postings → Period-End Closing → Distribution → Define Distribution	KSV1 (KSV2)
Actual Assessment:	
Actual Cost Assessment: IMG → Controlling → Cost Center Accounting → Actual Postings → Period-End Closing → Assessment → Maintain Assessment	KSU1 (KSU2)

TABLE 4.8

4.9 INTERNAL ORDER (CO-IO)

Internal order (IO) is a cost object that tracks the cost of a specific event. IO has a short life compared to a cost center. In SAP solutions, you will find two types of IO: (1) real IO and (2) statistical IO. Through real IO, you can track the cost of a particular event, and at the end you can settle the IO cost to the respective cost center. In statistical IO, you can only collect cost; you can't settle statistical IO to any other cost object.

Function Name and Path	T-code
Activate Order Management in CO Area: IMG → Controlling → Internal Orders → Activate Order Management in Controlling Area	OKKP
Order Types: IMG → Controlling → Internal Orders → Order Master Data → Define Order Types	KOT2_FUNCAREA

TABLE 4.9

Continued

Function Name and Path	T-code
Number Ranges for Order Types: IMG → Controlling → Internal Orders → Order Master Data → Maintain Number Ranges for Orders	KONK
Maintain Settlement Cost Elements: IMG → Controlling → Internal Orders → Actual Posting → Settlement → Maintain settlement cost element	KA01/KA06
Maintain Allocation Structures: IMG → Controlling → Internal Orders → Actual Posting → Settlement → Maintain Allocation Structures	SPRO
Maintain Settlement Profile: IMG → Controlling → Internal Orders → Actual Posting → Settlement → Maintain Settlement Profile	SPRO
Assignment of Settlement Profile to Order Type: IMG → Controlling → Internal Orders → Actual Posting → Settlement → Maintain Settlement Profile	SPRO
Number Ranges for CO Settlement Documents: IMG → Controlling → Internal Orders → Actual Postings → Settlement → Maintain Number Ranges for Settlement Documents	SNUM
Maintain Budget Profile: IMG → Controlling → Internal Orders → Budgeting and Availability Control → Maintain Budget Profile	OKOB
Maintain budget profile in order types: IMG → Controlling → Internal Orders → Budgeting and Availability Control → Maintain Budget Profile	OKOB
Define Tolerance Limits for Availability Control: IMG → Controlling → Internal Orders → Budgeting and Availability Control → Define Tolerance Limits for Availability Control	SPRO
Maintain Budget Manage: IMG → Controlling → Internal Orders → Budgeting and Availability Control → Maintain Budget Manager	OK14
Maintain Number Ranges for Budgeting: IMG → Controlling → Internal Orders → Budgeting and Availability Control → Maintain Number Ranges for Budgeting	OK11

TABLE 4.9

4.10 PROFIT CENTER ACCOUNTING (CO-PCA)

The following steps may be configured for profit center accounting.

Function Name and Path	T-code
Maintain CO Area: IMG → Controlling → General Controlling → Organization → Maintain Controlling Area	OKKP
Maintain Controlling Area Settings: IMG → Controlling → Profit Center Accounting → Basic Settings → Controlling Area Settings → Maintain Controlling Area Settings	0KE5
Create Dummy Profit Center: IMG → Controlling → Profit Center Accounting → Master Data → Profit Center → Create Dummy Profit Center	KE59
Set Control Parameters for Actual Data: IMG → Controlling → Profit Center Accounting → Basic Settings → Controlling Area Settings → Activate Direct Postings → Set Control Parameters for Actual Data	1KEF
Maintain Standard Hierarchy: IMG → Controlling → Profit Center Accounting → Master Data → Profit Center → Maintain Standard Hierarchy	KCH4
Maintain Profit Center Groups: IMG → Controlling → Profit Center Accounting → Master Data → Profit Center → Maintain Standard Hierarchy	KCH1
Create Profit Centers: IMG → Controlling → Profit Center Accounting → Master Data → Profit Center → Maintain Profit Center	KE51
Activate Inactive Profit Center: IMG → Controlling → Profit Center Accounting → Master Data → Profit Center → Activate Inactive Profit Center	KEOA2
Edit Automatic Account Assignments: IMG → Controlling → Profit Center Accounting → Actual Posting → Actual Postings → Maintain Automatic Account Assignment of Revenue Elements	OKB9

TABLE 4.10

4.11 PROFITABILITY ANALYSIS (CO-PA)

The following steps may be configured for profitability analysis.

Function Name and Path	T-code
Maintain Characteristics: IMG → Controlling → Profitability Analysis → Structures → Maintain Operating Concern → Maintain Characteristics	KEA5
Maintain Value Fields: IMG → Controlling → Profitability Analysis → Structures → Maintain Operating Concern → Maintain Value Fields	KEA6
Maintain Operating Concern: IMG → Controlling → Profitability Analysis → Structures → Define Operating Concern → Maintain Operating Concern	KEA0
Set Operating Concern: IMG → Controlling → Profitability Analysis → Structures → Set Operating Concern	KEBD
Assign CO Area to Operating Concern: IMG → Controlling → Profitability Analysis → Structures → Assign Controlling Area to Operating Concern	SPRO
Maintain Characteristic Values: IMG → Controlling → Profitability Analysis → Master Data → Characteristic Values → Maintain Characteristic Values	KES1
Define Characteristic Derivation: IMG → Controlling → Profitability Analysis → Master Data → Define Characteristic Derivation	KEDR
Define PA Transfer Structure for Settlement: IMG → Controlling → Profitability Analysis → Planning → Integrated Planning → Transfer Cost Center Planning/Process Planning → Assess Cost Center Costs/Process Costs → Define PA Transfer Structure for Assessment	KEI1

Continued

Function Name and Path	T-code
Assign PA Transfer Structure to Settlement Profile: IMG → Controlling → Profitability Analysis → Flows of Actual Values → Settlement of Production Variances → Assign PA Transfer Structure to Settlement Profile	SPRO
Create Profitability Report: IMG → Controlling → Profitability Analysis → Information System → Create Profitability Report	KE31

TABLE 4.11

4.12 PRODUCT COSTING (CO-PC)

The following steps may be configured for product costing.

Function Name and Path	T-code
Maintain Overhead Cost Elements: IMG → Controlling → Product Cost Controlling → Product Cost Planning → Basic Settings for Material Costing → Overhead → Maintain Overhead Cost Elements	KA06
Define Calculation Bases: IMG → Controlling → Product Cost Controlling → Product Cost Planning → Basic Settings for Material Costing → Overhead → Costing Sheet: Components → Define Calculation Bases	
Define Percentage Overhead Rates: IMG → Controlling → Product Cost Controlling → Product Cost Planning → Basic Settings for Material Costing → Overhead → Costing Sheet: Components → Define Percentage Overhead Rates	

TABLE 4.12

Continued

Function Name and Path	T-code
Define Quantity-based Overhead Rates: IMG → Controlling → Product Cost Controlling → Product Cost Planning → Basic Settings for Material Costing → Overhead → Costing Sheet: Components → Define Quantity-Based Overhead Rates	
Define Credits: IMG → Controlling → Product Cost Controlling → Product Cost Planning → Basic Settings for Material Costing → Overhead → Costing Sheet: Components → Define Credits	
Define Origin Groups: IMG → Controlling → Product Cost Controlling → Product Cost Planning → Basic Settings for Material Costing → Define Origin Groups	OKZ1
Define Costing Sheets: IMG → Controlling → Product Cost Controlling → Product Cost Planning → Overhead → Define Costing Sheets	
Define Overhead Keys: IMG → Controlling → Product Cost Controlling → Product Cost Planning → Overhead → Define Overhead Keys	
Define Overhead Groups: IMG → Controlling → Product Cost Controlling → Product Cost Planning → Overhead → Define Overhead Groups	
Define Cost Component Structure: IMG → Controlling → Product Cost Controlling → Product Cost Planning → Basic Settings for Material Costing → Define Cost Component Structure	

Continued

Function Name and Path	T-code
Define Costing Type: IMG → Controlling → Product Cost Controlling → Product Cost Planning → Material Cost Estimate with Quantity Structure → Costing Variant: Components → Define Costing Types	
Define Valuation Variant: IMG → Controlling → Product Cost Controlling → Product Cost Planning → Material Cost Estimate with Quantity Structure → Costing Variant: Components → Define Costing Variant	
Define Date Control: IMG → Controlling → Product Cost Controlling → Product Cost Planning → Material Cost Estimate with Quantity Structure → Costing Variant: Components → Define Date Control	
Define Quantity Structure Control: IMG → Controlling → Product Cost Controlling → Product Cost Planning → Material Cost Estimate with Quantity Structure → Costing Variant: Components → Define Quantity Structure Control	
Define Transfer Strategy: IMG → Controlling → Product Cost Controlling → Product Cost Planning → Material Cost Estimate with Quantity Structure → Costing Variant: Components → Define Transfer Strategy	
Define Costing Variants: IMG → Controlling → Product Cost Controlling → Product Cost Planning → Material Cost Estimate with Quantity Structure → Define Costing Variants	

TABLE 4.12

Chapter 5

USER TRANSACTION CODES

In this chapter, you will find frequently used transaction codes from the user's perspective. Unless specifically mentioned, you will find these transaction codes in the SAP Easy Access menu. Sometimes you will find user transaction codes in the IMG menu; these are provided for the convenience of consultants. For a complete list of transaction codes, refer to the CD-ROM distributed with this book.

5.1 GENERAL LEDGER (G/L) ACCOUNTING

The main activities in the G/L submodules involve: (1) maintenance of G/L master data, (2) business transactions, (3) period-end transactions, and (4) information systems. For your reference, some of the important transaction codes for General Ledger Accounting are provided in Table 5.1.

	Function Name and Path	T-code
Create G/L Master	**Create G/L Master:** SAP menu → Accounting → Financial Accounting → General Ledger → Master Records → G/L Accounts → Individual Processing → Centrally	FS00
	In Chart of Accounts (COA): SAP menu → Accounting → Financial Accounting → General Ledger → Master Records → G/L Accounts → Individual Processing → In Chart of Accounts	FSP0
	Create Company Code: SAP menu → Accounting → Financial Accounting → General Ledger → Master Records → G/L Accounts → Individual Processing → In Company Code	FSS0

TABLE 5.1

Continued

	Function Name and Path	T-code
Display Changes to G/L Master	**Display Changes Centrally:** SAP menu → Accounting → Financial Accounting → General Ledger → Master Records → G/L Accounts → Display Changes → Centrally	FS04
	Display Changes In COA: SAP menu → Accounting → Financial Accounting → General Ledger → Master Records → G/L Accounts → Display Changes → In Chart of Accounts	FSP4
	Display Changes In Company Code: SAP menu → Accounting → Financial Accounting → General Ledger → Master Records → G/L Accounts → Individual Processing → In Company Code	FSS4
Sample Account	**Creation of Sample Account:** SAP menu → Accounting → Financial Accounting → General Ledger → Master Records → G/L Accounts → Sample Account → Create	FSM1
	Change of Sample Account: SAP menu → Accounting → Financial Accounting → General Ledger → Master Records → G/L Accounts → Sample Account → Change	FSM2
	Display of Sample Account: SAP menu → Accounting → Financial Accounting → General Ledger → Master Records → G/L Accounts → Sample Account → Display	FSM3
	Display Changes of Sample Account: SAP menu → Accounting → Financial Accounting → General Ledger → Master Records → G/L Accounts → Sample Account → Display Changes	FSM4
	Delete of Sample Account: SAP menu → Accounting → Financial Accounting → General Ledger → Master Records → G/L Accounts → Sample Account → Delete	FSM5

Continued

	Function Name and Path	T-code
Posting to G/L Accounts	**GL Posting:** SAP menu → Accounting → Financial Accounting → General Ledger → Posting → Enter G/L Account Document	FB50
	General Posting: SAP menu → Accounting → Financial Accounting → General Ledger → Posting → General Posting	F-02
	Edit or Park G/L Document: SAP menu → Accounting → Financial Accounting → General Ledger → Posting → Edit or Park G/L Document	FV50
	General Document Parking: SAP menu → Accounting → Financial Accounting → General Ledger → Posting → General Document Parking	F-65
	Post with Clearing: SAP menu → Accounting → Financial Accounting → General Ledger → Posting → Post with Clearing	F-04
	Incoming Payments: SAP menu → Accounting → Financial Accounting → General Ledger → Posting → Incoming Payments	F-06
	Outgoing Payments: SAP menu → Accounting → Financial Accounting → General Ledger → Posting → Outgoing Payments	F-07
	Cash Journal Posting: SAP menu → Accounting → Financial Accounting → General Ledger → Posting → Cash Journal Posting	FBCJ
	Clear G/L Open Line Items: SAP menu → Accounting → Financial Accounting → General Ledger → Account → Clear	F-03
Posting with Reference Document	**Account Assignment Model:** SAP menu → Accounting → Financial Accounting → General Ledger → Posting → Reference Documents → Account Assignment Model	FKMT

TABLE 5.1

Continued

	Function Name and Path	T-code
	Recurring Document: SAP menu → Accounting → Financial Accounting → General Ledger → Posting → Reference Documents → Recurring Document	FBD1
	Sample Document: SAP menu → Accounting → Financial Accounting → General Ledger → Posting → Reference Documents → Sample Document	F-01
G/L Document	**Display Document Change:** SAP menu → Accounting → Financial Accounting → General Ledger → Document → Change	FB02
	Change Line Items: SAP menu → Accounting → Financial Accounting → General Ledger → Document → Change Line Items	FB09
	Display Document: SAP menu → Accounting → Financial Accounting → General Ledger → Document → Display	FB03
	Display Changes in Document: SAP menu → Accounting → Financial Accounting → General Ledger → Document → Display Changes	FB04
	Reset Cleared Items: SAP menu → Accounting → Financial Accounting → General Ledger → Document → Reset Cleared Items	FBRA
	Individual Reversal: SAP menu → Accounting → Financial Accounting → General Ledger → Document → Reverse → Individual Reversal	FB08
	Mass Reversal: SAP menu → Accounting → Financial Accounting → General Ledger → Document → Reverse → Mass Reversal	F.80
Cross- Company Posting	**Change Document:** SAP menu → Accounting → Financial Accounting → General Ledger → Document → Cross-CC Transaction → Change	FBU2

Continued

	Function Name and Path	T-code
	Display Document: SAP menu → Accounting → Financial Accounting → General Ledger → Document → Cross-CC Transaction → Display	FBU3
	Reverse Document: SAP menu → Accounting → Financial Accounting → General Ledger → Document → Cross-CC Transaction → Reverse	FBU8
Display G/L	**Display Balances:** SAP menu → Accounting → Financial Accounting → General Ledger → Account → Cross-CC Transaction → Display Balances	FS10N
	Display/Change Line Items: SAP menu → Accounting → Financial Accounting → General Ledger → Account → Cross-CC Transaction → Display/Change Line Items	FBL3N
Periodic Processing	**Account Balance Interest Calculation:** SAP menu → Accounting → Financial Accounting → General Ledger → Periodic Processing → Interest Calculation → Account Balance Interest Calculation	F.52
	Without Specification of Clearing Currency: SAP menu → Accounting → Financial Accounting → General Ledger → Periodic Processing → Automatic Clearing → Without Specification of Clearing Currency	F.13
	With Clearing Currency Specified: SAP menu → Accounting → Financial Accounting → General Ledger → Periodic Processing → Automatic Clearing → F13E – With Clearing Currency Specified	F13E
	Posting Recurring Entries: SAP menu → Accounting → Financial Accounting → General Ledger → Periodic Processing → Recurring Entries → F.14 – Execute	F.14

TABLE 5.1

Continued

Function Name and Path	T-code
Lists Recurring Entries: SAP menu → Accounting → Financial Accounting → General Ledger → Periodic Processing → Recurring Entries → F.15 – Lists	F.15
Valuate Foreign Currency: SAP menu → Accounting → Financial Accounting → General Ledger → Posting → Valuate Foreign Currency	F-05
Enter Accrual/Deferral Document: SAP menu → Accounting → Financial Accounting → General Ledger → Periodic Processing → Closing → Valuate → Enter Accrual/Deferral Doc.	FBS1
Reverse Accrual/Deferral Document: SAP menu → Accounting → Financial Accounting → General Ledger → Periodic Processing → Closing → Valuate → Reverse Accrual/Deferral Document	F.81

TABLE 5.1

5.2 ACCOUNTS PAYABLE (AP)

The main activities in the AP ledger submodules involve: (1) maintenance of AP master data, (2) business transactions, (3) period-end transactions, and (4) information systems. For your reference, some of the important transaction codes for accounts payable are listed in Table 5.2.

	Function Name and Path	T-code
Maintain Vendor Master	**Create Vendor Master:** SAP menu → Accounting → Financial Accounting → Accounts Payable → Master Records → Create Or	FK01
	SAP menu → Accounting → Financial Accounting → Accounts Payable → Master Records → Maintain centrally → Create	XK01

Continued

Function Name and Path	T-code
Change Vendor Master: SAP menu → Accounting → Financial Accounting → Accounts Payable → Master records → Change Or	FK02
SAP menu → Accounting → Financial Accounting → Accounts Payable → Master records → Maintain centrally → Create	XK02
Display Vendor Master: SAP menu → Accounting → Financial Accounting → Accounts Payable → Master records → Display Or	FK03
SAP menu → Accounting → Financial Accounting → Accounts Payable → Master records → Maintain centrally → Display	XK03
Block/Unblock Vendor Master: SAP menu → Accounting → Financial Accounting → Accounts Payable → Master records → Set Deletion Indicator Or	FK06
SAP menu → Accounting → Financial Accounting → Accounts Payable → Master records → Maintain centrally → Set Deletion Indicator	XK06
Display Vendor Master Changes: SAP menu → Accounting → Financial Accounting → Accounts Payable → Master records → Display changes Or	FK04
SAP menu → Accounting → Financial Accounting → Accounts Payable → Master records → Maintain centrally → Display changes	XK04
Vendor Master Change Confirmation: SAP menu → Accounting → Financial Accounting → Accounts Payable → Master records → Confirmation of change → Single	FK08

TABLE 5.2

Continued

	Function Name and Path	T-code
	Vendor Master Change Confirmation: SAP menu → Accounting → Financial Accounting → Accounts Payable → Master records → Confirmation of change → List	FK09
	Enhancing Vendor Master to Another Co. Code: SAP menu → Accounting → Financial Accounting → Accounts Payable → Master records → Compare → Company codes → Send	FK15
	Enhancing Vendor Master to Another Co. Code: SAP menu → Accounting → Financial Accounting → Accounts Payable → Master records → Compare → Company codes → Receive	FK16

Vendor Document:

Business Transaction with Vendor	**Invoice Posting (Enjoy Tran. code):** SAP R/3 System → Accounting → Financial Accounting → Accounts Payable → Document entry → Invoice	FB60
	Invoice Posting: SAP R/3 System → Accounting → Financial Accounting → Accounts Payable → Document entry → Invoice – general	F-43
	Credit Memo Posting: SAP R/3 System → Accounting → Financial Accounting → Accounts Payable → Document entry → Credit memo	FB65
	Credit Memo Posting: SAP R/3 System → Accounting → Financial Accounting → Accounts Payable → Document entry → Credit memo – general	F-41

Document Parking:

	Park/Edit Invoice: SAP R/3 System → Accounting → Financial Accounting → Accounts Payable → Document entry → Document Parking → Park/edit invoice	FV60

Continued

Function Name and Path	T-code
Invoice Parking—General: SAP R/3 System → Accounting → Financial Accounting → Accounts Payable → Document entry → Document Parking → Invoice parking – general	F-63
Park/Edit Credit Memo: SAP R/3 System → Accounting → Financial Accounting → Accounts Payable → Document entry → Document Parking → Park/edit credit memo	FV65
Credit Memo Parking—General: SAP R/3 System → Accounting → Financial Accounting → Accounts Payable → Document entry → Document Parking → Credit memo parking – general	F-66

Down Payment:

Request: SAP R/3 System → Accounting → Financial Accounting → Accounts Payable → Document entry → Down payment → Request	F-47
Down Payment: SAP R/3 System → Accounting → Financial Accounting → Accounts Payable → Document entry → Down payment → Down payment	F-48
Clearing: SAP R/3 System → Accounting → Financial Accounting → Accounts Payable → Document entry → Down payment → Clearing	F-54

Outgoing Payment:

Post Outgoing Payment: SAP R/3 System → Accounting → Financial Accounting → Accounts Payable → Document entry → Outgoing payment → Post	F-53

TABLE 5.2

Continued

Function Name and Path	T-code
Post + print forms: SAP R/3 System → Accounting → Financial Accounting → Accounts Payable → Document entry → Outgoing payment → Post + print forms	F-58
Payment Request: SAP R/3 System → Accounting → Financial Accounting → Accounts Payable → Document entry → Outgoing payment → Payment request	F-59
Automatic Payment Programs: SAP R/3 System → Accounting → Financial Accounting → Accounts Payable → Periodic Processing → F-110 – Payments	F110

Document Management:

Change a Document: SAP R/3 System → Accounting → Financial Accounting → Accounts Payable → Document → Change	FB02
Change Line Items: SAP R/3 System → Accounting → Financial Accounting → Accounts Payable → Document → Change line items	FB09
Display Document: SAP R/3 System → Accounting → Financial Accounting → Accounts Payable → Document → Display	FB03
Display Changes: SAP R/3 System → Accounting → Financial Accounting → Accounts Payable → Document → Display changes	FB04
Reset Cleared Items: SAP R/3 System → Accounting → Financial Accounting → Accounts Payable → Document → Reset cleared items	FBRA

Continued

	Function Name and Path	T-code
Period-end Transactions	**Interest Balance:** SAP R/3 System → Accounting → Financial Accounting → Accounts Payable → Periodic processing → Interest calculation → Balance	**F.44**
	Dunning Run: SAP R/3 System → Accounting → Financial Accounting → Accounts Payable → Periodic processing → Dunning	**F150**
	Execute Recurring Entries: SAP R/3 System → Accounting → Financial Accounting → Accounts Payable → Periodic processing → Recurring entries → Execute	**F.14**
	Open Items in Foreign Currency: SAP R/3 System → Accounting → Financial Accounting → Accounts Payable → Periodic processing → Closing → Valuate → Open items in foreign currency	**F.05**
	Regrouping Receivables/Payables: SAP R/3 System → Accounting → Financial Accounting → Accounts Payable → Periodic processing → Closing → Regroup → Receivables/payables	**F101**
	AP Balance Carry Forward: SAP R/3 System → Accounting → Financial Accounting → Accounts Payable → Periodic processing → Closing → Carry forward → Balance Carry forward	**F.07**
Information Systems	**Transaction Figures: Account Balance:** SAP R/3 System → Accounting → Financial Accounting → Accounts Payable → Information system → Reports for Accounts Payable Accounting → Vendor Balances → Transaction Figures: Account Balance	**S_ALR_87012079**

TABLE 5.2

Continued

Function Name and Path	T-code
Due Date Analysis for Open Items: SAP R/3 System → Accounting → Financial Accounting → Accounts Payable → Information system → Reports for Accounts Payable Accounting → Vendors: Item → Due Date Analysis for Open Items	S_ALR_87012078
List of Vendor Line Items: SAP R/3 System → Accounting → Financial Accounting → Accounts Payable → Information system → Reports for Accounts Payable Accounting → Vendors: Item → List of Vendor Line Items	S_ALR_87012103
Payment List: SAP R/3 System → Accounting → Financial Accounting → Accounts Payable → Information system → Reports for Accounts Payable Accounting → Payment Transactions → Payment List	S_P99_41000099
Check Register: SAP R/3 System → Accounting → Financial Accounting → Accounts Payable → Information system → Reports for Accounts Payable Accounting → Payment Transactions → Check Register	S_P99_41000101
Cashed Checks: SAP R/3 System → Accounting → Financial Accounting → Accounts Payable → Information system → Reports for Accounts Payable Accounting → Payment Transactions → Cashed Checks	S_ALR_87012119
Number Ranges for Checks: SAP R/3 System → Accounting → Financial Accounting → Accounts Payable → Information system → Reports for Accounts Payable Accounting → Payment Transactions → Number Ranges for Checks	S_P99_41000102

TABLE 5.2

5.3 ACCOUNTS RECEIVABLE (AR)

The main activities in the AR submodules involve: (1) maintenance of customer master data, (2) business transactions with customers, (3) period-end transactions, and (4) information systems. For your reference, some of the important transaction codes for AR are listed in Table 5.3.

	Function Name and Path	T-code
Maintenance of Customer Master Data	**Create Customer Master:** SAP R/3 System → Accounting → Financial Accounting → Accounts Receivable → Master records → Create Or	FD01
	SAP R/3 System → Accounting → Financial Accounting → Accounts Receivable → Master records → Maintain centrally → Create	XD01
	Change Customer Master: SAP R/3 System → Accounting → Financial Accounting → Accounts Receivable → Master records → Change Or	FD02
	SAP R/3 System → Accounting → Financial Accounting → Accounts Receivable → Master records → Maintain centrally → Change	XD02
	Display Customer Master: SAP R/3 System → Accounting → Financial Accounting → Accounts Receivable → Master records → Display Or	FD03

TABLE 5.3

Continued

Function Name and Path	T-code
SAP R/3 System → Accounting → Financial Accounting → Accounts Receivable → Master records → Maintain centrally → Display	XD03
Block/Unblock Customer Master: SAP R/3 System → Accounting → Financial Accounting → Accounts Receivable → Master records → Block/unblock Or	FD05
SAP R/3 System → Accounting → Financial Accounting → Accounts Receivable → Master records → Maintain centrally → Block/unblock	XD05
Set Deletion Indicator in Customer Master: SAP R/3 System → Accounting → Financial Accounting → Accounts Receivable → Master records → Set Deletion Indicator Or	FD06
SAP R/3 System → Accounting → Financial Accounting → Accounts Receivable → Master records → Maintain centrally → Set Deletion Indicator	XD06
Confirmation of Change in Customer Master—Single: SAP R/3 System → Accounting → Financial Accounting → Accounts Receivable → Master records → Confirmation of change → Single	FD08
Confirmation of Change in Customer Master—Single List: SAP R/3 System → Accounting → Financial Accounting → Accounts Receivable → Master records → Confirmation of change → List	FD09
Display Changes in Customer Master: SAP R/3 System → Accounting → Financial Accounting → Accounts Receivable → Master records → Display changes Or	FD04

Continued

	Function Name and Path	T-code
	SAP R/3 System → Accounting → Financial Accounting → Accounts Receivable → Master records → Maintain centrally → Display changes	XD04

Document Posting:

	Function Name and Path	T-code
Business Transactions with Customers	**Posting Customer Invoice:** SAP R/3 System → Accounting → Financial Accounting → Accounts Receivable → Document entry → Invoice	FB70
	Posting Customer Invoice—General: SAP R/3 System → Accounting → Financial Accounting → Accounts Receivable → Document entry → Invoice – general	F-22
	Posting Credit Memo: SAP R/3 System → Accounting → Financial Accounting → Accounts Receivable → Document entry → Credit memo	FB75
	Posting Credit Memo—General: SAP R/3 System → Accounting → Financial Accounting → Accounts Receivable → Document entry → Credit memo – general	F-27
	Posting Incoming Payment: SAP R/3 System → Accounting → Financial Accounting → Accounts Receivable → Document entry → Incoming payment	F-28

Document Parking:

	Function Name and Path	T-code
	Park/Edit Invoice: SAP R/3 System → Accounting → Financial Accounting → Accounts Receivable → Document entry → Document Parking → Park/edit invoice	FV70
	Invoice Parking—General: SAP R/3 System → Accounting → Financial Accounting → Accounts Receivable → Document entry → Document Parking → Invoice parking – general	F-64

TABLE 5.3

Continued

Function Name and Path	T-code
Park/Edit Credit Memo: SAP R/3 System → Accounting → Financial Accounting → Accounts Receivable → Document entry → Document Parking → Park/edit credit memo	FV75
Credit Memo Parking—General: SAP R/3 System → Accounting → Financial Accounting → Accounts Receivable → Document entry → Document Parking → Credit memo parking – general	F-67

Down Payment:

Down Payment Request: SAP R/3 System → Accounting → Financial Accounting → Accounts Receivable → Document entry → Down payment → Request	F-37
Down Payment: SAP R/3 System → Accounting → Financial Accounting → Accounts Receivable → Document entry → Down payment → Down payment	F-29
Down Payment Clearing: SAP R/3 System → Accounting → Financial Accounting → Accounts Receivable → Document entry → Down payment → Clearing	F-39

Reference Documents:

Recurring Entry Document: SAP R/3 System → Accounting → Financial Accounting → Accounts Receivable → Document entry → Reference documents → Recurring Entry Document	FBD1
Account Assignment Model: SAP R/3 System → Accounting → Financial Accounting → Accounts Receivable → Document entry → Reference documents → Account assignment model	FKMT

Continued

	Function Name and Path	T-code
	Sample Document: SAP R/3 System → Accounting → Financial Accounting → Accounts Receivable → Document entry → Reference documents → Sample document	F-01
Period-end Transactions	**Running Dunning:** SAP R/3 System → Accounting → Financial Accounting → Accounts Receivable → Periodic processing → Dunning	F150
	Running Balance Interest Calculation: SAP R/3 System → Accounting → Financial Accounting → Accounts Receivable → Periodic processing → Interest calculation → Balance interest	F.26
	Recurring Entry Posting: SAP R/3 System → Accounting → Financial Accounting → Accounts Receivable → Periodic processing → Recurring entries → Execute	F.14
	Open Items in Foreign Currency: SAP R/3 System → Accounting → Financial Accounting → Accounts Receivable → Periodic processing → Closing → Valuate → Open items in foreign currency	F.05
	Reserve for Bad Debt (Gross): SAP R/3 System → Accounting → Financial Accounting → Accounts Receivable → Periodic processing → Closing → Valuate → Reserve for bad debt (gross)	F104
	Regrouping Receivables/Payables: SAP R/3 System → Accounting → Financial Accounting → Accounts Receivable → Periodic processing → Closing → Regroup → Receivables/payables	F101

TABLE 5.3

Continued

	Function Name and Path	T-code
	Balance Carry Forward Account Receivable: SAP R/3 System → Accounting → Financial Accounting → Accounts Receivable → Periodic processing → Closing → Carry forward → Balance Carry forward	F.07
Information Systems	**Customer Balances in Local Currency:** SAP R/3 System → Accounting → Financial Accounting → Accounts Receivable → Information system → Reports for Accounts Receivable Accounting → Customer Balances → Customer Balances in Local Currency	S_ALR_87012172
	Due Date Analysis for Open Items: SAP R/3 System → Accounting → Financial Accounting → Accounts Receivable → Information system → Reports for Accounts Receivable Accounting → Customers: Items → Due Date Analysis for Open Items	S_ALR_87012168
	List of Customer Line Items: SAP R/3 System → Accounting → Financial Accounting → Accounts Receivable → Information system → Reports for Accounts Receivable Accounting → Customers: Items → List of Customer Line Items	S_ALR_87012197
	Customer Open Item Analysis by Balance of Overdue Items: SAP R/3 System → Accounting → Financial Accounting → Accounts Receivable → Information system → Reports for Accounts Receivable Accounting → Customers: Items → Customer Open Item Analysis by Balance of Overdue Items	S_ALR_87012178

TABLE 5.3

5.4 ASSETS MANAGEMENT (AM)

The main activities in the assets accounting submodules involve: (1) maintenance of AA master data, (2) business transactions, (3) period-end transactions, and (4) information systems. For your reference, some of the important transaction codes for Assets Management are provided in Table 5.4.

	Function Name and Path	T-code
Assets Master Maintenance	**Create Assets Master:** SAP R/3 System → Accounting → Fixed Assets → Asset → Create → Asset	AS01
	Create Group Assets Master: SAP R/3 System → Accounting → Fixed Assets → Asset → Create → Group Asset	AS21
	Create Sub Assets Master: SAP R/3 System → Accounting → Fixed Assets → Asset → Create → Sub-Number → Asset	AS11
	Create Group Sub Assets Master: SAP R/3 System → Accounting → Fixed Assets → Asset → Create → Sub-Number → Group Asset	AS24
	Change Assets Master: SAP R/3 System → Accounting → Fixed Assets → Asset → Change → Asset	AS02
	Change Group Assets Master: SAP R/3 System → Accounting → Fixed Assets → Asset → Change → Group Asset	AS22
	Display Assets Master: SAP R/3 System → Accounting → Fixed Assets → Asset → Display → Asset	AS03
	Display Group Assets Master: SAP R/3 System → Accounting → Fixed Assets → Asset → Display → Group Asset	AS23

TABLE 5.4

Continued

	Function Name and Path	T-code
	Lock Assets Master: SAP R/3 System → Accounting → Fixed Assets → Asset → Lock → Asset	AS05
	Lock Group Assets Master: SAP R/3 System → Accounting → Fixed Assets → Asset → Lock → Group Asset	AS25
	Delete Assets Master: SAP R/3 System → Accounting → Fixed Assets → Asset → Delete → Asset	AS06
	Delete Group Assets Master: SAP R/3 System → Accounting → Fixed Assets → Asset → Delete → Group Asset	AS26
Assets **Acquisition**	**External Acquisition:** SAP R/3 System → Accounting → Fixed Assets → Asset → Posting → Acquisition → External Acquisition → With Vendor	F-90
	Acquisition with Automatic Offsetting Entry: SAP R/3 System → Accounting → Fixed Assets → Asset → Posting → Acquisition → External Acquisition → Acquis. w/Autom. Offsetting Entry	ABZON
	Clearing Offsetting Entry: SAP R/3 System → Accounting → Fixed Assets → Asset → Posting → Acquisition → External Acquisition → Clearing Offsetting Entry	F-91
	From Affiliated Company: SAP R/3 System → Accounting → Fixed Assets → Asset → Posting → Acquisition → External Acquisition → From Affiliated Company	ABZP
	Credit Memo for Current Year Invoice Year: SAP R/3 System → Accounting → Fixed Assets → Asset → Posting → Acquisition → Credit Memo → ABGL – ... in Invoice Year	ABGL

Continued

	Function Name and Path	T-code
	Credit Memo for Previous Year Invoice Year: SAP R/3 System → Accounting → Fixed Assets → Asset → Posting → Acquisition → Credit Memo → ABGF – ... in Next Year	ABGF
	In-House Production: SAP R/3 System → Accounting → Fixed Assets → Asset → Posting → Acquisition → ABZE – In-House Production	ABZE
	Capitalization of AUC via Distribute: SAP R/3 System → Accounting → Fixed Assets → Asset → Posting → Capitalize Asset u. Const. → AIAB – Distribute	AIAB
	Capitalization of AUC via Settle: SAP R/3 System → Accounting → Fixed Assets → Asset → Posting → Capitalize Asset u. Const. → AIBU – Settle	AIBU
Assets Retirement/ Transfer	**Transfer within Company Code:** SAP R/3 System → Accounting → Fixed Assets → Posting → Transfer → Transfer within Company Code	ABUMN
	Intercompany Asset Transfer: SAP R/3 System → Accounting → Fixed Assets → Posting → Transfer → Intercompany Asset Transfer	ABT1N
	Retirement with Customer: SAP R/3 System → Accounting → Fixed Assets → Posting → Retirement → Retirement w/Revenue → With Customer	F-92
	Asset Sale without Customer: SAP R/3 System → Accounting → Fixed Assets → Posting → Retirement → Retirement w/Revenue → Asset Sale Without Customer	ABAON
	Asset Retirement by Scrapping: SAP R/3 System → Accounting → Fixed Assets → Posting → Retirement → Asset Retirement by Scrapping	ABAVN

TABLE 5.4

	Function Name and Path	T-code
	Subsequent Revenue: SAP R/3 System → Accounting → Fixed Assets → Posting → Retirement → Subsequent Revenue	ABNE
	Subsequent Costs: SAP R/3 System → Accounting → Fixed Assets → Posting → Retirement → Subsequent Costs	ABNK
Period-end Transactions	**Execute Depreciation Run:** SAP R/3 System → Accounting → Fixed Assets → Periodic Processing → Depreciation Run → Asset Explorer	AFAB
	Fiscal Year Change: SAP R/3 System → Accounting → Fixed Assets → Periodic Processing → Fiscal Year Change	AJRW
	Execute: SAP R/3 System → Accounting → Fixed Assets → Periodic Processing → Year-End Closing → Execute	AJAB
Information Systems	**Asset Explorer:** SAP R/3 System → Accounting → Fixed Assets → Reports on Asset Accounting → Individual Asset → AW01N – Asset Explorer	AW01N
	... by Asset Number: SAP R/3 System → Accounting → Fixed Assets → Reports on Asset Accounting → Asset Balances → Balance Lists → Asset Balances → by Asset Number	S_ALR_87011963
	... by Asset Class: SAP R/3 System → Accounting → Fixed Assets → Reports on Asset Accounting → Asset Balances → Balance Lists → Asset Balances → by Asset Class	S_ALR_87011964
	Leasing: SAP R/3 System → Accounting → Fixed Assets → Reports on Asset Accounting → Asset Balances → Leased Assets → Leasing	S_ALR_87010139

Continued

Function Name and Path	T-code
Liabilities from Leasing Agreements: SAP R/3 System → Accounting → Fixed Assets → Reports on Asset Accounting → Asset Balances → Leased Assets → Liabilities from Leasing Agreements	S_ALR_87010141

TABLE 5.4

5.5 COST ELEMENT ACCOUNTING (CO-CEL)

The main activities in the CO-CEL submodules involve: (1) maintenance of cost element master data and (2) information systems. For your reference, some of the important transaction codes for Cost Element Accounting are listed in Table 5.5.

	Function Name and Path	T-code
Master Maintenance	**Create Primary Cost Element:** SAP R/3 System → Accounting → Controlling → Cost Element Accounting → Master Data → Cost Element → Individual Processing → Create Primary	KA01
	Create Secondary Cost Element: SAP R/3 System → Accounting → Controlling → Cost Element Accounting → Master Data → Cost Element → Individual Processing → Create Secondary	KA06
	Change Cost Element Master Data: SAP R/3 System → Accounting → Controlling → Cost Element Accounting → Master Data → Cost Element → Individual Processing → Change	KA02
	Display Cost Element Master Data: SAP R/3 System → Accounting → Controlling → Cost Element Accounting → Master Data → Cost Element → Individual Processing → Display	KA03

TABLE 5.5

Continued

	Function Name and Path	T-code
	Delete Cost Element Master Data: SAP R/3 System → Accounting → Controlling → Cost Element Accounting → Master Data → Cost Element → Individual Processing → Delete	KA04
	Display Changes in Cost Element Master Data: SAP R/3 System → Accounting → Controlling → Cost Element Accounting → Master Data → Cost Element → Individual Processing → Display Changes	KA05
	Create Cost Element Group: SAP R/3 System → Accounting → Controlling → Cost Element Accounting → Master Data → Cost Element Group → Create	KAH1
	Change Cost Element Group: SAP R/3 System → Accounting → Controlling → Cost Element Accounting → Master Data → Cost Element Group → Change	KAH2
	Display Cost Element Group: SAP R/3 System → Accounting → Controlling → Cost Element Accounting → Master Data → Cost Element Group → Display	KAH3
Information Systems	**CO/FI Reconciliation in CoCd Currency:** SAP R/3 System → Accounting → Controlling → Cost Element Accounting → Information System → Reports for Cost and Revenue Element Accounting → Reconciliation → - CO/FI Reconciliation in CoCd Currency	S_ALR_87013603
	Overview of Cost Flows: SAP R/3 System → Accounting → Controlling → Cost Element Accounting → Information System → Reports for Cost and Revenue Element Accounting → Cost Flow → - Overview of Cost Flows	KAL7
	Reconciliation Ledger: SAP R/3 System → Accounting → Controlling → Cost Element Accounting → Information System → Reports for Cost and Revenue Element Accounting → Reconciliation → - Reconciliation Ledger: CO Line Items	KALR

Continued

Function Name and Path	T-code
Cost Element Master Data Reports: SAP R/3 System → Accounting → Controlling → Cost Element Accounting → Information System → Reports for Cost and Revenue Element Accounting → Master Data Indexes → – Cost Elements: Master Data Report	KA23

TABLE 5.5

5.6 COST CENTER ACCOUNTING (CO-CCA)

The main activities in the CO-CCA submodules involve: (1) maintenance of cost center master data, (2) CO internal posting, (3) period-end processing, and (4) information systems. For your reference, some of the important transaction codes for Cost center accounting are provided in Table 5.6.

	Function Name and Path	T-code
Master Maintenance	**Create Cost Center Master:** SAP R/3 System → Accounting → Controlling → Cost Center Accounting → Master Data → Cost Center → Individual Processing → KS01 – Create	KS01
	Change Cost Center Master: SAP R/3 System → Accounting → Controlling → Cost Center Accounting → Master Data → Cost Center → Individual Processing → Change	KS02
	Display Cost Center Master: SAP R/3 System → Accounting → Controlling → Cost Center Accounting → Master Data → Cost Center → Individual Processing → Display	KS03

TABLE 5.6

Continued

Function Name and Path	T-code
Delete Cost Center Master: SAP R/3 System → Accounting → Controlling → Cost Center Accounting → Master Data → Cost Center → Individual Processing → Delete	KS04
Display Changes to Cost Center Master: SAP R/3 System → Accounting → Controlling → Cost Center Accounting → Master Data → Cost Center → Individual Processing → Display Changes	KS05
Create Cost Center Group: SAP R/3 System → Accounting → Controlling → Cost Center Accounting → Master Data → Cost Center → Cost Center Group → Create	KSH1
Change Cost Center Group: SAP R/3 System → Accounting → Controlling → Cost Center Accounting → Master Data → Cost Center → Cost Center Group → Change	KSH2
Display Cost Center Group: SAP R/3 System → Accounting → Controlling → Cost Center Accounting → Master Data → Cost Center → Cost Center Group → Display	KSH3
Create Activity Type: SAP R/3 System → Accounting → Controlling → Cost Center Accounting → Master Data → Activity Type → Individual Processing → Create	KL01
Change Activity Type: SAP R/3 System → Accounting → Controlling → Cost Center Accounting → Master Data → Activity Type → Individual Processing → Change	KL02
Display Activity Type: SAP R/3 System → Accounting → Controlling → Cost Center Accounting → Master Data → Activity Type → Individual Processing → Display	KL03

Continued

Function Name and Path	T-code
Delete Activity Type: SAP R/3 System → Accounting → Controlling → Cost Center Accounting → Master Data → Activity Type → Individual Processing → Delete	KL04
Create Activity Group: SAP R/3 System → Accounting → Controlling → Cost Center Accounting → Master Data → Activity Type → Activity Type Group → KLH1 – Create	KLH1
Change Activity Group: SAP R/3 System → Accounting → Controlling → Cost Center Accounting → Master Data → Activity Type → Activity Type Group → KLH2 – Change	KLH2
Display Activity Group: SAP R/3 System → Accounting → Controlling → Cost Center Accounting → Master Data → Activity Type → Activity Type Group → KLH3 – Display	KLH3
Create Statistical Key Figure: SAP R/3 System → Accounting → Controlling → Cost Center Accounting → Master Data → Statistical Key Figures → Individual Processing → Create	KK01
Change Statistical Key Figure: SAP R/3 System → Accounting → Controlling → Cost Center Accounting → Master Data → Statistical Key Figures → Individual Processing → Change	KK02
Display Statistical Key Figure: SAP R/3 System → Accounting → Controlling → Cost Center Accounting → Master Data → Statistical Key Figures → Individual Processing → Display	KK03
Delete Statistical Key Figure: SAP R/3 System → Accounting → Controlling → Cost Center Accounting → Master Data → Statistical Key Figures → Individual Processing → Delete	KK03DEL

TABLE 5.6

Continued

	Function Name and Path	T-code
	Create Statistical Key Figure Group: SAP R/3 System → Accounting → Controlling → Cost Center Accounting → Master Data → Statistical Key Figures → Statistical Key Figure Group → Create	KBH1
	Change Statistical Key Figure Group: SAP R/3 System → Accounting → Controlling → Cost Center Accounting → Master Data → Statistical Key Figures → Statistical Key Figure Group → Change	KBH2
	Display Statistical Key Figure Group: SAP R/3 System → Accounting → Controlling → Cost Center Accounting → Master Data → Statistical Key Figures → Statistical Key Figure Group → Display	KBH3
Transactions	**Manual Reposting of Costs:** SAP R/3 System → Accounting → Controlling → Cost Center Accounting → Actual Postings → Manual Reposting of Costs → Enter	KB11N
	Display Manual Reposting of Costs: SAP R/3 System → Accounting → Controlling → Cost Center Accounting → Actual Postings → Manual Reposting of Costs → Display	KB13N
	Reverse Manual Reposting of Costs: SAP R/3 System → Accounting → Controlling → Cost Center Accounting → Actual Postings → Manual Reposting of Costs → Reverse	KB14N
	Manual Reposting of Revenues: SAP R/3 System → Accounting → Controlling → Cost Center Accounting → Actual Postings → Manual Reposting of Revenues → Reverse	KB41N
	Display Manual Reposting of Revenues: SAP R/3 System → Accounting → Controlling → Cost Center Accounting → Actual Postings → Manual Reposting of Revenues → Display	KB43N

Continued

Function Name and Path	T-code
Reverse Manual Reposting of Revenues: SAP R/3 System → Accounting → Controlling → Cost Center Accounting → Actual Postings → Manual Reposting of Revenues → Reverse	KB44N
Reposting of Line Items: SAP R/3 System → Accounting → Controlling → Cost Center Accounting → Actual Postings → Repost Line Items → Enter	KB61
Display Reposting of Line Items: SAP R/3 System → Accounting → Controlling → Cost Center Accounting → Actual Postings → Repost Line Items → Display	KB63
Reverse Reposting of Line Items: SAP R/3 System → Accounting → Controlling → Cost Center Accounting → Actual Postings → Repost Line Items → Reverse	KB64
Enter Activity Allocation: SAP R/3 System → Accounting → Controlling → Cost Center Accounting → Actual Postings → Activity Allocation → Enter	KB21N
Display Activity Allocation: SAP R/3 System → Accounting → Controlling → Cost Center Accounting → Actual Postings → Activity Allocation → Display	KB23N
Reverse Activity Allocation: SAP R/3 System → Accounting → Controlling → Cost Center Accounting → Actual Postings → Activity Allocation → Reverse	KB24N
Enter Manual Cost Allocation: SAP R/3 System → Accounting → Controlling → Cost Center Accounting → Actual Postings → Manual Cost Allocation → Enter	KB15N

TABLE 5.6

Continued

Function Name and Path	T-code
Display Manual Cost Allocation: SAP R/3 System → Accounting → Controlling → Cost Center Accounting → Actual Postings → Manual Cost Allocation → Display	KB16N
Reverse Manual Cost Allocation: SAP R/3 System → Accounting → Controlling → Cost Center Accounting → Actual Postings → Manual Cost Allocation → Reverse	KB17N
Enter Statistical Key Figures: SAP R/3 System → Accounting → Controlling → Cost Center Accounting → Actual Postings → Statistical Key Figures → Enter	KB31N
Display Statistical Key Figures: SAP R/3 System → Accounting → Controlling → Cost Center Accounting → Actual Postings → Statistical Key Figures → Display	KB33N
Reverse Statistical Key Figures: SAP R/3 System → Accounting → Controlling → Cost Center Accounting → Actual Postings → Statistical Key Figures → Reverse	KB34N
Periodic Reposting: SAP R/3 System → Accounting → Controlling → Cost Center Accounting → Period-End Closing → Single Functions → Periodic Reposting	KSW5
Accrual Calculation: SAP R/3 System → Accounting → Controlling → Cost Center Accounting → Period-End Closing → Single Functions → Accrual Calculation	KSA3
Distribution: SAP R/3 System → Accounting → Controlling → Cost Center Accounting → Period-End Closing → Single Functions → Allocations → Distribution	KSV5

Continued

	Function Name and Path	T-code
	Assessment: SAP R/3 System → Accounting → Controlling → Cost Center Accounting → Period-End Closing → Single Functions → Allocations → Assessment	KSU5
Information Systems	**Range: Cost Centers:** SAP R/3 System → Accounting → Controlling → Cost Center Accounting → Information System → Reports for Cost Center Accounting → Plan/Actual Comparisons → Cost Centers: Actual/Plan/Variance	S_ALR_87013612
	Range: Cost Elements: SAP R/3 System → Accounting → Controlling → Cost Center Accounting → Information System → Reports for Cost Center Accounting → Plan/Actual Comparisons → Range: Cost Elements	S_ALR_87013613
	Cost Centers: Actual Line Items: SAP R/3 System → Accounting → Controlling → Cost Center Accounting → Information System → Reports for Cost Center Accounting → Line items → Cost Centers: Actual Line Items	KSB1
	Cost Center Master Data: SAP R/3 System → Accounting → Controlling → Cost Center Accounting → Information System → Reports for Cost Center Accounting → Line items → Cost Centers: Actual Line Items → Cost Centers: Master Data Report	KS13

TABLE 5.6

5.7 INTERNAL ORDER (CO-IO)

The main activities in the CO-IO sub-modules involve: (1) maintenance of internal order (IO) master data, (2) CO internal posting, (3) period-end processing, and (4) information systems. For your reference, some of the important transaction codes for Internal Order are provided in Table 5.7.

	Function Name and Path	T-code
Master Data	**Create IO:** SAP R/3 System → Accounting → Controlling → Internal Orders → Master Data → Special Functions → Order → Create	KO01
	Change IO: SAP R/3 System → Accounting → Controlling → Internal Orders → Master Data → Special Functions → Order → Change	KO02
	Display IO: SAP R/3 System → Accounting → Controlling → Internal Orders → Master Data → Special Functions → Order → Display	KO03
	Create IO Group: SAP R/3 System → Accounting → Controlling → Internal Orders → Master Data → Order Group → Create	KOH1
	Change IO Group: SAP R/3 System → Accounting → Controlling → Internal Orders → Master Data → Order Group → Change	KOH2
	Display IO Group: SAP R/3 System → Accounting → Controlling → Internal Orders → Master Data → Order Group → Display	KOH3
Transactions	**Manual Reposting of Cost:** SAP R/3 System → Accounting → Controlling → Internal Orders → Actual Postings → Manual Reposting of Costs → Enter	KB11N
	Displaying Manual Reposting of Cost: SAP R/3 System → Accounting → Controlling → Internal Orders → Actual Postings → Manual Reposting of Costs → Display	KB13N
	Reversing Manual Reposting of Cost: SAP R/3 System → Accounting → Controlling → Internal Orders → Actual Postings → Manual Reposting of Costs → Reverse	KB14N

Continued

Function Name and Path	T-code
Manual Reposting of Revenues: SAP R/3 System → Accounting → Controlling → Internal Orders → Actual Postings → Manual Reposting of Revenues → Enter	KB41N
Displaying Manual Reposting of Revenues: SAP R/3 System → Accounting → Controlling → Internal Orders → Actual Postings → Manual Reposting of Revenues → Display	KB43N
Reversing Manual Reposting of Revenues: SAP R/3 System → Accounting → Controlling → Internal Orders → Actual Postings → Manual Reposting of Revenues → Reverse	KB44N
Reposting Line Items: SAP R/3 System → Accounting → Controlling → Internal Orders → Actual Postings → Repost Line Items → Enter	KB61
Displaying Manual Reposting of Line Items: SAP R/3 System → Accounting → Controlling → Internal Orders → Actual Postings → Repost Line Items → Display	KB63
Reversing Manual Reposting of Line Items: SAP R/3 System → Accounting → Controlling → Internal Orders → Actual Postings → Repost Line Items → Reverse	KB64
IO Individual Settlement: SAP R/3 System → Accounting → Controlling → Internal Orders → Period-End Closing → Settlement → Individual Processing	KO88
IO Collective Settlement: SAP R/3 System → Accounting → Controlling → Internal Orders → Period-End Closing → Settlement → Collective Processing	KO8G

TABLE 5.7

Continued

Function Name and Path		T-code
	Line Item Settlement of Investment Order: SAP R/3 System → Accounting → Controlling → Internal Orders → Period-End Closing → Settlement → Investment Order: Line Items	KOB5
Information Systems	**Orders: Actual Line Items:** SAP R/3 System → Accounting → Controlling → Internal Orders → Information System → Reports for Internal Orders → Orders: Actual Line Items	KOB1
	CO Documents: Actual Costs: SAP R/3 System → Accounting → Controlling → Internal Orders → Information System → Reports for Internal Orders → CO Documents: Actual Costs	KSB5
	Display Budget Document: SAP R/3 System → Accounting → Controlling → Internal Orders → Information System → Reports for Internal Orders → Display Budget Document	KO2B

TABLE 5.7

5.8 PROFIT CENTER ACCOUNTING (CO-PCA)

The main activities in the CO-PCA submodules involve: (1) maintenance of profit center master data, (2) CO internal posting, (3) period-end processing, and (4) information systems. For your reference, some of the important transaction codes for Profit Center Accounting are provided in Table 5.8.

Function Name and Path		T-code
Master Data	**Create Profit Center:** SAP R/3 System → Accounting → Controlling → Profit Center Accounting → Master Data → Profit Center → Individual Processing → Create	KE51

Continued

	Function Name and Path	T-code
	Change Profit Center: SAP R/3 System → Accounting → Controlling → Profit Center Accounting → Master Data → Profit Center → Individual Processing → Change	KE52
	Display Profit Center: SAP R/3 System → Accounting → Controlling → Profit Center Accounting → Master Data → Profit Center → Individual Processing → Display	KE53
	Delete Profit Center: SAP R/3 System → Accounting → Controlling → Profit Center Accounting → Master Data → Profit Center → Individual Processing → Delete	KE54
	Display Changes in Profit Center: SAP R/3 System → Accounting → Controlling → Profit Center Accounting → Master Data → Profit Center → Individual Processing → Display Changes	6KEA
Standard Hierarchy	**Create Standard Hierarchy:** SAP R/3 System → Accounting → Controlling → Profit Center Accounting → Master Data → Standard Hierarchy → Create	KCH1
	Change Standard Hierarchy: SAP R/3 System → Accounting → Controlling → Profit Center Accounting → Master Data → Standard Hierarchy → Change	KCH5N
	Display Standard Hierarchy: SAP R/3 System → Accounting → Controlling → Profit Center Accounting → Master Data → Standard Hierarchy → Display	KCH6N
Profit Center Group	**Create Profit Center Group:** SAP R/3 System → Accounting → Controlling → Profit Center Accounting → Master Data → Profit Center Group → Create	KCH1

TABLE 5.8

Continued

	Function Name and Path	T-code
	Change Profit Center Group: SAP R/3 System → Accounting → Controlling → Profit Center Accounting → Master Data → Profit Center Group → Change	KCH2
	Display Profit Center Group: SAP R/3 System → Accounting → Controlling → Profit Center Accounting → Master Data → Profit Center Group → Display	KCH3
Actual Postings	**Enter Actual Posting:** SAP R/3 System → Accounting → Controlling → Profit Center Accounting → Actual Postings → Profit Center Document → Enter	9KE0
	Display Actual Posting: SAP R/3 System → Accounting → Controlling → Profit Center Accounting → Actual Postings → Profit Center Document → Display	9KE9
	Change Actual Posting: SAP R/3 System → Accounting → Controlling → Profit Center Accounting → Actual Postings → Statistical Key Figures → Change	9KE5
	Display Statistical Key Figure: SAP R/3 System → Accounting → Controlling → Profit Center Accounting → Actual Postings → Statistical Key Figures → Display	9KE6
	Assessment: SAP R/3 System → Accounting → Controlling → Profit Center Accounting → Actual Postings → Period-End Closing → Assessment	3KE5
	Distribution: SAP R/3 System → Accounting → Controlling → Profit Center Accounting → Actual Postings → Period-End Closing → Distribution	4KE5

Continued

	Function Name and Path	T-code
	Transferring Payables/Receivables: SAP R/3 System → Accounting → Controlling → Profit Center Accounting → Actual Postings → Period-End Closing → Distribution	1KEK
	Balance Carry Forward: SAP R/3 System → Accounting → Controlling → Profit Center Accounting → Actual Postings → Period-End Closing → Balance Carry Forward	2KES
Information Systems	**Profit Center: Actual Line Items:** SAP R/3 System → Accounting → Controlling → Profit Center Accounting → Information System → Reports for Profit Center Accounting → Line Item Reports → Profit Center: Actual Line Items	KE5Z
	Profit Center: Receivables: SAP R/3 System → Accounting → Controlling → Profit Center Accounting → Information System → Reports for Profit Center Accounting → Line Item Reports → Open Items → Profit Center: Receivables	S_ALR_87013343
	Profit Center: Payables: SAP R/3 System → Accounting → Controlling → Profit Center Accounting → Information System → Reports for Profit Center Accounting → Line Item Reports → Open Items → Profit Center: Payables	S_ALR_87013344
	Profit Centers: Customers (Transferred Periodically): SAP R/3 System → Accounting → Controlling → Profit Center Accounting → Information System → Reports for Profit Center Accounting → Line Item Reports → Balance Sheet Items Transferred Periodically → Profit Centers: Customers (Transferred Periodically)	S_ALR_87013345

TABLE 5.8

Continued

Function Name and Path	T-code
Profit Centers: Vendors (Transferred Periodically): SAP R/3 System → Accounting → Controlling → Profit Center Accounting → Information System → Reports for Profit Center Accounting → Line Item Reports → Balance Sheet Items Transferred Periodically → Profit Centers: Vendors (Transferred Periodically)	S_ALR_87013346
Profit Centers: Assets (Transferred Periodically): SAP R/3 System → Accounting → Controlling → Profit Center Accounting → Information System → Reports for Profit Center Accounting → Line Item Reports → Balance Sheet Items Transferred Periodically → Profit Centers: Assets (Transferred Periodically)	S_ALR_87013347
Profit Centers: Materials (Transferred Periodically): SAP R/3 System → Accounting → Controlling → Profit Center Accounting → Information System → Reports for Profit Center Accounting → Line Item Reports → Balance Sheet Items Transferred Periodically → Profit Centers: Materials (Transferred Periodically)	S_ALR_87013348

TABLE 5.8

5.9 PROFITABILITY ANALYSIS (CO-PA)

The main activities in the CO-PA submodules involve: (1) maintenance of PA master data, (2) CO internal posting, (3) period-end processing, and (4) information systems. For your reference, some of the important transaction codes for Profitability Analysis are provided in Table 5.9.

Function Name and Path	T-code
Change Characteristic Values: SAP R/3 System → Accounting → Controlling → Profitability Analysis → Master Data → Characteristic Values → Change Characteristic Values	KES1
Define Characteristics Hierarchy: SAP R/3 System → Accounting → Controlling → Profitability Analysis → Master Data → Characteristic Values → Define Characteristics Hierarchy	KES3
Maintain Derivation Rules: SAP R/3 System → Accounting → Controlling → Profitability Analysis → Master Data → Maintain Derivation Rules	KEDE
Maintain Realignments: SAP R/3 System → Accounting → Controlling → Profitability Analysis → Master Data → Maintain Realignments	KEND
Assessment: SAP R/3 System → Accounting → Controlling → Profitability Analysis → Actual Postings → Period-End Closing → Transfer Cost Center Costs/Process Costs → Assessment	KEU5
Execute Report: SAP R/3 System → Accounting → Controlling → Profitability Analysis → Information System → Execute Report	KE30
Display Line Items—Actual: SAP R/3 System → Accounting → Controlling → Profitability Analysis → Information System → Display Line Item List → Actual	KE24

TABLE 5.9

Continued

Function Name and Path	T-code
Summarization Level Data Refresh: SAP R/3 System → Accounting → Controlling → Profitability Analysis → Tools → Summarization Levels → Refresh	KEDU
External Data Transfer: SAP R/3 System → Accounting → Controlling → Profitability Analysis → Tools → External Data Transfer → Execute	KEFC

TABLE 5.9

5.10 PRODUCT COSTING (CO-PC)

The main activities in the CO-PC submodules involve the calculation of cost and analysis. For your reference, some of the important transaction codes for product costing are listed in Table 5.10.

Function Name and Path	T-code
Display Materials to be Costed: SAP R/3 System → Accounting → Controlling → Product Cost Controlling → Product Cost Planning → Material Costing → Display Materials to be Costed	CKAPP01
Edit Costing Run: SAP R/3 System → Accounting → Controlling → Product Cost Controlling → Product Cost Planning → Material Costing → Costing Run → Selection List → CKMATSEL – Create	CKMATSEL

Continued

Function Name and Path	T-code
Create Cost Estimate with Quantity Structure: SAP R/3 System → Accounting → Controlling → Product Cost Controlling → Product Cost Planning → Material Costing → Cost Estimate with Quantity Structure → Create	CK11N
Create Cost Estimate without Quantity Structure: SAP R/3 System → Accounting → Controlling → Product Cost Controlling → Product Cost Planning → Material Costing → Cost Estimate Without Quantity Structure → KKPAN – Create	KKPAN
Price Update: SAP R/3 System → Accounting → Controlling → Product Cost Controlling → Product Cost Planning → Material Costing → Price Update	CK24
Create Product Cost Estimate: SAP R/3 System → Accounting → Controlling → Product Cost Controlling → Product Cost Planning → Material Costing → Production Lot Cost Estimate → Create	CKW1
Create Base Planning Object: SAP R/3 System → Accounting → Controlling → Product Cost Controlling → Product Cost Planning → Reference and Simulation Costing → Create Base Planning Object	KKE1
Edit Costing Model: SAP R/3 System → Accounting → Controlling → Product Cost Controlling → Product Cost Planning → Easy Cost Planning and Execution Services → CKCM – Edit Costing Model	CKCM

TABLE 5.10

Continued

Function Name and Path	T-code
Results of Costing Run: SAP R/3 System → Accounting → Controlling → Product Cost Controlling → Product Cost Planning → Information System → Summarized Analysis → Analyze Costing Run → Results of Costing Run	S_ALR_87099930
Price vs. Cost Estimate: SAP R/3 System → Accounting → Controlling → Product Cost Controlling → Product Cost Planning → Information System → Summarized Analysis → Analyze Costing Run → Price vs. Cost Estimate	S_ALR_87099931
Variances between Costing Runs: SAP R/3 System → Accounting → Controlling → Product Cost Controlling → Product Cost Planning → Information System → Summarized Analysis → Analyze Costing Run → Variances Between Costing Runs	S_ALR_87099932

TABLE 5.10

Chapter 6

FICO QUICK TOUR

This chapter covers, in bullet-point style, the FICO submodules. Note that this chapter has an important role from an interview perspective. It is impossible to cover all of the submodules of the SAP software in such a small number of pages, but this chapter does cover the most important points of the SAP FICO submodules.

6.1 SAP GENERAL

- The client is an independent unit within a system. For example, an SAP server may have more than one client. Each client has its data environment and the SAP solution stores all master data within a client's environment. When you log into the SAP server, you will select your client. However, some tables as well as configuration and customization are client independent. Because of client dependence and independence, it is not desirable to keep different components of the system landscape in the same system.

- Operating concerns: Operating concerns represent an organization entity from the market segment point of view. You can assign several controlling areas to one operating concern. CO-PA operates within an operating concern.

- The controlling area: The controlling area is the basic organizational unit in Controlling (CO). You may assign more than one company code to a controlling area. As a period-end activity, you allocate expenses from one cost object to another.

- Company code: The company code is an independent account unit for which you maintain books of account for external reporting.
- In SAP R/3 or mySAP Financial, you follow the variant principle to simplify the configuration, The variant principle is a three-step process: (1) Create the variant, (2) populate the variant with data, and (3) assign the variant to business objects.

6.2 FI GENERAL

- The term "accounting" is used to capture day-to-day business transactions for various purposes. You can broadly classify accounting information users as (1) external users, i.e., Internal Accounting Standards (IAS), International Financial Reporting Standards (IFRS), stockholders, and other legal authorities and (2) internal users, i.e., the management of a company.
- The Financial Information (FI) modules take care of external reporting by providing information in the form of a balance sheet and P&L account.
- The Controlling (CO) module takes care of management's reporting requirements. It offers a variety of reporting tools that handle different reporting requirements for the effective management of an entity. FI is the main source of data for CO; however, sometimes the CO module generates FI postings, such as reconciliation posting initiated by the reconciliation ledger.
- To post business transactions to a period, you must define or maintain an accounting year or financial year. In SAP R/3 or in mySAP Financial, this is called the fiscal year. There are two types of fiscal year: (1) year independent and (2) year dependent.
- A year-dependent fiscal year is valid for a particular year that you are defining (see Figure 6.1). If you are using a year-dependent fiscal year, then each and every year you have to maintain the definition of the fiscal year. For an example of a shortened fiscal year, is year dependent fiscal year.

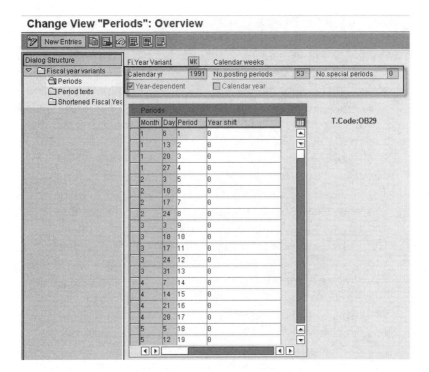

FIGURE 6.1   Year-dependent fiscal year

■ The second type of fiscal year is a year-independent fiscal year. A year-independent fiscal year is not relevant to a particular year. The year-independent fiscal year is further subdivided into a calendar year and a noncalendar year. A calendar year always starts on January 1 and ends on December 31, while a noncalendar year can start in any month.

FV	Description	Year-depend	Calendar yr	Number of posting	
V3	Apr.- March, 4 special periods	☐	☐	12	
V6	July - June, 4 special periods	☐	☐	12	
V9	Oct.- Sept., 4 special periods	☐	☐	12	

FIGURE 6.2   Noncalendar fiscal year

In Figure 6.2, the fiscal years are noncalendar years because they start on dates other than January 1.

- A fiscal year variant contains the definition of posting periods. Generally, a posting period represents a month. In Figure 6.2, you defined how many posting periods a fiscal year will have. There are two types of posting period; (1) normal posting period and (2) special posting period. A normal posting period represents a month of a fiscal year, while a special posting period is a virtual posting period. Special posting periods are used to track year-end activities.
- While posting a transaction, you enter the document posting date. Based upon the document posting date, the system determines the posting period and the fiscal year to be posted.
- To record transactions in foreign currencies, you maintain translation ratios through various tools in mySAP Financial. These are (1) inversion, (2) base currency, and (3) exchange rate spreads. With the exchange rate spread, you will maintain an average rate, and the system will derive the buying rate and selling rate. With base currency, you will maintain an exchange rate between the base currency and foreign currencies.

6.3 GENERAL LEDGER (G/L) ACCOUNTING

- Each G/L is set up according to a chart of accounts (COA). The COA contains the definitions of all G/L accounts. The definitions consist mainly of the account number, account name, and the type of G/L account, i.e., whether the account is a P&L type account or a balance sheet type account.
- Each company code uses one COA for the G/L. This COA is assigned to the company code, and a COA can be used by multiple company codes. This means that the G/L of these company codes have an identical structure. A COA is an index of G/L accounts. Since the COA is a client-dependent master, you have two views for a G/L account master: (1) general data,

which is client dependent, and (2) company code data, which is company code specific.

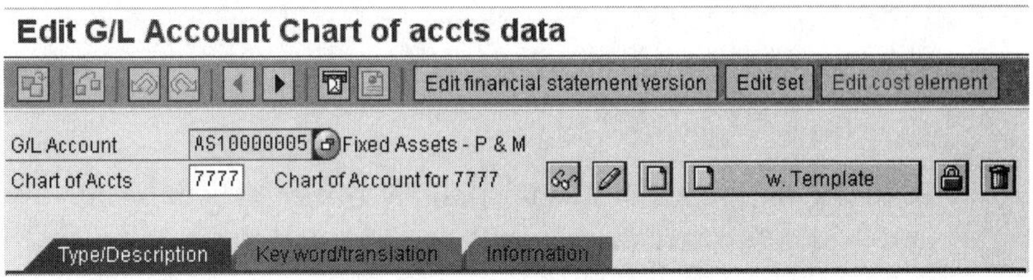

Edit G/L Account Chart of accts data

FIGURE 6.3   G/L master general data segment

Edit G/L Account Company code data

FIGURE 6.4   G/L master company code segments

- To organize a large number of G/L accounts and their presentation, you will group together G/L accounts through account groups. At a minimum, you should have two account groups: (1) balance sheet accounts and (2) profit and loss (P&L) accounts.
- A COA broadly consists of balance sheet accounts and P&L accounts. During year end, these are treated differently. Year-end balances of the balance sheet accounts will be carried over to the next year, while year-end balances of the P&L accounts will be transferred to retain earning accounts.
- A COA also consists of some special accounts: reconciliation accounts and retain earning accounts.

- ◻ A reconciliation account is a control account of subsidiary ledgers for accounts payable (AP), accounts receivable (AR), and assets management (AM). You will maintain at least one reconciliation account for each category. Subsidiary ledgers are connected to G/Ls through reconciliation ledgers.
- ◻ Retain earning accounts are used to carry over the net result of business activities to subsequent years.

- Account groups control various parameters for G/L account masters. These are: the field status variant and the number range of the G/L master.
- The field status controls the maintenance and display of G/L masters. The fields of the G/L master will have one of the following status indicators: Hide, Display, Required Entry, or Optional Entry.
- The G/L account master also controls how the business transaction will be displayed and managed. These are controlled through the open item management attribute, the line item display attribute, and account currency.
- Open item management: Open items are treated as incomplete transactions, which will be offset by another open item(s).
- Line item management: If this attribute is switched on, you can detail line items while viewing a ledger in the G/L master. Otherwise, the system will only display the G/L balance.
- By default, all accounts are managed at the company code level in company code currency; however, you can maintain a G/L account in a foreign currency. If you are maintaining a G/L account in a currency other than company code currency, you can only post a transaction in that currency. With a company code–managed currency G/L account, you can post in any currency.
- To meet various legal and management requirements, you can present your account in different ways. You will often use more than one COA. At best, you can use three COAs for a company code: (1) operational COA, (2) group COA, and (3) country COA.

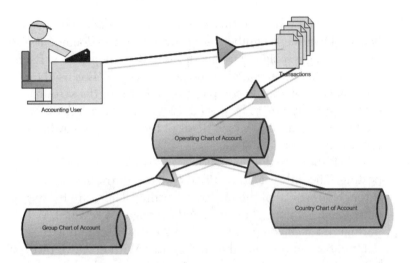

FIGURE 6.5   COA

- While posting business transactions, a user selects the operational COA G/L account. From the operational COA G/L accounts, information flows to other G/L accounts of other COAs.
- To present a financial statement, you maintain financial statement versions with mySAP Financial. You may create any number of financial statement versions to meet your requirements.
- To classify and store business transactions, you use document types. Document types control the number range of accounting documents and allowed account types. mySAP Financial comes with standard document types. If these standard document types do not meet your requirements, you can create your own through transaction code OBA7.
- Accounting documents contain a document header and line items. A document header holds information that is applicable to the entire document, e.g., company code, document types, posting date, document date, etc.
- In order to distinguish between the various FI documents, document types are used. Each document is assign to

one document type, and this is entered in the document header. Document numbers are provided by the document number ranges assigned to one or more document types. Each document line item contains one posting key. This is used for internal control; during complex postings it tells the system: (1) the account type to be posted, (2) whether it is a debit or credit posting, and (3) which fields of the line item may have or require an entry.

- The SAP software does not allow you to delete an incorrect posting. The only way to rectify the incorrect transaction is through a reversal of the incorrect posting. There are two types of reversal: (1) normal reversal and (2) negative reversal. With normal reversal, you post the reversal entry by crediting the debit entry and debiting the credit entry. With negative reversal, you post the reversal entry by posting entries on both the debit and credit sides with the opposite sign.

- If you are working in a corporate group environment, you will often come across cross-company code transactions. A cross-company code transaction involves more than one company code. This situation arises when one company code makes purchases for other company codes, one company code pays invoices for other company codes, or one company code sells goods to other company codes.

- Through transaction code OBYA, you can customize clearing accounts in both company codes.

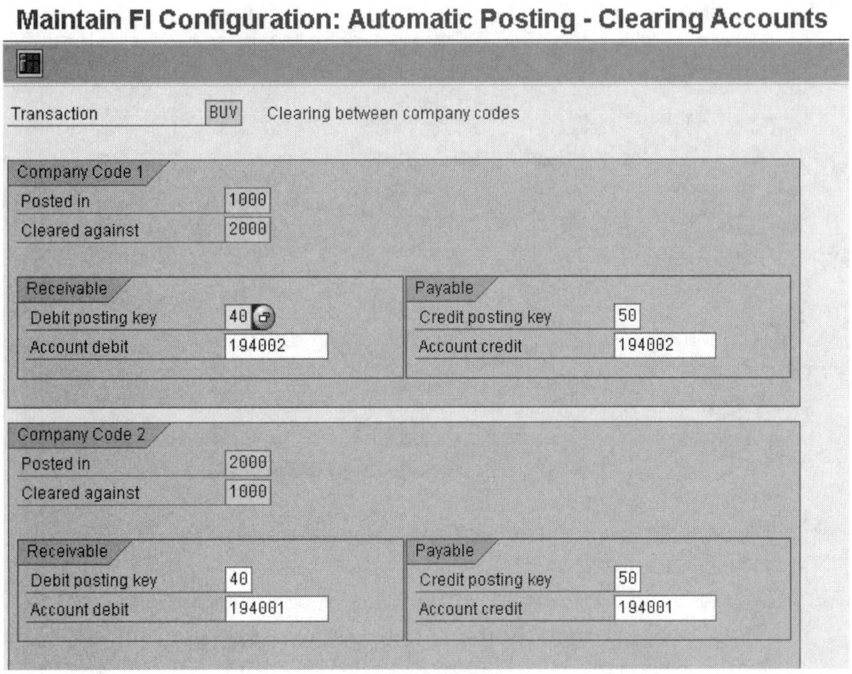

Maintain FI Configuration: Automatic Posting - Clearing Accounts

Transaction	BUV Clearing between company codes

Company Code 1

Posted in	1000
Cleared against	2000

Receivable

Debit posting key	40
Account debit	194002

Payable

Credit posting key	50
Account credit	194002

Company Code 2

Posted in	2000
Cleared against	1000

Receivable

Debit posting key	40
Account debit	194001

Payable

Credit posting key	50
Account credit	194001

FIGURE 6.6   Cross-company code configuration

- Cross-company code transactions will create a cross-company code document, which is a combination of the document number of the first company code, the first company code number, and the fiscal year. It is stored in the document header of all of the documents created so you have a complete audit trail.

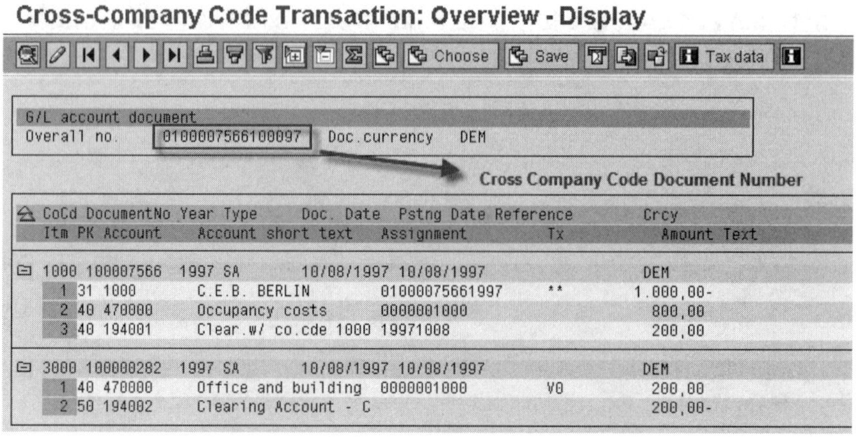

Cross-Company Code Transaction: Overview - Display

FIGURE 6.7   Cross-company code document

- Through transaction code FBU3, you can view cross-company code documents.
- mySAP Financial provides two types of clearing open items: (1) clearing open items and (2) posting with clearing. In the former case, you will clear existing debits with credits. In the latter case, you will clear one or more open items while posting another business transaction, e.g., payment for invoice. In this case, the invoice is an open item and you are clearing it while making payment.
- There are two ways to clear transactions: (1) manual clearing and (2) automatic clearing.
- When handling payment differences, the system always looks for two types of tolerance: (1) tolerance group for employees and (2) tolerance group for vendor/customer. The payment difference has to be within both tolerances to be handled automatically.
- Payment differences arise while clearing open items. Figure 6.8 shows how to handle payment differences. The system will take into consideration employee tolerance and customer/vendor tolerance and determine whether or not this payment difference is within the limit.

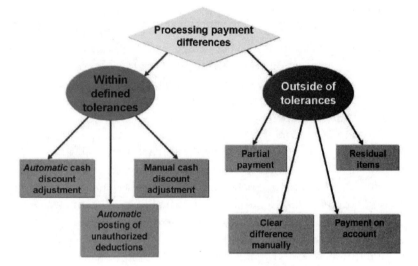

FIGURE 6.8   Payment difference

- If the payment difference is within the limit, a cash discount will be posted automatically and the payment difference will be either treated as an additional cash discount or charged to an expenses account.
- If the payment difference is outside of the tolerance limit, the payment will be processed as a partial payment, a residual payment, or a payment on account. You can also process the payment difference manually.
- In case of partial payment, all line items will remain as open items. With a residual payment, the system will clear an invoice with payment and create a new open item for the differential amount.

6.4 AP AND AR

- Like a G/L account group, you can create a vendor group (through transaction code OBD2 and OBD3). The vendor group/customer group controls the field status and number range of the vendor master, and whether the vendor/customer is a one-time vendor/customer.
- The vendor/customer master is a client-dependent master. Any company code within that client may use that master. The vendor master has three views or segments: (1) general data, (2) company code data, and (3) purchase organization/sales organization data. General data is available to all company codes within the client, company code data is company code dependent and contains all information relating to accounting, and purchase sales organization data is purchase sales organization specific.
- You will maintain a master record for your regular vendors. The master for one-time vendors does not contain any vendor-specific information. A one-time vendor master will be used for more than one vendor. You will maintain vendor-specific data while posting to a one-time vendor at the transaction level.
- A vendor may also be a customer. In this case, you will maintain a vendor master as well as a customer master. If you want to clear the vendor against the customer or vice versa, you have to fill out the highlighted fields in both masters, shown in Figures 6.9 and 6.10.

Display Vendor: Control

| Vendor | 1994 | IDES Canada | Toronto |

Account control

| Customer | | Authorization | |
| Trading Partner | 4000 | Corporate Group | |

FIGURE 6.9   Vendor master control

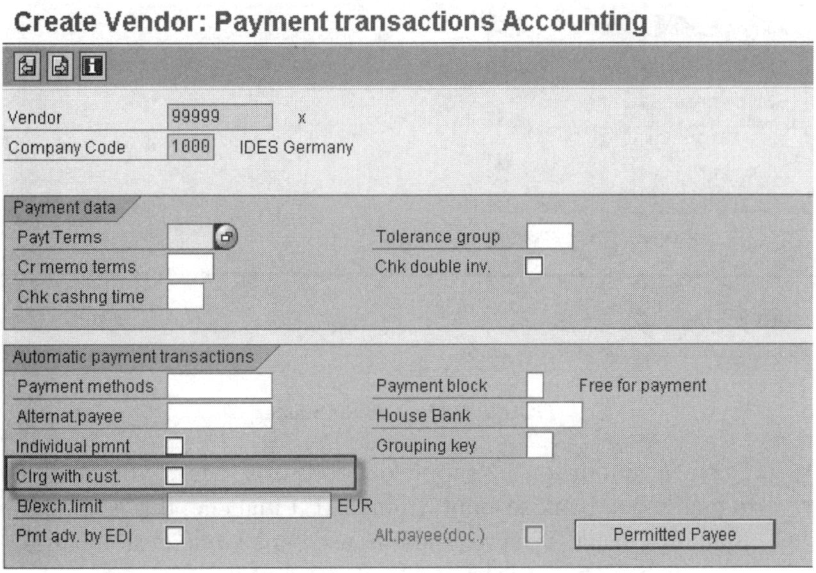

Create Vendor: Payment transactions Accounting

| Vendor | 99999 | x |
| Company Code | 1000 | IDES Germany |

Payment data

Payt Terms		Tolerance group	
Cr memo terms		Chk double inv.	
Chk cashng time			

Automatic payment transactions

Payment methods		Payment block		Free for payment
Alternat.payee		House Bank	
Individual pmnt		Grouping key	
Clrg with cust.	
B/exch.limit		EUR
Pmt adv. by EDI		Alt.payee(doc.)		Permitted Payee

FIGURE 6.10   Vendor master payment transaction

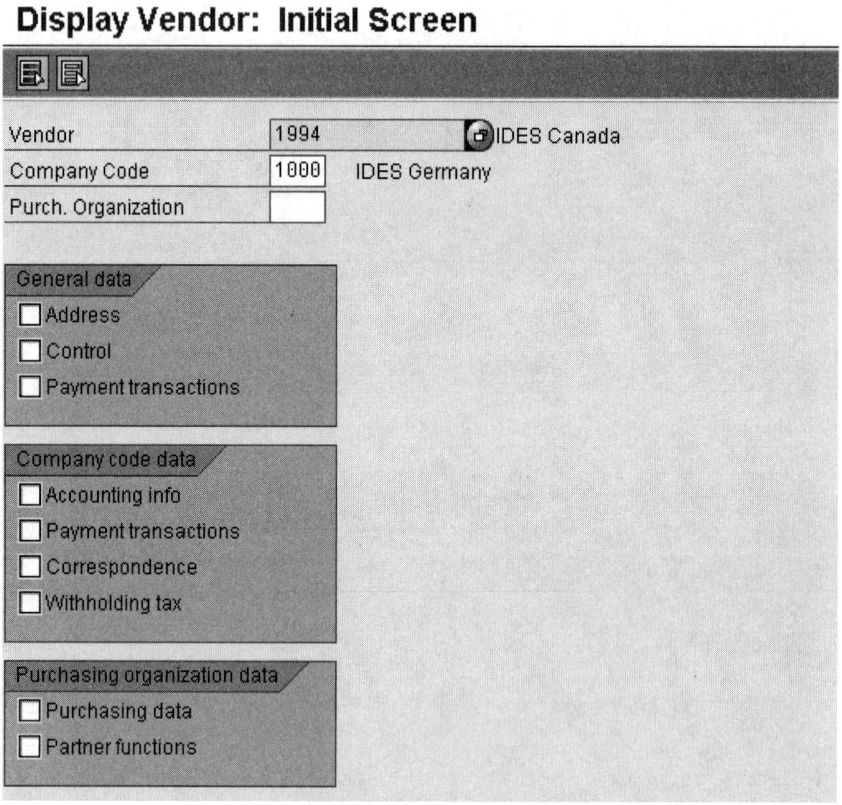

Display Vendor: Initial Screen

Vendor   1994   IDES Canada
Company Code   1000   IDES Germany
Purch. Organization

General data
- [ ] Address
- [ ] Control
- [ ] Payment transactions

Company code data
- [ ] Accounting info
- [ ] Payment transactions
- [ ] Correspondence
- [ ] Withholding tax

Purchasing organization data
- [ ] Purchasing data
- [ ] Partner functions

FIGURE 6.11   **Vendor master**

- To pay a vendor for the supply of goods or services, you need to maintain a bank account. In mySAP Financial, this is known as a house bank. You create the house bank while customizing. A house bank has at least one bank account in which you maintain bank master data.
- When dealing with the customer and vendor, you use payment terms. In SAP solutions, payment terms determine the baseline date for due date calculation, the cash discount period, and the cash discount percentage.
- You assign default payment terms to the customer or vendor at the master level, which can be overwritten while posting a transaction.

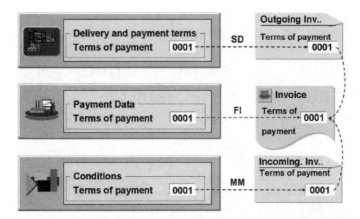

FIGURE 6.12   **Transfer of payment terms**

- You can enter the payment terms in the company code segment and the purchase organization segment. Now the question arises of which payment term holds priority over the other. The logic is very simple here: If the transaction originates from MM, the MM payment term has priority. If the transaction originates from FI, the FI payment term has priority.
- You can use one payment term for both the customer and the vendor. While customizing the payment term through transaction code OBB8, you will configure whether a payment term is applicable to receivable and/or payable.

Change View "Terms of Payment": Details

| | New Entries | | | | | | | |

| Payt Terms | 0002 | Sales text | |
| Day limit | 0 | Own explanation | |

Account type		Baseline date calculation	
☑ Customer		Fixed day	
☑ Vendor		Additional months	

FIGURE 6.13   **Assigning payment term**

- You can block a particular vendor or customer at the company code level or at the client level, i.e., for all company codes.

You can carry out this activity through transaction code XK02/ MK02/FK02 and XD02/VD02/FD02.

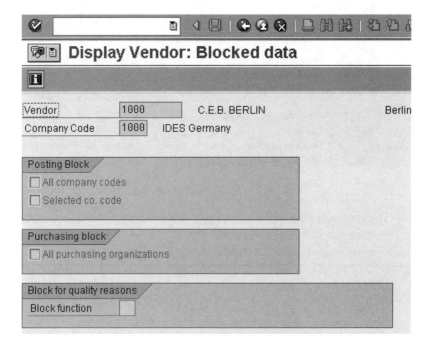

FIGURE 6.14   **Blocking the vendor master**

- A payment term determines the baseline date. In turn, the baseline date determines the starting date for due date calculation, interest calculation, and dunning.
- You have four baseline date options to choose from while customizing payment terms. These are: (1) No default (to be entered while posting a transaction), (2) Document date, (3) Posting date, and (4) Entry date.

FIGURE 6.15   **Setting the baseline date**

- In Figure 6.16, a percentage has been entered with relation to days. If the customer pays the amount due within the defined number of days, the system will calculate a cash discount subject to vendor/customer tolerance.

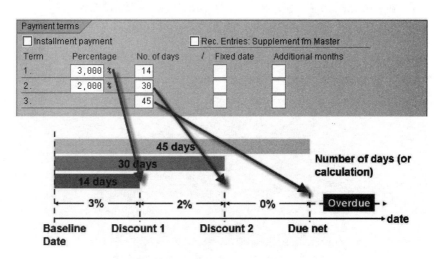

FIGURE 6.16 **Cash discount determination**

- Certain business transactions will be shown separately from normal transactions. These types of transactions are called special G/L transactions. They are: down payment, bills of exchange, and guarantee of payment
- While dealing with day-to-day business, you may enter certain types of special transactions called statistical entry and noted items. From an accounting point of view, these transactions do not affect your financial statement. However, to comply with various legal requirements, you need to show them in your financial statement.
- Statistical entry: At some point, you may offer a guarantee to a third person on behalf of your customer. In this case, you are liable to the third party. At the same time, your customer will pay you the same amount in case of breach of contract. These types of transactions either appear on both sides of your balance sheet or appear as notes in your financial statement.

■   Noted items: Noted items are special G/L transactions that only reminds the user about payments that are due or payments to be made. A noted item will not update the G/L account. A down payment request is a noted item. While displaying the vendor/customer balance, mySAP ERP provides you functionality to choose one of these transactions or all transactions with a business partner.

■   Figure 6.17 is from transaction code FBL1N—Vendor Line item display. It allows you to select various types of items for line item display.

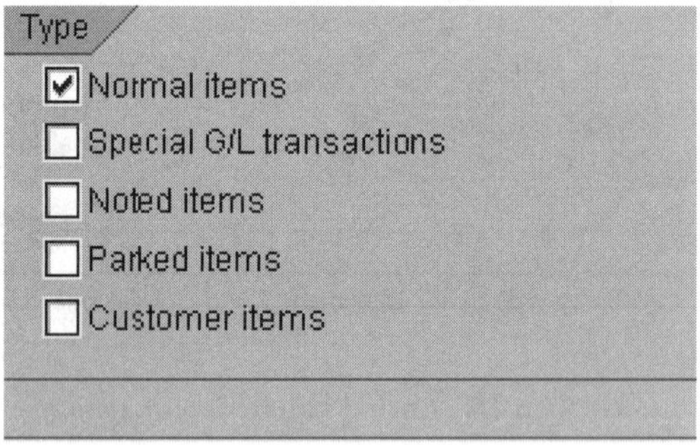

FIGURE 6.17   **Display options for vendor line items**

■   While entering a business transaction, a user may not be able to post a document because he does not have enough information, he is not authorized to post that entry, or he may have posted an incomplete entry.

To handle these types of situations, mySAP ERP provides you with hold documents and park documents.

□   Hold document: Say a user has a business transaction that has 100 line items. He entered 10 line items and realized that he has to address some other critical issue. In this situation, since the document is incomplete, he cannot post it. He has two options: (1) Come out of the entry screen and enter all of the line items again or (2) temporarily save it. The latter action is called a hold document. When you have a hold document, the system will not check that debits equals credits.

- □ Park document: This functionality also relates to temporarily storing a document. The major difference between parking and holding is the debit and credit check. When a document is parked, debits should equal credits.

6.5 ASSET ACCOUNTING (AA)

- The AM module is a submodule of the FI module. Like AP and AR, AA also serves as a subsidiary ledger.

- In AA you are using a chart of depreciation (COD), which is an index of depreciation areas. The COD is client dependent, and can be assigned to more than one company code. Unlike a COA, you cannot create a COD. You can draw your own COD by copying the standard COD template provided by SAP.

- To accommodate different depreciation rules for different purposes, you can use more than one depreciation area. In SAP R/3, you can configure up to 99 depreciation areas.

- The assignment of a COA to a company code is independent from the assignment of a COD.

- Since SAP R/3 is an integrated system, the AA module transfers data to other modules and receives data from other modules.

  a. When you purchase assets through the MM module, the MM module passes data to the FI-AA module.
  b. When you run depreciation, the FI-AA module passes this information to CO modules.
  c. Through the Plant Maintenance (PM) module, you can settle the maintenance cost that is to be capitalized.
  d. You use the asset class as selection criteria for various reports in FI-AA.

- For controlling purposes, you need to transfer depreciation expenses from the FI-AA module to the CO module. Depending on business requirements, you can define the cost center at either the assets master level or the depreciation cost element level.

- If you want to distribute depreciation expenses to various cost centers, you can achieve this with a distribution cost center and distribution cycle.

- During the depreciation run, depreciation expenses and CO interest are always posted to default cost center.

- The asset class represents the classification criteria of assets. The utmost care has to be taken while deciding asset classification. The asset class controls the number range of assets, account determination, screen layout of the asset master, and maintenance level.

- Generally, you classify assets on the basis of the presentation of your financial statement.

- The AA module does not differentiate between tangible assets and intangible assets.

- In the AA module, you have the option to maintain complex assets individually by their components. For example, a desktop consists of a PC, a monitor, a mouse, and a keyboard. Now here you have two options: (1) simple assets—treat the entire desktop package as one asset or (2) complex assets—treat each individual component as an asset within an asset. In the latter case, you will maintain individual components of your desktop through subassets. Subassets have the following advantages: You can depreciate different components at different rates and you can track your individual subassets through a subassest's number.

- Assets under construction (AUC) is a special class of tangible assets. Because of its special nature, it appears separately in financial statements. You can manage AUC through individual management and collective management. After completion of the project, you will settle to assets either through line item settlement or through distribution.

Like AUC, Low Value Assets (LVA) is also a special class of assets. Generally, you maintain this asset class for those assets that need to depreciate in the same year. In the depreciation area at the company code level, you set your maximum amount for low value for assets acquisition and purchase orders.

- Due to special accounting requirements, leased assets are also considered special assets. During the lease period, the leased asset is the property of the lessee or the manufacturer. From the lease and accounting point of view, there are two kinds of lease: (1) capital lease and (2) operating lease. With a capital lease, the lesser will break the total lease cost into capital costs and interest. The capital cost will be capitalized and depreciation will be calculated. The interest component will be charged to the P&L account as a financial cost of the financing activities. With an operating lease, the lesser will charge the lease payment as a periodic cost in the P&L account.

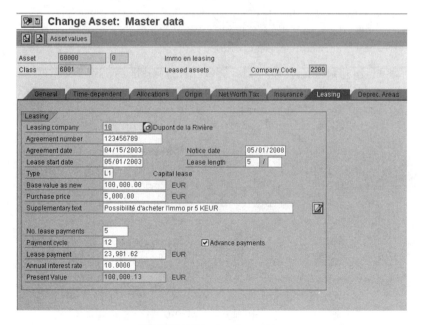

FIGURE 6.18   Leasing assets

- To comply with different legal and managerial requirements, you often adopt different methods of calculating depreciation. Depreciation areas take care of this requirement. One depreciation area takes care of one type of depreciation. In SAP R/3, you can define up to 99 depreciation areas. Through transaction code OADB you can add and delete depreciation areas.

- When you have parallel currencies, you have to define one depreciation area for each currency. These depreciation areas should be identical to the book depreciation areas.

- Derived depreciation areas are special depreciation areas that derive their values from one or more.

- You can add or delete depreciation areas in AA. However, if you want to delete a depreciation area from a COD, the depreciation area in question should fulfill the following preconditions:

  □ The depreciation area should not be a master depreciation area.

  □ There should not be any posting in that depreciation area.

  □ The depreciation area should not be a reference depreciation area for a derived depreciation area.

- Through transaction code AS90, you can determine various accounts to be used for G/L account posting. This automatic account determination happens based on the COD, COA, account determination, and depreciation area.

- Transactions posted in the AA module update the APC cost in the book depreciation area and change the forecast depreciation in real time. Periodically, you will run a depreciation run, which posts APC costs to other depreciation areas and updates depreciation.

  Due to changes in the business process, you may find that depreciation was understated or overstated. To handle this type of situation, SAP solutions provide two methods: (1) the catch-up method and (2) smoothing. With the catch-up method, the system will calculate the differential depreciation by reducing posted depreciation from planned depreciation and post the differential depreciation in the current period. With smoothing, the differential depreciation will be spread over the remaining posting period.

- You can assign depreciation keys for depreciation areas through transaction code OAYZ. In addition to other parameters, you are assigning five calculation methods to depreciation keys. These are: (1) base method, (2) declining-balance method, (3) maximum amount method, (4) multilevel method, and (5) period control method.

- Base method: The base method contains general control parameters the system needs for calculating depreciation. With this method, you specify the depreciation type, the depreciation calculation method, and the treatment of the end of depreciation.

- Declining-balance method: The declining-balance method includes both the declining-balance method and the sum-of-the-years-digits method. The normal declining-balance method of depreciation multiplies the straight-line percentage rate resulting from the useful life by a given factor.

- Maximum amount method: You use the maximum amount method to specify the maximum amount up to which the system should calculate depreciation until a certain calendar date.

- Multi-Level method: Base methods for certain depreciation calculation methods use either a total percentage rate or a periodic percentage rate to calculate depreciation.

- Period control method: To determine the depreciation start and end dates for asset transactions, you can set an appropriate period control in the period control method for these four transaction categories: (1) acquisitions, (2) subsequent acquisitions/post-capitalization, (3) intracompany transfers, and (4) retirements.

- Sometimes it is necessary to depreciate assets up to a scrap value. To handle this type of situation, SAP R/3 has provided two different approaches: (1) by assigning a scrap value key to the depreciation key used in the depreciation area or (2) by explicitly entering an absolute scrap value in the asset master data for the depreciation area.

6.6 CO GENERAL

- If you divide accounting into internal and external accounting, FI represents external accounting, while CO represents internal reports. CO has a management-oriented approach. It is a tool in the hand of management for effective control of an entity. Like the company code, in CO your highest entity is the controlling area. Depending upon company code assignment, your controlling area may be a cross-company code controlling area or the company code = controlling area. This configuration is done through transaction code OKKP. You can perform cross-company code cost accounting by assigning more than one company code to one controlling area. You may assign multiple company codes to a controlling area under these conditions:

  - A company code may have different operating currencies. In this case, you may choose either one of the company code currencies as the controlling area's currency or you may choose a different currency as the controlling area's currency.

  - A company code may use different fiscal year variants, but they should have the same number of posting periods.

  - All company codes within a controlling area use the same COA.

- The CO module consists of the following submodules, which handle different user requirements.

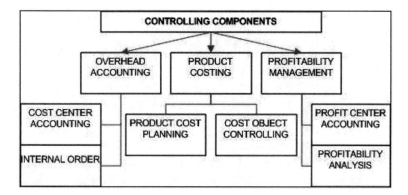

FIGURE 6.19   **CO module components**

- Cost Center Accounting (CEL): Cost element is the carrier of cost between FICO and within the CO module. It classifies costs and revenues posted to CO according to their origin. Through the cost element, you can reconcile cost flows between FI and CO.

- Overhead Accounting: Cost center accounting (CCA), along with internal order, takes care of those costs that are not directly attributable to any product or service, i.e., indirect costs. This is essential, as you have to track these costs from the control point of view.

- Product Cost Planning (PCC) is used for evaluating the cost of a product. This submodule provides various types of information about product costs, which leads toward a decision about producing a product or manufacturing in-house.

- Profitability Analysis (PA) deals with market segments and provides various reports for analyzing the results of enterprise activities on the external market. Through this module, you can determine how successful the enterprise is in different market segments, i.e., products, divisions, and customers.

- Profit Center Accounting (PCA): This module plays an important role from a responsibility point of view. It takes care of P&L analysis of the subareas in the enterprise that are responsible for profits.

- All the CO submodules described here have their master data, i.e., cost element, cost center, profit center, characteristics, etc. In CO you will also have various master data groups, which are used for easy reporting and to process more than one set of master data at a time. Master data groups are cost center groups, cost element groups, and IO groups. Master data groups make analysis and reporting easier. Instead of processing master data individually, you select a master data group to process all of the master data at one time. When reporting at each hierarchical level, the system will generate an automatic total, making reporting easier. Within a client, you can use each master data name once.

- When indirect expenses are posted in FI using cost element, the system will post a one-sided entry through the CO document.

- While posting FI transactions, CO is being populated through various default assignments or manual assignment. When posting happens to CO, SAP R/3 will generate a CO document. When posting happens to more than one cost object, true posting happens to one-cost objects and posting to other cost objects are statistical.

- You cannot settle statistical posting. Statistical posting is for informational purposes only.

6.7 CEL

- Cost Element Accounting (CEA) is a submodule of CO. Cost flows between FI and CO and within CO through cost element and/or revenue. When cost flows from FI to CO, it flows through the primary cost element. When cost flows within CO, it flows through the primary cost element as well as a secondary cost element. Through cost element, you can track the point of origination of expenses.

■ If you have an expense account for which CO posting is required, a cost element has to be created for cost accounting purposes. While posting within CO, you will create a secondary cost element for which there will not be any FI posting.

6.8 COST CENTER ACCOUNTING (CCA)

■ Costs directly attributable to a product and services are assigned to product/services. Costs other than direct costs, i.e., personnel costs or rental costs, are captured through the Cost Center Accounting module and later on assigned to different CCA modules according to their consumption.

■ Posting expenses to cost centers enables internal accounting. Before creating cost center master data and the cost center hierarchy, you have to plan the organization structure. The organization structure of the cost center may depend upon allocation criteria, geographical requirements, etc. The highest node of the cost center organization structure is called the standard hierarchy.

■ Within CCA, cost center master data controls setup parameters. You can create cost center master data through transaction codes KS01 (Create), KS02 (Change), and KS03 (View). These are:

  □ Header information: This includes the cost center number and the controlling area for which this is created.

  □ Basic data: This contains cost center manager and cost center type.

  □ Hierarchy area: Here you are assigning the cost center to a group note in order to create the organization hierarchy.

  □ Company: Since cost centers are company code dependent, when you are working in cross-company code controlling areas, you have to assign the cost center to one of the company codes.

■ Within CCA, you use a statistical key figure (SKF) to distribute/allocate one or more cost center costs to various cost centers, e.g., the number of employees in the IT department.

- The SKF may be a fixed value or a total value. With a fixed value SKF, values will carry over to a future period, while a total value SKF is valid for a particular period.

- A purchase order does not create an FI document. However, if a commitment is active, a purchase order will create a commitment posting.

- Once you receive goods, the SAP R/3 system will clear commitment postings and post actual cost.

- Sometimes, some of the costs accrue in FI in a random fashion, which makes period comparison questionable. You can configure the accrual concept in CO to overcome this difficulty. The CO module provides two types of accrual calculation: (1) percentage method and (2) target = actual method.

- Through the accrual process, you can accumulate certain costs periodically in CO, which will be offset by an FI transaction.

- In CCA, you have various methods to transfer cost from one cost center to other cost objects. These are: reposting, assessment, and distribution.

  □ Reposting enables you to correct posting errors. It transfers costs from the cost center to other cost objects, while retaining original cost elements. There are two types of reposting: (1) manual reposting and (2) line item reposting. With manual reposting, you transfer cost (or revenue) from cost centers to other objects based on certain distribution rules. With line item reposting, you repost or transfer line items from cost centers to other cost objects with reference to an FI document.

  □ Distribution is another method of transferring cost from a cost center to other cost objects. Sometimes, while incurring costs in FI, you do not have enough information to distribute your expenses to other cost centers. In this situation, you could collect these costs in a cost center and later on distribute them to other cost centers. As with reposting, distribution also retains the original cost element. You can reverse and repeat distribution as often as desired.

  □ Assessment is used to allocate primary and secondary costs from one cost center to other cost objects. In the assessment process, you will use assessment cost element as a carrier of cost. During this process, you will lose the original cost element.

- In CO, you observed that you are following various methods to transfer cost from one cost object to others. Some of these transfers are within the CO, and some are within the company code level. At the end of the month, it is essential to reconcile data for internal accounting with data for external accounting. The reconciliation ledger facilitates this reconciliation.

6.9 IO

- All indirect costs flow either to cost centers or to overhead IO. IO holds cost and/or revenue for short periods. You can divide IO into the following categories: (1) overhead order, (2) accrual order, and (3) order with revenue.

  - Overhead order captures indirect costs not directly attributable to any product or services for a short period.

  - Accrual order accumulates certain costs that will be offset by another entry at a particular interval.

  - Order with revenue is used to track costs and revenue for a particular object.

- IOs normally act as an interim cost collector and a tool for planning, monitoring, and reporting transactions. Once the objective of the IO is complete, the costs captured in IO have to be settled to their cost center/IO or to a G/L.

- IO is used in the SAP R/3 system for planning, monitoring, controlling, and settling a particular project. You use different types of IO as mentioned earlier to capture different types of requirements.

- You will create an IO with reference to order type. Order type controls the number range of the IOs, types of orders, settlement profile, and budget profile.

- Depending upon master data attributes, the SAP R/3 system posts transactional data either as real postings or as statistical postings.

- When the IO is statistical and you are posting FI transactions, if you are assigning expenses to IO and cost centers, then the real posting goes to the cost center and the statistical posting happens to IO.

- Real postings always happen to real IO.

- Like assessment or distribution for cost centers, you transfer the IO cost from IO to other cost objects through settlement. After completion of the IO life cycle, you can settle IO to its original cost center. In the case of external IO settlement, the settlement process will create an FI posting.

- You run order settlement to settle transfer IO cost to its final destination. You can run settlement either at the period end or at the end of the order life.

- In the SAP R/3 system, you can settle IOs (CO component), sales orders (SD component), projects (PS component), and production orders with product cost collectors (PP component) to profitability segments.

6.10 PA

PA provides various reports for analyzing the results of enterprise activities on the external market. Through this module, you can determine how successful the enterprise is in different market segments, i.e., products, divisions, and customers.

- The PA module (CO-PA) is used to measure the profitability of segments. A market segment may be a product, customer, geographical area, company code, or business areas. This is a good tool to monitor marketing activities with a market-oriented approach.

- PA is one of the most important submodules of CO and is widely used. There are two types of PA: (1) costing-based PA and (2) account-based PA.

- Among the two types of PA, costing-based CO-PA is more widely used.

- Costing-based CO-PA generates reports based on segments. Segments represent one characteristic or a combination of characteristics.

- Table 6.1 lists the differences between costing-based CO-PA and account-based CO-PA.

Costing-based CO-PA	Account-based CO-PA
1. Uses characteristics and value fields to display reports.	1. Uses cost and revenue elements to display reports.
2. In costing-based CO-PA, you can calculate anticipated cost.	2. Takes real cost and revenue from FI; hence you cannot calculate anticipated cost.
3. Uses tables specific to CO-PA, which may or may not agree with FI.	3. Uses CO application tables.
4. Revenue and cost of sales are posted when the billing document is posted.	4. Revenues are posted when the billing document is posted, while cost of sales is posted when FI posting occurs for goods issue.
5. At a given point in time, it may or may not reconcile with FI.	5. Always reconciles with FI.

TABLE 6.1   Costing-based CO-PA versus account-based CO-PA

- In costing-based CO-PA, CO-PA stores its data in a separate set of tables. While generating operating areas, the system will create these tables. These tables are CE1XXXX, CE2XXXX,

CE3XXXX, and CE4XXXX, where XXXX represents the operating concern. Figure 6.20 shows how data is organized into different tables in CO-PA.

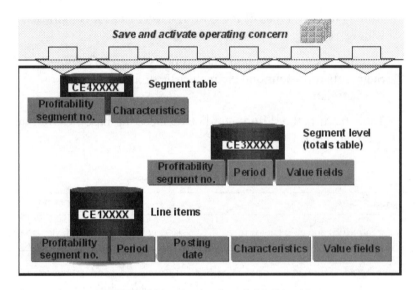

FIGURE 6.20 Costing-based CO-PA tables

- CO-PA gets its data from the SD, MM, and FI modules and from overhead controlling through cost center assessment and IO settlement.

- When you make sales through the SD module, depending on the sales order status, the SD module passes all information relating to sales to FI as well as to CO.

- Figure 6.21 shows when the FI and CO modules are updated. At the point of delivery and at the point of billing, the SD module passes information to FI, which creates the FI document as well as the CO document.

- Account-based CO-PA is updated with the cost of material when delivery occurs from the SD module, while revenue is updated when the SD module passes the billing document to FI. However, with costing-based CO-PA, both revenue and cost are updated when the SD module passes billing document information.

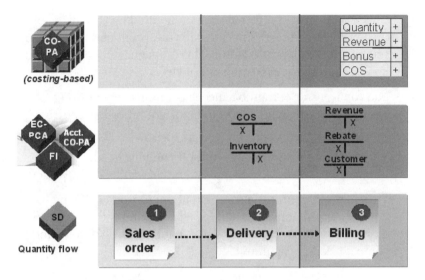

FIGURE 6.21   Time of posting into CO-PA from the SD module

- CO-PA gets its data from various modules as follows:

    □ From SD: With costing-based CO-PA, sales data passes to CO-PA when the order is created or changed, or during billing. With account-based CO-PA, CO-PA gets it data when goods are issued or during billing.

    □ From FI: Direct costs that are attributable to a particular segment are transferred directly from FI.

    □ From CO: Indirect costs can be periodically transferred into CO-PA, using allocations, settlements, and assessments.

6.11 PCA

The PCA module plays an important role from a responsibility point of view. Along with PA, this module plays a leading role in profitability management for an enterprise. It takes care of P&L analysis of the subareas in the enterprise that are responsible for profits.

- This module tracks internal profit generated by various responsibility centers. You can map your product, branches, and functionality as a profit center. This is a management-oriented approach from the control point of view.

- You can transfer certain balance sheet items, which along with cost and revenue give you important ratios like return on investment (ROI).

- The cost center profit center master contains header information, basic data, group assignment, and validity period.

- Since a profit center is a component of enterprise CO, by default a profit center is valid for all company codes assigned to a controlling area. However, you can limit this by deselecting company code assignment.

- Assets, cost centers, business processes, IOs, projects, production orders, and cost objects have a field for profit center assignments in their master records. When you post any transaction to one of these objects, the profit center is populated with data.

- Based on configuration, PCA facilitates profit center valuation. When a goods movement takes place between profit centers, it can be treated as a sale in PCA and the goods valued based on either legal valuation or profit center valuation.

- If the selling profit center and the buying profit center belong to the same company code, then valuation takes place based on profit center valuation. Otherwise, legal valuation is used.

- In profit center valuation, you can determine the transfer price, which is generally cost + margin.

- Profit center accounts get their data from FI and CO posting in the following ways:

  □ All postings for revenue and cost elements (assignment to profit center using CO account assignment object)

  □ Expense and revenue accounts that are posted using logistic transactions

- Balance sheet accounts and other expense and revenue accounts (optional)

- Like cost center assessment and distribution, you can use profit center assessment and distribution to transfer costs from one service cost center to other cost center.

6.12 PCC

PCC is used for evaluating the cost of a product. This submodule gives various types of information about product costs that lead toward a decision about whether to produce a product or manufacture in-house. It analyzes the actual cost and the planned cost for producing a product.

- In product costing, the material master, BOM, work center, and routing are important:

  - The material master controls attributes of materials, i.e., raw materials, assemblies, and products.

  - A BOM represents a list of materials used to produce a product.

  - A work center is the location where you are producing your product.

- An order is related to the product and holds and supplies information about the planned order cost and the actual cost incurred while producing the product. It facilitates the comparison of planned cost and actual cost at a detailed level. Once you have completed production, you may settle production order to finished stock.

- A sales order collects cost and revenue for a particular sales order and facilitates the comparison of actual and planned cost and revenue.

Chapter 7

SPECIAL AREAS

Some of the areas in the FICO modules are complex, and deserve special attention from an interview and consulting point of view. This chapter discusses some of these important areas.

7.1 FOREIGN CURRENCIES

You carry out accounting for a company code in the country currency (local currency) of the company code. Therefore, you must specify the local currency in the system for each company code. All other currencies used are indicated as foreign from the point of view of the company code. There are several situations in which you need foreign currencies: (1) to post and save receivables and payables in foreign currency, (2) to make payments in foreign currency, (3) to manage accounts in foreign currency (foreign currency balance sheet accounts), and (4) to carry out consolidation and prepare corporate group reports.

These are the following *configuration* steps for foreign currencies:

1. **Check Currency Codes (SPRO):**
   SAP solutions come with standard currency codes for the ISO company codes. Sometimes circumstances arise in which you have to define new currency. You can do so through this step.
2. **Set Decimal Places for Currencies (OY04):**
   In this step, you will define the number of decimal places for the currency.
3. **Check Exchange Rate Types (SPRO):**
   In this step, you will define exchange rate types, which you will use later on for various transactions.

4. **Define Valuation Methods (OB59):**
   To valuate foreign currencies, you need at least one valuation method. With the valuation methods, you will define how to handle foreign currency valuation methods and the exchange rate types you are going to use. In a high-level valuation method, you will hold various parameters for foreign currency valuations.

5. **Prepare Automatic Postings for Foreign Currency Valuation (OBA1):**
   In this step, you will assign various G/L accounts to record foreign valuation differences.

   These are the following *application* steps for foreign currencies:

6. **Enter Exchange Rates (SPRO):**
   In this step, you will enter exchange rates to convert one currency to another.

7. **Foreign Currency Valuation (F.05):**
   This transaction code is used to valuate foreign currencies. Foreign currency income and expenses will be recorded in the respective account defined through transaction code OBA1.

7.2 INTERCOMPANY TRANSACTIONS

In today's complex business world, a corporate group may have more than one legal entity. When these legal entities make transactions between themselves, these transactions are called intercompany transactions. Here are some examples of intercompany transactions:

- One entity makes payments for other entities.
- One entity incurs expenses for other entities.
- One entity sells its products or services to other entities.
- One entity purchases goods or services from other entities.

To deal with these kinds of expenses, you need to carry out the following steps in your SAP solutions:

1. Create customer and/or vendor master in the respective company codes.
2. Set this relation in transaction code OBYA.

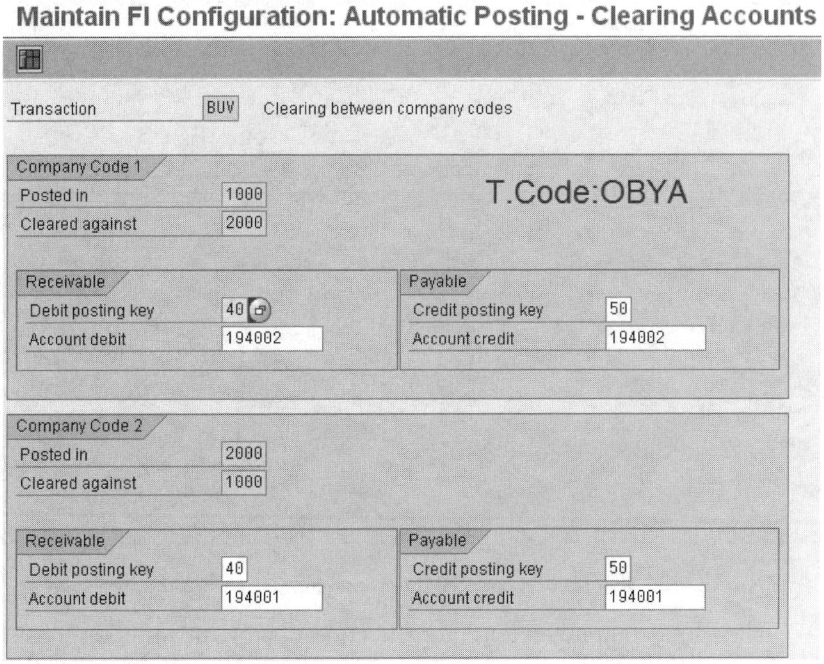

Maintain FI Configuration: Automatic Posting - Clearing Accounts

FIGURE 7.1   Transaction code OBYA—cross-company transaction configuration

When you post an intercompany transaction, the SAP system will generate three accounting documents: (1) an FI document for the first company code, (2) an FI document for the second company code, and (3) a inter-company document.

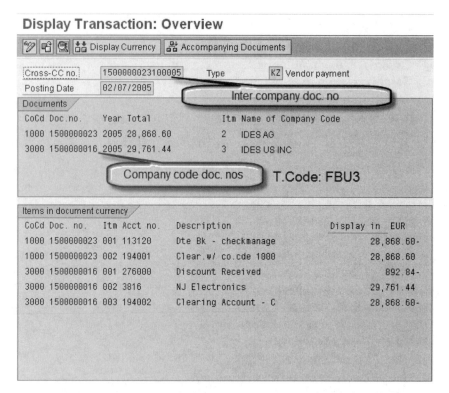

FIGURE 7.2   Transaction code FBU3—cross-company transaction display

The cross-company/inter-company code document number consists of the first company code document number, plus the company code, plus the last two digits of the fiscal year. Table 7.1 lists some commonly used transaction codes for cross-company/inter-company posting.

T-Code/Programs	Description
FBU3	Display cross-company document
FBU8	Cross-company reversal
RFBVOR00	Report on cross-company transactions

TABLE 7.1   Transaction codes for cross-company/inter-company documents

7.3 BANK RECONCILIATION

Bank reconciliation is a process whereby you are matching your accounting records with the bank record. At a particular point in time, your accounting record may or may not match the bank record. This is due to the time difference between recording transactions in the company's books of account and the bank's transaction postings. At the end of the month or at a particular time interval agreed to with the bank, the bank sends a bank statement to the company.

The company compares the bank statement with the transactions recorded in its books of account. This process may bring up the true balance with the bank, a transaction the company failed to record, or a transaction recorded by the bank that does not pertain to the company. There are two approaches to remedy this: (1) adjusting the balance per bank or (2) adjusting the balance per books.

The steps involved in each of these approaches are presented in Table 7.2.

Adjusting the Balance per Bank	Adjusting the Balance per Books
Balance per Bank Statement on MM/DD/YY	Balance per Books on MM/DD/YY
Add: Deposits in transit	Deduct: Deposits in transit
Deduct: Outstanding checks	Add: Outstanding checks
Add or Deduct: Bank errors	Add or Deduct: Bank errors
Adjusted/Corrected Balance per Book	Adjusted/Corrected Balance per Bank

TABLE 7.2   Bank reconciliation

In SAP solutions, when the bank reconciliation process is implemented, you will have a minimum of three G/L accounts: (1) incoming clearing account, (2) outgoing clearing account, and (3) main account.

Once the company has issued checks to their vendors, it will pass the following entries:

> Debit Vendor Account
> Credit Outgoing clearing account

When receiving checks, the company will pass the following entries:

> Debit Incoming clearing account
> Credit Customer Account

When the company receives a bank statement from its bank, it passes the following accounting entries:

For incoming payment:

> Debit Bank main account
> Credit Incoming clearing account

For outgoing payment:

> Debit Outgoing clearing account
> Credit Bank main account

When the company passes these entries, the main bank account balance will agree with the bank balance as per bank.

To carry out automatic/manual bank reconciliation, you need to configure the following steps:

- **Create Account Symbol (OT53):** In this step, you will create various IDs for banking transactions, such as the following: (1) CI—Check Issues, (2) CR—Check Receipts, (3) BD—Bank Debits, (4) BC—Bank Credits, and (5) BM—Bank Main Accounts.
- **Assign Account to Account Symbol (OT53):** In this step, you will assign G/L accounts to account symbols.
- **Create Keys for Posting Rule (OT53):** In this step, you will create posting rules and IDs.
- **Define Posting Rules (OT53):** In this step, you will assign posting keys, account symbols, document types, and posting types to posting rules.
- **Define Variant for Manual Bank Statement (OT43):** In this step, you will define a screen variant for data entry for bank reconciliation.

Using transaction code FF67 from the application menu, you can input data for manual bank reconciliation statements. You can upload a BAI file for electronic bank statements through T-code FF.5.

7.4 LOCKBOX CONFIGURATION

A lockbox is an arrangement with a bank under which payments are mailed to a strategically located post office box that is serviced by the bank. The bank picks up the payments from the post office several times a day and accelerates the processing of the checks to make funds available to the customer. Lockboxes enhance the security and control of funds and can reduce workloads in customer service offices.

The following steps need to be carried out to use a lockbox:

1. **Define House Bank (FI12):** In this step, you will create a house bank, bank ID, and account ID. Each house bank of a company code is represented by a bank ID in the SAP system, and every account at a house bank is represented by an account ID. In the SAP system, you use the bank ID and the account ID to specify bank details. These specifications are used, for example, for automatic payment transactions to determine the bank details for payment.
   Path: SAP Customizing Implementation Guide → Financial Accounting → Bank Accounting → Bank Accounts → Define House Banks

2. **Define Lockboxes for House Bank (SPRO):** In this step, you define your lockbox accounts at the house banks. Thus, on the outgoing invoice you can inform your customer of the lockbox to which payment is to be made. By specifying this, you can optimize the payment transactions. The lockbox procedure is currently used only in the United States.
   Path: SAP Customizing Implementation Guide → Financial Accounting → Bank Accounting → Bank Accounts → Define House Banks

3. **Define Lockboxes for House Banks (SPRO):** In this activity, you store control data for the lockbox procedure. This data is needed for importing lockbox files sent by banks. Currently, only BAI and BAI2 file formats are supported by SAP solutions.
   Path: SAP Customizing Implementation Guide → Financial Accounting → Bank Accounting → Bank Accounts → Define Lockboxes for House Banks

4. **Define Posting Data (SPRO):** In this activity, you store information needed to process particular lockbox data and generate postings. The Destination and Origin are routing information and defined by your bank. For every unique destination/origin, posting information is needed to create the following postings:

   □ G/L posting—Debit bank account (incoming checks) and credit payment clearing account
   □ A/R posting—Debit payment clearing account and credit customer account

   Path: SAP Customizing Implementation Guide → Financial Accounting → Bank Accounting → Business Transactions → Payment Transactions → Lockbox → Define Posting Data

The following steps need to be carried out from the application side:

1. **Main Lockbox Program to Upload Data (FLB2):**
2. **Post Processing of Lockbox Data (FLB1):**

7.5 REVENUE RECOGNITION

The revenue recognition principle arises from accrual accounting and the matching principle. Accrual accounting and the matching principle help the user determine how a business entity will determine whether a particular transaction will be treated as an expense or revenue.

In accrual accounting, revenues are recognized when you have realized and you have performed, i.e., when goods are transferred or services rendered, no matter when cash is received.

In cash accounting, revenues are recognized when you have received cash, regardless of the timing of goods or services sold. Revenue recognition depends upon the nature of the transaction. From an academic point of view, transactions can be broadly divided into four types: (1) selling inventory, (2) selling services, (3) leasing activities, and (4) selling of assets other than inventory.

Revenue recognition occurs from four types of transactions:

1. Revenue from selling inventory is recognized at the date of sale, which is often interpreted as the date of delivery.
2. Revenue from rendering services is recognized when services are completed and billed.
3. Revenue from permission to use a company's assets (e.g., interest for using money, rent for using fixed assets, and royalties for using intangible assets) is recognized as time passes or as assets are used.
4. Revenue from selling an asset other than inventory is recognized at the point of sale when it takes place.

Revenue recognition mostly applies when you are billing your customer in advance. For example, you entered a service contract (such as a maintenance contract) with your customer for $12,000 for one year. As per payment terms, you billed your customer in advance. Therefore, as of January 1, you billed your customer for an entire year and the customer paid. At the end of January, you can treat $1,000 as your income and the remaining $11,000 remains as a liability.

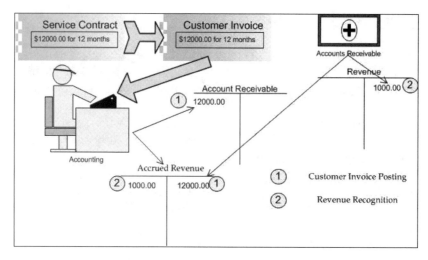

FIGURE 7.3   **Revenue recognition**

To handle revenue determination in an SAP solution, you need the following configuration:

1. **Set Revenue Recognition for Item Categories:** In this step, you will maintain two fields: (1) your revenue recognition method and (2) the start date. These configuration steps are in the following path: *Sales and Distribution → Basic Functions → Account Assignment/Costing → Revenue Recognition →*

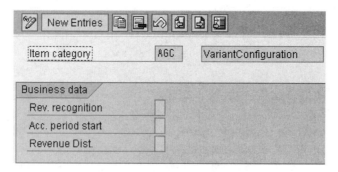

FIGURE 7.4   **Revenue recognition**

□ Rev. recognition: Here you specify the revenue recognition category. There are four types of revenue recognition categories: (1) No value, (2) A, (3) B, and (4) D. This designates how you are going to determine your revenue.
□ Acc. period start: This indicator determines the start date of revenue recognition.

2. **Maintain Account Determination:** In this IMG step, you will assign various G/L accounts to which transactions will be posted.

□ Determine the revenue account: The revenue account is maintained in the first column. This is configured through transaction code VKOA.
□ Assign account for unbilled receivables: In this step, you will assign G/L accounts for the deferred revenue account (special G/L account) and the unbilled receivable account.

After configuration, the SD user will post the customer invoice for the full amount in the SD module. Once you run transaction code VF44, the system will list the transactions that need to be considered as revenue for the said period.

7.6 AUTOMATIC PAYMENT PROGRAM

Through an automatic payment program, you can pay both vendors and customers to whom you owe money. The transaction code for the configuration of an automatic payment program is FBZP. To execute the program, you would use transaction code F110. There are five steps to configure an automatic payment program:

1. **All Company Code:** Enter the sending and paying company codes, outgoing payment with cash discount from. In this step, you will define the sending and paying company code relation.
2. **Paying Company Code:** Enter the minimum amount of the incoming and outgoing payments and the form for the payment advice.
3. **Country Payment Methods:** Select Check will be created, Allowed for personal payments, Street, P.O. box or No. (bank details for wire transfer), or RFFOUS_C (RFFOUS_T for wire transfer) as the print (payment) program.
4. **Company Code Payment Methods:** Enter minimum and maximum amounts and the form for payment transfer. The payment per due day, optimized by bank group or postal code, can also be selected.

5. **Bank Determination:** If there is more than one house bank, a ranking order can be given. Under Amounts, specify the amount available for outgoing payment. Under Accounts, enter the bank clearing account for the bank subaccount.

After configuring the automatic payment program, you will run it using transaction code F110. Follow these steps:

1. Enter the Run Date and Identification and go to the Parameters tab.
2. Enter company codes, payment methods, the next pay date, and vendor accounts.
3. Go to the Additional Log tab and select due date check, payment method selection in all cases, and line items of the payment documents.
4. Go to the Printout/data medium tab, enter the variant against the payment program, and select **Maintain Variants**.
5. Enter the paying company code, house bank details, and check lot number.
6. Select **Print Checks** and **Print payment summary** for checks and **Print payment advice notes** for wire transfers (enter the printer and select **Print** immediately). Also set the number of sample printouts to zero.
7. Then execute **Proposal**, **Payment run**, and **Printout**.

7.7 THREE-WAY MATCH

The three-way match is part of the procure to pay (P2P) process. Refer to the SAP Business process section for details of the P2P. The P2P process involves various steps depending on configuration and the SAP modules implemented. Out of all the steps involved in the P2P process, these three steps are components of the three-way match:

- Creation of PO (T-code ME21N)
- Goods receipt (T-code MIGO)
- LIS invoice receipts (T-code MIRO)

1. After sorting the list of vendors, the purchase department will create a purchase order through transaction code ME21N. In this step, there is no accounting impact, but in Controlling (CO), the PO will create a commitment posting if you have activated commitment management. This commitment item will be converted into an actual posting once you have received material.

2. Once you have received goods, the goods receiving clerk will enter the goods receipts into the SAP system through transaction code MIGO. While posting the goods receipt, the system will check quantity, goods, and price against the PO. If you have partial goods against a PO, the goods receiving clerk will modify the quantity, which will leave the PO open until the next goods receipt. The G/L is automatically updated with postings made to the G/L, cost centers, or asset accounts, while an offsetting posting will be made to a new general account called the GR/IR account. The accounting will be as follows:

Expenses Accounts	Debit
Inventory	Debit
Assets	Debit
GR\IR	Credit

3. The accounting department will receive an invoice from the vendor. Invoice verification is the last step in the three-way match. While posting the invoice, the system will check goods receipts for quantity and price with PO. The following entry is posted once you save the invoice:

GR/IR	Debit
Vendor	Credit

7.8 P2P

An organization sells goods and services. To sell goods and services, naturally, it will have to procure these goods and services or produce them. The procurement part of goods and services is handled by the purchasing department of an organization. Although the procurement process starts with the purchase department, it flows to various departments and ultimately ends with a payment to the vendor. In SAP solutions, the P2P cycle may be simple or complex, depending on the modules implemented and the client's business process. The following shows how the P2P process can be viewed using different modules.

- P2P process with FICO module: When you are only working with the FICO module, the P2P process is pretty simple. In this case, the recording of goods movement will be taken care of outside of the SAP solution.

  □ Vendor invoice posting
  □ Payment to vendor

- P2P process with FICO and MM modules:

  □ Source determination
  □ Purchase order
  □ Goods receipt
  □ Invoice verification
  □ Payment to vendor

7.9 VENDOR DOWN PAYMENT AND CLEARING

"Down payment" is the term used when you are entering into agreement with your vendor to purchase an expensive item or capital assets. It means an upfront payment to the vendor before delivery of goods and services, and is also called an "advance payment." According to the accrual concept, a down payment or advance payment is not a liability but rather an asset. Since the down payment is treated as an asset for your financial statement, it cannot be mixed with normal transactions with vendors. In SAP solutions, a down payment is treated as a special G/L transaction. Down payment transactions are shown and recorded in a different reconciliation (control) account called an alternative reconciliation account. As per SAP standards, a vendor down payment process involves the following steps:

1. Down payment request (T-code F-37)
2. Down payment (T-code F-29 or F110)
3. Invoice (T-code FB70)
4. Down payment clearing (T-code F-39)

The down payment request is an optional step, but the advantage of this step is that you can make payment to your vendor through an automatic payment program.

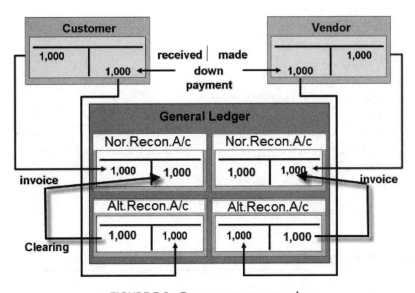

FIGURE 7.5   Down payment processing

When clearing the down payment, the system will do a transfer posting from the alternative reconciliation account to the normal reconciliation account. For this automatic account determination, you need to configure the vendor down payment through transaction code OBYR.

7.10 ORDER TO CASH (OTC)

The order to cash (OTC) process covers all to the steps related to placing an order from customer purchase order to cash collection from the customer. During this process, the user has to go through various steps for successful processing of a business transaction. Before delivering material to a customer, the company has to check the customer's credit and the availability of the material. This process involves the SD, MM, and FICO modules. Generally, the following steps are involved in a typical situation:

- Sales quotation
- Standard order
- Shipping
- Delivery
- Picking
- Posting goods issue
- Warehouse picking execution
- Packing
- Billing: Using transaction code VF01, the SD user will create a billing document, which will trigger an FI document to record the FI transaction.
- Payment of customer: This is a FI process. Through various FI transaction codes, you can record incoming payments.

7.11 MAKE TO ORDER

Sometimes a customer requests a specific product that is not a generally available product line of your vendor. This circumstance requires the make to order process.

Make to order is initiated after receiving a customer order. The sales department receives the customer's make to order and passes the sales order to the material department, as well as the purchasing department, which checks for the required materials. The material requirement analysis is carried out through the SAP solution. In the material requisition planning (MRP) run, the SAP software explodes the Bills of Material (BOM) for all levels. If the required materials are not available, the MRP will create planned orders.

Planned orders for materials produced in-house will be converted into production orders, while planned orders for materials procured from outside will be converted into purchase orders.

The availability of material produced in-house and procured from outside will be decided through the replenishment time mentioned in the material master. In the case of in-house produced goods, the route time will take precedence over the replenish date mentioned in the material master.

The cycle of made to order is as follows:

- Create material for make to order
- Route creation
- Create BOM
- Sales order
- Production order
- Recording of finished goods
- Delivery against sales order
- Invoicing

7.12 SUMMARIZATION LEVELS IN CO-PA

To satisfy various business needs, CO-PA deals with large data to produce segment reports, i.e., reports based on customer hierarchy, product group, or geographical location. Due to the large volume of data handling, the user may question system performance. To increase response time, the SAP R/3 system provides a summarization concept in CO-PA.

Summarization means the system aggregates data based on required segments and stores the data in a different set of tables. Since the system holds data in summary form in different tables, it provides quick access to the user.

When the user runs a particular CO-PA report, the system looks for the most suitable summarization table instead of the CE1XXXX table (where XXXX is the operating concern name).

In the absence of the summarization level, the system always looks for CE3XXXX and CE4XXXX tables for each and every run. A summarization level stores the original dataset in a reduced form.

From a technical point of view, a summarization consists of two tables that have just been generated, the key table and the totals table. The key table corresponds to the segment table and contains the pseudosegments produced from the reduced characteristics. The totals table corresponds to the segment level and contains the associated value fields.

Figure 7.6 shows the summarization levels. From top to bottom, it goes from more specific segments to less specific segments.

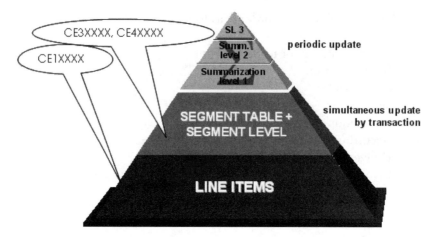

FIGURE 7.6   **Summarization levels**

In the absence of the summarization level, the SAP R/3 system will return the following types of warnings shown in Figures 7.7 and 7.8:

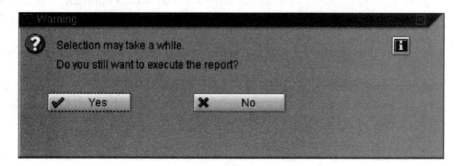

FIGURE 7.7   **CO-PA reporting error**

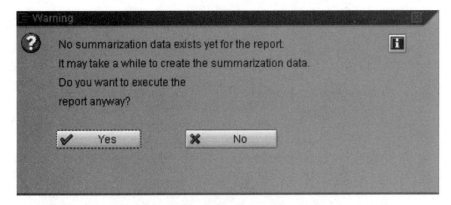

FIGURE 7.8   CO-PA reporting error

To avoid these messages and increase system performance, you have to build a summarization level following these steps:

1. **Create Automatic Proposal for Summarization Levels (T-code KEDVP):** In this step, the data system will propose new summarization levels according to CO-PA usage. SAP R/3 allows you to create up to 5,000 summarization levels.
2. **Define/Change Summarization Levels (T-code KEDV):** Once summarization levels are proposed, you can change the attributes of the summarization level in this step. The summarization level status will be active without data.
3. **Build Summarization Levels (T-code KEDU):** Once you build your summarization level, you need to populate it with data. The summarization level holds historical data; to use it properly, you need to execute this transaction at the proper interval to populate the summarization level with recent data.

Chapter 8   NEW G/L

To satisfy a broader range of internal and external requirements, the mySAP ERP application combines all general ledger functionality under one roof. mySAP ERP also streamlines various functions of earlier versions, which makes reporting easier and meets all internal and external reporting requirements. Now New G/L provides a unified structure for cost of sales accounting, profit center accounting (PCA), and segment reporting. The New G/L ledger has the following advantages:

- Accelerates period-end processing
- Makes reporting easier by providing real-time reconciliation between FI and CO
- Lets an entity report in multiple ways by providing multiple ledgers within G/L accounting
- Has an extended data structure so the customer can add new fields to standard tables

Refer to OSS: 756146 for a more complete list of advantages.

mySAP combines the following features of older versions into the New G/L concept:

- General ledger (G/L)
- PCA
- Reconciliation ledger
- Special-purpose ledger (SPL)
- Business area
- Cost of sales accounting

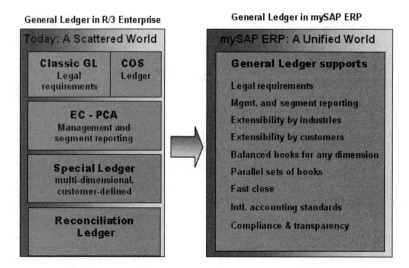

FIGURE 8.1   Comparing R/3 Enterprise and mySAP ERP

Implementation of New G/L is compulsory for newer customers and optional for existing SAP customers. If existing customers want to use this functionality, they can activate it by using transaction code FAGL_ACTIVATION. New G/L activation is client specific, not company code specific. After activation of New G/L, you will find some new paths for New G/L, in addition to the old paths. See Figure 8.2.

▷	📄	Financial Accounting
▽		Financial Accounting (New)
	▷	Financial Accounting Global Settings (New)
	▷	General Ledger Accounting (New)
	▷ 📄	Accounts Receivable and Accounts Payable
	▷ 📄	Contract Accounts Receivable and Payable
	▷	Bank Accounting
	▷	Consolidation Preparation (New)
	▷ 📄	Asset Accounting
	▷ 📄	Lease Accounting
	▷ 📄	Special Purpose Ledger
	▷ 📄	Travel Management

FIGURE 8.2   New G/L menus

After activating New G/L, you will have two views for document display: (1) Data Entry View and (2) General Ledger View as shown in figures 8.3 and 8.4.

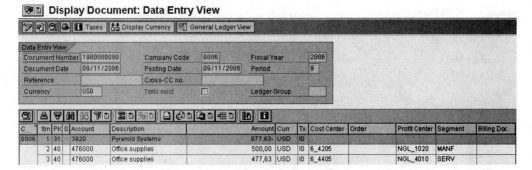

FIGURE 8.3 Data Entry View

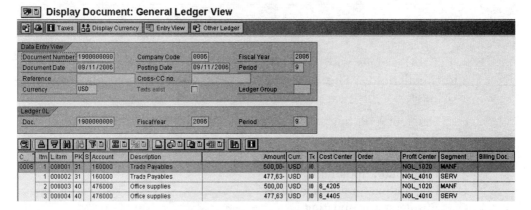

FIGURE 8.4 General Ledger View

Since New G/L substitutes FI_SPL, it comes with leading and nonleading ledger concepts. For the time being, think of leading ledgers as your G/L and non-leading ledgers as your FI_SPL. Table 8.1 points out the differences between leading ledgers and nonleading ledgers.

	Leading Ledger	Nonleading Ledger
Existence	Required	Optional
Transaction Posting	All FI transactions will be updated	May or may not be posted with all FI transactions
Currencies	Takes currencies from company code	Can maintain currencies different from company code
Fiscal Year	Same as company code	Can be different from company code
Accounting Principle	Follow basic accounting principle	May follow different accounting principle
Number of ledgers	One leading ledger for a given company code	May have zero or more

TABLE 8.1   Leading ledger versus nonleading ledger

mySAP comes with a brand-new table (FAGLFLEXT) that contains additional fields. The FSGLFEXT table thus supports the following activities:

- Segment reporting
- Profit center updating
- Cost of sales accounting
- Cost center updating
- Preparation for consolidation
- Business-area updating

You can add new fields to this table to capture different scenarios.

8.1 DOCUMENT SPLITTING

The main functionality of New G/L is document splitting. You use document splitting to capture additional missing accounting assignments by which each and every document is balanced individually. As an example, say you are entering a cost center while posting an expense. From the cost center, expenses are posted to the profit center. Is the payable also assigned to the profit center? The answer is "No" if you are using an old version of SAP software, but it is "Yes" if you are using mySAP. If document splitting is active in mySAP, the system will transfer the profit center from expense line items to payable line items.

There are three types of document splitting: (1) active (rule-based) split, (2) passive split, and (3) clearing lines/zero balance formation by balancing dimensions.

1. Active split: This is a configuration step in which the system will split the document. Active splitting is applicable for original entries, i.e., vendor invoice posting and customer invoice posting.
2. Passive split: This is the default setting. Passive splitting is applicable for subsequent transactions, i.e., clearing of vendor invoice with payment, etc.
3. Clearing lines/zero balance formation by balancing char. (and document): This occurs when a transfer is made between two segments.

8.2 TRANSACTION CODES

mySAP ERP comes with several new transaction codes that replace existing transaction codes:

- FAGLB03: Display Balances (New); replaces FS10N
- FAGLL03: Display Line Items (New); replaces FBL3N
- FB50L/FB01L: G/L Document Posting for a Ledger Group; replaces FB50/FB01
- FAGL_FC_VAL: Foreign Currency Valuation (New); replaces F.05
- FAGLF101: Sorting/Reclassification (New); replaces F101
- FAGLGVTR: Balance Carry-forward (New), replaces F.16, GVTR, and 2KES

Chapter **9**

TABLES IN THE SAP SYSTEM

Whenever you enter data in a screen, the data is stored in a table. Sometimes there may be more than one table linked to a particular screen. As a FICO functional consultant, you should be aware of important tables in the SAP software and their data structure. You can use transaction code SE11 to see the field structure of a table. By invoking transaction code SE16 or SE16N, you can browse the data in a particular table.

The tables provided in this chapter

9.1 ENTERPRISE STRUCTURE (FI-ES)

The following is an important SAP table for FI enterprise structure:

Table	Description
T001	Company code
T005	Countries
TCURC	Currency codes
TCURR	Exchange rate
TCURT	Currency name
T077S	Account group (G/L accounts)
T009	Fiscal year variants
T880	Global company data
T014	Credit control area

TABLE 9.1   FI-G/L tables

291

Table	Description
T004	Chart of accounts (COA)
T077S	Account group (G/L accounts)
T009	Fiscal year variants
T880	Global company data
T014	Credit control area
T010O	Posting period variant
T010P	Posting period variant names
T001B	Permitted posting periods
T003	Document types
T012	House banks

TABLE 9.1   FI-G/L tables

9.2 GENERAL LEDGER ACCOUNTING (FI-G/L)

The following is an important SAP table for FI G/L Accounting:

Table	Description
SKA1	G/L master—Chart of accounts segment
SKB1	G/L master—Company code segment
BNKA	Bank master record
BKPF	Accounting documents header

Continued

Table	Description
BSEG	Accounting documents item level
BNKA	Bank master record
BSAD	Accounting: Index for customers (cleared items)
BSAK	Accounting: Index for vendors (cleared items)
BSAS	Accounting: Index for G/L accounts (cleared items)

TABLE 9.2   FI-G/L tables

9.3 ACCOUNTS RECEIVABLE (FI-AR)

The following is an important SAP table for FI Accounts Receivable:

Table	Description
KNA1	Customer master—General data
KNB1	Customer master—Company code data
KNVV	Customer master—Sales data
KNBK	Bank details
KNVH	Customer hierarchy
KNVP	Customer partners
KNVS	Shipment data for customer
KNVK	Contact persons
KNVI	Customer master tax indicator

TABLE 9.3   FI-AR tables

9.4 ACCOUNTS PAYABLE (FI-AP)

The following is an important SAP table for FI Accounts Payable:

Table	Description
LFA1	Vendor master—General data
LFB1	Vendor master—Company code data
LFM1	Purchasing organization data
LFM2	Purchasing data
LFB5	Vendor dunning data
LFBK	Bank details

TABLE 9.4   FI-AP tables

9.5 ASSETS MANAGEMENT (FI-AA)

The following is an important SAP table for FI Assets Management:

Table	Description
ANKA	Asset classes: General data
ANKT	Asset classes: Description
ANLU	Asset master record user fields
ANLZ	Time-dependent asset allocations
ANEK	Document header asset posting
ANEP	Asset line items
ANKB	Asset classes: Depreciation area

TABLE 9.5   FI-AA tables

9.6 GENERAL (CO)

The following is an important SAP table for Controlling:

Table	Description
TKA01	Controlling (CO) areas
TKA02	CO area assignment
KEKO	Product costing header
KEPH	Cost components for cost of goods manufacturing
KALO	Sales order items—costing objects
KANZ	Accounting: Index for G/L accounts (cleared items)

TABLE 9.6   CO tables

9.7 COST CENTER ACCOUNTING (CO-CCA)

The following is an important SAP table for CO Cost Center Accounting:

Table	Description
CSKS	Cost center master data
CSKT	Cost center texts
CRCO	Assignment of work center to cost center
COSP	CO object: Cost totals for external postings
COEP	CO object: Line items (by period)
COBK	CO object: Document header
COST	CO object: Price totals

TABLE 9.7   CO-CCA tables

9.8 PROFIT CENTER ACCOUNTING (CO-PCA)

The following is an important SAP table for CO Profit Center Accounting:

Table	Description
CEPC	Profit center master data table
CEPCT	Texts for profit center master data
GLPCA	EC-PCA: Actual line items
GLPCC	EC-PCA: Transaction attributes
GLPCO	EC-PCA: Object table for account
GLPCP	EC-PCA: Plan line items

TABLE 9.8   CO-PCA tables

9.9 PROFITABILITY ANALYSIS (CO-PA)

The following is an important SAP table for CO Profitability Analysis:

Table	Description
CE1XXXX	CO-PA—Actual line items (where XXXX represents operating concern)
CE2XXXX	CO-PA—Plan line items
CE3XXXX	Total records—make time-based classification possible
CE4XXXX	PA segment definition: higher level table used to assign segment number to each combination of characteristic values

TABLE 9.9   CO-PA tables

10 SAP MM CONFIGURATION

The Material Management (MM) module is integrated with the SD, PP, QM, WM, FI, and CO modules. The MM module is part of the logistic menu in SAP software. The MM module takes care of inventory management and the procurement process.

Along with other master data, this module controls two main data masters, i.e., vendor master and material master.

Similar to the FI and CO modules, you will maintain the organizational hierarchy while implementing the MM module. This chapter provides an overview of the MM module and describes the minimum configuration steps. As a FICO functional consultant, it is necessary that you understand MM flow if you are working in an implementation site where MM is part of the implementation.

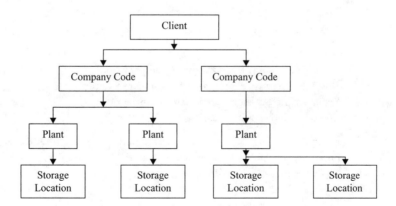

FIGURE 10.1   SAP MM organizational structure

Figure 10.1 shows a straightforward MM organizational structure. Depending upon client requirements, your MM organization may be simple or complex. Note that this chapter describes configuration steps for a simple MM module.

In Figure 10.1, observe that the MM module is dependent on the company code, which is the highest organizational entity in FI. FICO configuration is not discussed here, so before configuring MM, make sure that FI and CO configuration have already taken place.

	Description and Path	T-code
1	Define, Copy, Delete, Check Plant: SPRO → Enterprise Structure → Definition → Logistics (General) → Define, Copy, Delete, Check Plant	OX10
2	Maintain Storage Location: SPRO → Enterprise Structure → Definition → Materials Management → Maintain Storage Location	OX09
3	Maintain Purchase Organization: SPRO → Enterprise Structure → Definition → Materials Management → Maintain Purchase Organization	OX08
4	Assign Plant to Company Code: SPRO → Enterprise Structure → Assignment → Logistics (General) → Assign Plant to Company Code	SPRO
5	Assign Purchasing Organization to Company Code: SPRO → Enterprise Structure → Assignment → Materials Management → Assign Purchasing Organization to Company Code	OX18
6	Assign Purchasing Organization to Plant: SPRO → Enterprise Structure → Assignment → Materials Management → Assign Purchasing Organization to Plant	OX01
7	Define Industry Sectors and industry sector-specific field section: SPRO → Logistics (General) → Material Master → Field Selection → Define Industry Sectors and industry sector-specific field section	SPRO

Continued

	Description and Path	T-code
8	Define Attributes of Material Type: SPRO → Logistics (General) → Material Master → Basic Settings → Material Types → Define Attributes of Material Type	SPRO
9	Define Number Ranges for Each Material Type: SPRO → Logistics (General) → Material Master → Basic Settings → Material Types → Define number ranges for each material type	SPRO
10	Maintain Company Codes for Material Master: SPRO → Logistics (General) → Material Master → Basic Settings → Material Types → Maintain Company Codes for Material Master	OMSY
11	Set Tolerance Limit for Price Variance: SPRO → Materials Management → Purchasing → Purchase Order → Set Tolerance Limit for Price Variance	SPRO
12	Set Tolerance Limits: SPRO → Materials Management → Logistics Invoice Verification → Invoice Block → Set tolerance limits	SPRO
13	Group Together Valuation Areas: SPRO → Materials Management → Valuation and Account Assignment → Account Determination without Wizard → Group Together Valuation Areas	SPRO
14	Configure Automatic Posting: SPRO → Materials Management → Valuation and Account Assignment → Account Determination without Wizard → Configure Automatic Posting	SPRO

TABLE 10.1   MM configuration steps

11 SAP SD CONFIGURATION

The Sales and Distribution (SD) module is part of a logistic module that supports customers starting from accepting a quotation from the customer until billing the customer for products or services sold. This module is tightly integrated with other modules like MM, PP, FI, etc.

Figure 11.1 shows a simple SD business process, where the SD, MM, and FI modules are involved. In a complex business process, other SAP modules are involved and integrated with the SD module to carry out the sales cycle.

FIGURE 11.1   SD business process

Table 11.1 lists simple SD configuration steps.

	Description and Path	T-code
1	IMG → Enterprise Structure → Definition → Sales and Distribution → Define, copy, delete, check Sales organization → Define Sales Organization	SPRO
2	IMG → Enterprise Structure → Definition → Sales and Distribution → Define, copy, delete, check distribution channel → Define Distribution Channel	SPRO
3	IMG → Enterprise Structure → Assignment → Sales and Distribution → Assign sales organization to company code	OVX3
4	IMG → Enterprise Structure → Assignment → Sales and Distribution → Assign distribution channel to sales organization	OVXK
5	IMG → Enterprise Structure → Definition → Logistics–General → Define, copy, delete, check division	SPRO
6	IMG → Enterprise Structure → Assignment → Sales and Distribution → Assign division to sales organization	OVXA
7	IMG → Enterprise Structure → Assignment → Sales and Distribution → Set up sales area	OVXA
8	IMG → Enterprise Structure → Assignment → Sales and Distribution → Assign sales organization → Distribution channel → Plant	OVXG
9	IMG → Enterprise Structure → Definition → Logistics Execution → Define, copy, delete, check shipping point	SPRO
10	IMG → Enterprise Structure → Assignment → Logistics Execution → Assign shipping point to plant	OVXC
11	IMG → Sales and Distribution → Master Data → Define Common Distribution Channels	VOR1
12	IMG → Sales and Distribution → Master Data → Define Common Divisions	VOR2

Continued

	Description and Path	T-code
13	IMG → Sales and Distribution → Basic Functions → Pricing → Pricing Control → Define Condition Tables	**V/03**
14	IMG → Sales and Distribution → Basic Functions → Pricing → Pricing Control → Define Condition Types	**SPRO**
15	IMG → Sales and Distribution → Basic Functions → Pricing → Pricing Control → Define Access Sequences	**SPRO**
16	IMG → Sales and Distribution → Basic Functions → Pricing → Pricing Control → Define And Assign Pricing Procedures	**SPRO**
17	IMG → Sales and Distribution → Sales → Sales Documents → Sales Document Header → Define Sales Document Types	**VOV8**
18	IMG → Sales and Distribution → Sales → Sales Documents → Sales Document Header → Define Number Ranges For Sales Documents	**VN01**
19	IMG → Sales and Distribution → Sales → Sales Documents → Sales Document Header → Assign Sales Area To Sales Document Types	**SPRO**
20	IMG → Sales and Distribution → Sales → Sales Documents → Sales Document Item → Define Item Categories	**SPRO**
21	IMG → Sales and Distribution → Sales → Sales Documents → Sales Document Item → Assign Item Categories	**SPRO**
22	IMG → Sales and Distribution → Sales → Sales Documents → Schedule Lines → Define Schedule Line Categories	**VOV6**

TABLE 11.1   SD configuration steps

Continued

	Description and Path	T-code
23	IMG → Sales and Distribution → Sales → Sales Documents → Schedule Lines → Assign Schedule Line Categories	SPRO

TABLE 11.1   SD configuration steps

INDEX